Managing Change
A strategic approach to organisational development and renewal

Managing Change

A strategic approach to
organisational development and renewal

Bernard Burnes

University of Manchester Institute
of Science and Technology

Pitman Publishing
128 Long Acre, London WC2E 9AN

A Division of Longman Group Limited

First published in 1992
Reprinted 1993 (twice)
Reprinted 1994 (twice)

© Bernard Burnes 1992

A CIP catalogue record for this book can be obtained from the
British Library.

ISBN 0 273 03376 X

Printed in Great Britain by Bell and Bain Ltd, Glasgow

Contents

Part Two   Strategic management – Theory and practice

Part Three   The management of change – Theory and practice

Part Four   Managing change and changing managers – Conclusions

9   Managing change: lessons and guidelines   241

10   Changing managers: management competence and organisational culture   274

Bibliography   302

Index   314

To Sue, Duncan and Stuart

Acknowledgements

This book is the product of nearly a decade of researching into, teaching about and advising organisations. During that period many people have generously given of their time and knowledge to assist me in my work; without them, this book would not have been possible. Space does not permit me to name them all, but I am nevertheless extremely grateful to them, one and all.

There are, however, some who deserve a special mention. One of these is Hakeem James, whose PhD I am supervising. Many of the ideas and observations in this book are the product of our joint collaboration. In particular, Hakeem's assistance with Chapters 3 and 10 was invaluable.

The National Economic Development Office (NEDO), especially Brian Weekes and Penny David, have been a source of support and encouragement for many years. For that, and especially Brian and Penny's advice on this book, I am extremely grateful. I must also express my thanks to NEDO for permission to reproduce case studies two and three in Chapter 4.

My publishers, Pitman, have been very encouraging and patient. Penelope Woolf's comments on drafts of this book have helped to improve it enormously.

Lastly, and mostly, I am irredeemably indebted to my wife, Sue. Her painstaking reading and rewriting of draft after draft of this book have improved it beyond recognition. It is not too much to say that she deserves as much credit as I do for what is good about this book.

Nevertheless, despite all the help and assistance I have received, any faults or shortcomings in the final product are mine and mine alone.

Introduction

Whatever type of organisation people work in, and whatever type of job they do, the one fact that can be relied on is that the organisation and their job will change, sometimes quite dramatically, and not always for the better. It follows that the ability to initiate and manage change is one that all managers need to possess. It could even be argued that what distinguishes the successful manager and the successful organisation from their less successful counterparts is the ability to manage change. The primary aim of this book is to give students and practising managers a clear view of the theory and practice of managing change, in order to equip them with this ability.

The last 200 years could well be labelled: 'The Age of the Organisation'. The organisation in its many forms – from giant industrial conglomerates to small one-person businesses – is one of the dominant features of modern societies. Yet organisations are not static or uniform entities. The world and our expectations of it are changing in a rapid and unpredictable manner. Organisations have to respond to these changing circumstances, or risk being left behind in the increasingly competitive environment of the 1990s.

In this situation, the ability to understand the choices and dilemmas which face organisations, and to make sense of the plethora of advice, theories and beliefs that are on offer to them, is crucial. However, it is also important to recognise that these theories and beliefs have developed in particular circumstances and at particular points in time. As such, they reflect conditions, and incorporate assumptions, which are not necessarily appropriate to the needs of organisations in the 1990s. In particular, as Part One shows, the view of human beings as unreliable and lazy, which prevailed in the early years of the Industrial Revolution and later became enshrined in the Classical approach to organisations, does not fit in with the needs of organisations today.

Therefore, in order for managers to make informed choices for their organisations, they must understand the nature and history of the theories and beliefs which are available to guide their actions. One of the purposes of this book is to do just that: to bring into the open the history, development and nature of the theories and approaches which govern, often at the level of the subconscious, the way organisations are structured, managed and, when necessary, changed. These theories and beliefs influence the routine way that organisations operate and are managed, particularly at times of change, as will be illustrated by the case studies in this book.

This does not mean that everyone, or indeed anyone, in an organisation is necessarily aware of any particular theory or set of beliefs. Nevertheless, as Part One will demonstrate, and as Mintzberg and Quinn (1991:xii) recently noted:

> *Whether we realize it or not, our behavior is guided by the systems of ideas that we have internalized over the years. Much can be learned by bringing these out into the open, examining them more carefully, and comparing them with alternative ways to view the world – including ones based on systematic study (that is, research).*

These 'systems of ideas', or organisation theories as they are more commonly called, are crucial to change management in two respects. Firstly, they provide models of how organisations should be structured and managed. Secondly, they provide guidelines for judging and prescribing the behaviour and effectiveness of individuals and groups in an organisation.

As Mintzberg and Quinn indicate, it is clear that in many organisations there is no clear understanding of these theories. It follows that choices with regard to the appropriateness of structures and practices, and the way these are implemented, are founded on limited knowledge and perhaps false assumptions. Change cannot hope to be fully successful under these circumstances. Consequently, a full understanding of these theories is necessary if informed choices are to be made when instigating and implementing change. For this reason, these will be examined critically in relation to each other, and also in comparison with how organisations are, rather than how theorists suppose them to be. The aim is to provide a practical guide to organisational change, an understanding of the approaches to change, and methods of identifying, planning and implementing change.

The book is organised into four parts. **Part One The develop-ment of organisation theory** comprises three chapters. Chapter 1 deals with the history and emergence of modern forms of organisation in the Industrial Revolution, and the first attempts in the early years of the twentieth century to provide a theory of how organisations should operate – the Classical approach. This was an approach which portrayed organisations as machines, and people as mere cogs in them.

Chapter 2 reviews the two main challengers to the Classical school: the Human Relations approach and Contingency Theory. These emerged in the 1930s and 1960s respectively. The former makes the case for seeing organisations as social systems, which rely for their success on the co-operation and commitment of their personnel. The latter, Contingency Theory, argues against there being one theory or approach for all organisations and all situations. Instead, it proposes that the approach an organisation adopts should be dependent (i.e. contingent) on its particular circumstances.

Chapter 3 examines new organisational paradigms which are emerging in response to the rapid changes that have taken place in recent years. These visions of the future are seen through the work of leading management thinkers from both sides of the Atlantic, namely Tom Peters and Robert Waterman, Rosabeth Moss Kanter, and Charles Handy.

Part Two Strategic management – Theory and practice com-prises two chapters. This part examines both the literature on strategic management, and how individual companies undertake it in practice. Chapter 4 traces the origins and development of strategy. It shows that although strategy was originally conceived as a quantitative approach concerned primarily with product-market issues, this has changed considerably. Strategy is now seen as a qualitative process embracing the full range of organisational issues and situations, in-cluding internal arrangements as well as external market and other concerns.

Chapter 5 illustrates how the theory of strategic management is put into practice. This is shown through the differing experiences of four real companies; only their names have been changed. These case studies show not only the complexity and difficulties involved in strategy formulation, but also that even the best strategies can fail if their implementation, the management of change, is deficient.

Part Three The management of change – Theory and prac-tice comprises three chapters. It covers the literature on and ap-proaches to change management, and, through six case studies, the reality. Chapter 6 examines the various conflicting and confusing theories and approaches to managing change which have emerged over the years. In particular, it shows how different approaches and theories relate to different types and levels of change (the individual, the work group and the organisational levels).

Chapters 7 and 8 present six case studies of change management. As with Chapter 5, these are real companies; again only their names have been changed. The three case studies in Chapter 7 deal with change projects which arose from strategic decisions. However, they show that even projects initiated in this way still have to be planned and executed in a systematic manner: one which involves, rather than excludes, those most closely affected. As the three case studies in Chapter 8 reveal, this does not mean that the strategic element can be ignored. In these companies, the lack of a strategic approach to change can be seen to have led to disappointment and demoralisation.

Part Four Managing change and changing managers – Conclusions comprises the concluding two chapters of the book. This part presents guidelines for initiating and executing change, and also discusses the competence of managers to undertake this process. Chapter 9 reviews the process of change as described in the previous chapters. It then presents an approach to change management which sets the planning and management of individual projects in the context of the strategic and cultural circumstances of the organisation concerned. It also provides detailed guidelines for undertaking actual change projects. Nevertheless, it is argued that managing change is a complex and potentially perilous task, which relies to a large extent on the competence and commitment of managers for its success.

For this reason, Chapter 10 reviews the case for considering managerial competence to be the key factor in successful change. The conclusion reached is that whilst managerial competence is important, managers do not operate in a vacuum; they are constrained or assisted by the culture of the organisation in which they work. It follows that to create the conditions for successful change, managers may need to bring about cultural change. This poses a dilemma for managers: they are both the guardians and the beneficiaries of the existing culture. To bring about such a change will require them to transform the beliefs and values they have grown up with and cherish, and perhaps also to threaten their own position. However, if they do not create the conditions for and bring about change, the result may be their dismissal due to the poor performance of their companies. Therefore, in the competitive world of the 1990s, for organisations who need to replace outmoded values and practices, managing change successfully will depend upon changing managers, through improvement if possible – or replacement if necessary.

Part One

The development of organisation theory

1

From trial and error to the science of management: *the rise of organisation theory*

Introduction

In Britain and the rest of the industrial world today, it is almost impossible to imagine life without the plethora of organisations which make up and facilitate our everyday existence. Yet organisations in their modern form – indeed, in any form – were virtually unknown before the Industrial Revolution, 200 years ago. In the intervening period, not only have organisations, in their many shapes, sizes and manifestations, come to reach into every facet of our lives, but they have also acquired an equally diverse range of theories, nostrums and semi-sacrosanct beliefs about how they should be structured and managed.

This chapter sets out to explore and discuss the origins of organisations, from the Industrial Revolution to the early years of the twentieth century, when the first detailed and comprehensive theory of organisations began to take shape. The chapter begins by showing how the rise of commerce created the conditions for the emergence of the factory system, the precursor of all modern organisations. It is argued that the driving force behind this development was the merchant class. It will also be stressed that two key features of the early factory system were its ad hoc, trial-and-error nature, and the antagonistic relationship between owners and employees, or – to use the terminology of the period – masters and servants.

The chapter then goes on to show that, as the nineteenth century progressed and organisations grew in number and size, trial and error increasingly gave way to more considered and consistent approaches to work organisation. This development was especially pronounced in the USA and continental Europe, as industrial leadership moved away from Britain and towards these areas.

What emerged, separately, were three different but complementary attempts by Frederick Taylor in the USA, Henri Fayol in France and Max Weber in Germany to replace the ad hoc, rule-of-thumb approach to organisations with a universally-applicable blueprint or theory for how they should operate. These three approaches later coalesced into what became known as the Classical school of organisation theory. This approach to organisations is characterised by the horizontal and hierarchical division of labour, the minimisation of human skills and discretion, and the attempt to construe organisations as rational-scientific entities.

The chapter concludes by arguing that the Classical approach, whilst being a significant advance on what went before, was badly flawed. In particular, its view of human nature and motivation was not only inaccurate, but also alienated workers from, and made them resentful of the organisations which employed them.

The rise of commerce and the birth of the factory

The pivotal event which shaped the world into the form we now see around us was the British Industrial Revolution, which began in the late eighteenth century. Before it, most societies were based on small-scale, self-sufficient agricultural production, with the vast majority of the population, some 80–90 per cent, living in the countryside. By the end of the nineteenth century, after the Industrial Revolution had run its course, the reverse became the case, in the industrialised countries at least, with most people living in urban centres and depending on industrial and commercial activities for their livelihood (Landes, 1969).

The key development of the Industrial Revolution towards this pro-cess of change was the creation of the factory system. It was this that gave the impetus to, and created the model for all that was to follow. As Weber (1928:302) pointed out, the factory's distinguishing charac-teristic was 'in general ... not the implements of work applied but the concentration of ownership of workplace, means of work, source of power and raw materials in one and the same hand, that of the entre-preneur'. Or, to put it another way, it was the way the entrepreneur 'organised' the elements of production which distinguished it from what went before.

This tells us what changed, but it does not explain why or how in a few score years organisations came to dominate our lives. To answer this, it is necessary to appreciate the great surge of economic activity – especially the international trade in textile products – which arose in the seventeenth and eighteenth centuries. This trade gave an enormous impetus to textile production, which in turn had a knock-on effect in all other spheres of economic activity (Mathias, 1969).

Before and during the early part of the Industrial Revolution, textile production was carried out as an agricultural by-occupation based on family units. However, as demand increased in the eighteenth century, some 'men and women [became] specialist spinners or weavers, thinking first of wool, treating work on the land as, at most, a by-occupation' (Ashton, 1948:23). Allied to this, a new mechanism sprang up to link producer and consumer: the 'putting-out' system, whereby a large merchant would 'put out' work to a number of independent domestic producers.

The advantage to the merchant was threefold: it was cheap – there were few overheads; it was flexible – production could be easily expanded or contracted; and it avoided the difficulties involved in directly employing a workforce. However, as demand continued to increase in the late eighteenth century, this system became more complex and more costly, and eventually it became too cumbersome (Pollard, 1965). The chain of intermediaries linking producer to consumer became increasingly difficult for the large merchant to control. There were many problems with the putting-out mechanism: dishonesty (on both sides) was rife; deliveries were late; and quality often poor. Laws attempting to control producers could do nothing to rectify the fundamental weaknesses in the system. The incompatibility between the large and complex organisation of distribution and the multitude of tiny domestic workshop units, unsupervised and unsupervisable, was bound to set up tensions and drive merchants to seek new ways of production – ways whereby they could establish their own managerial control over the production process (Pollard, 1965).

There was also an incompatibility between different cultures. For the merchant, the expansion of markets was a chance to increase profits in order to live in the grand style. For the rural domestic producer, involved in long hours of backbreaking work, it created the conditions for increased leisure. As Marglin (1976:35) commented: 'wages rose and workers insisted on taking out a portion of their gains in the form of greater leisure. However sensible this may have been from their own point of view, it is no way for an enterprising capitalist to get ahead.'

Therefore, it was the merchant who began the move towards the factory system – not because the merchant had an innate desire to run factories or exercise direct control over labour, but in order to take full advantage of expanding market opportunities to reap greater rewards.

Nevertheless, there was no headlong rush to create a new economic order overnight. The earliest factories, if that is not too grand a word for them, were small, unpowered weaving or spinning sheds which used existing technology and methods. A few very large factories – such as Wedgwood's Etruria Works in Stoke-on-Trent – were established, but these were the rare exceptions. Indeed, in 1780, the investment in fixed equipment and stock in the textile industry, which was the leading edge of the Industrial Revolution, was only £10 per worker, and the average factory employed no more than 10 or 12 people. By 1830, when the textile industry had grown to employ 100,000 people and the average factory size was 137 workers, the investment in fixed equipment and stock had only increased to £15 per worker, and 50 per cent of the workforce were still home-based (Hobsbawm, 1968; Pollard, 1965; Tillett, 1970). Given this situation, it is hardly surprising that capital investment was quickly recovered and that it was running expenses, mainly wages and raw materials, which formed the bulk of manufacturing costs. It is this, and the original motive for moving to the factory system in the first place (to have greater control over labour), which explains the prevailing attitude of employers towards labour in the nineteenth century.

The relationship between employers and employees

Employers based their attitude towards employees on two basic propositions:

1 Labour is unreliable, lazy and will only work when tightly controlled and closely supervised.
2 The main controllable business cost is labour; therefore the key to increased profits is to cheapen its cost, and/or increase its productivity, by getting employees to work harder, or for longer hours, for the same, or less, money.

In this respect, as contemporary writers such as Babbage (1835) and Ure (1835) observed, workers' skill was seen as at best an inconvenience and at worst a threat, because it could be scarce, costly and allow workers a strong bargaining position.

As might be expected, employers' hostility was reciprocated by labour. Workers exhibited a strong dislike for, and reluctance to become part of the factory system. As Pollard (1965) noted, this was for three main reasons:

1 It involved a wholesale change of culture and environment and the destruction of small, tightly-knit communities in which they lived. Hard though the life of cottage industry was, it had given workers a measure of independence and some control over what they did, when they did it and how.
2 The discipline of the factory was harsh and unremitting with men, women and small children all expected to work long hours, often seven days a week, in appalling conditions.
3 Given the lack of alternative organisational forms on which to establish factory life, employers often modelled them on workhouses or prisons. Indeed, to square the circle, some workhouses and prisons turned themselves into factories and their inmates into little more than slaves. Thus, factories acquired the same stigma as was attached to prisons and workhouses.

Thus, the antagonism that existed between owners and workers was based on a genuine clash of interests – one which has echoed through British industrial relations ever since.

If this picture of the factory system in the nineteenth century seems bleak to us, it is nevertheless accurate, as is shown in the work of its proponents such as Charles Babbage and Andrew Ure, social reformers such as Seebohm Rowntree, political activists such as Frederick Engels and contemporary novelists such as Charles Dickens. In defence of the factory owners, who must take responsibility for what emerged, it must be said that their own experience was limited and there were no textbooks to guide them. That they should 'copy' what models existed reflected both the common view of labour amongst the owning classes, and a lack of alternative organisational forms on which to base the emergent factory system.

However, the nineteenth century can be seen as a time when managers in industry and commerce began to develop a more systematic and less harsh and arbitrary approach to the organisation of work. Nevertheless, the developing factory system could not shake off the legacy of its origins or ignore the continuing battle between labour and management over control, rewards and skill.

Organisation of work

The system of organising work which came to characterise industrial life at the end of the nineteenth century was based on the hierarchical division of labour, and owed much to the work of Adam Smith, enshrined in his book: *The Wealth of Nations* (1776). Smith used the now famous example of pin-making to illustrate what he saw as the advantages of the division of labour. He pointed out that a pin could be made entirely by one person doing everything, or by a number of different people each specialising in one aspect of its production. He believed the latter was more efficient, for three reasons:

1 A worker who constantly performs one simple task will quickly acquire greater dexterity than one who performs a variety of tasks.
2 It avoids the loss of time necessitated by one person moving from one task to another.
3 The concentration of attention on one special task leads to the invention of machines which aid the productivity of labour and allow one person to do the work previously performed by many.

Smith's ideas were given flesh and form by pioneering factory owners such as Josiah Wedgwood, and Matthew Boulton and James Watt. At his Etruria pottery works, Wedgwood developed a production system which split the work process into separate departments, each with its own specialist supervisor. Work was organised almost on a flow-line basis with the skill involved in each operation reduced to a minimum in order, in Wedgwood's own words, 'to make machines of men as cannot err' (quoted in Tillett, 1970:37). Matthew Boulton and James Watt developed a similar approach at their Soho Works in Birmingham in the 1770s. They also kept detailed production records, a practice virtually unknown at the time (Roll, 1930). Wedgwood, Boulton, Watt, and a few others were the architects of the factory system. By their organisation of work on and off the shopfloor, they created models which later managers would copy and adapt to their own needs and circumstances.

Charles Babbage (1835) put forward a method of applying the division of labour principle to the detailed analysis of any job. He emphasised the need for, and advantage of dividing tasks between and within mental and manual labour. He envisaged three 'classes' employed in the work process: the entrepreneur and his technical specialists who would design machines and plan the form of work organisation; operative engineers and managers who would be responsible for executing such plans and designs, based on only partial knowledge of the processes involved; and the mass of employees, needing only a low level of skill, who would undertake the actual work. Thus, in Babbage's (1835: vii) view:

> ... *the master manufacturer, by dividing the work to be executed into different processes, each requiring different degrees of skill or force, can purchase exactly the precise quality of both which is necessary for each process* ...

Andrew Ure (1836:viii – ix), one of Babbage's contemporaries, drew special attention to the role that technology could play in this process:

> *By developing machines ... which require only unskilled instead of skilled labour, the cost of labour can be reduced [and] the bargaining position of the worker reduced.*

It becomes clear why workers not only opposed the factory system, but, even when it became established, continued to oppose strongly changes in work practices and the introduction of new equipment. Even in the present day, the tendency is for workers to feel apprehensive towards – if not downright resistant to – change (Smith *et al.*, 1982). Nevertheless, despite the increasing opposition of 'organised' labour, the work practices associated with the factory system gradually permeated every aspect of industrial and commercial life, albeit only on a piecemeal basis. Even by the end of the nineteenth century, there was no unified or accepted approach which managers could apply to organisations in their entirety. Those who created and controlled the large business organisations which were becoming the norm in many industrial countries, especially the USA, still had to rely on their own experience and judgment, but with growing frustration over their inability to control and organise these bodies fully and effectively.

The USA

In the USA, for a number of reasons, the need for a workable, overall approach to organisational design and control was perhaps more acute than anywhere else. The USA had industrialised far more rapidly and on a larger scale than any other nation. Only in the 1860s, after the Civil War, did the USA begin to industrialise in earnest; but by the end of the nineteenth century it was well on its way to becoming the premier industrial nation, leaving Britain and Germany struggling in its wake. In addition, the size of organisations was typically vast compared to those in Europe. Whilst the average British business was still the small, family-owned firm, in the USA it was the monopoly, which dominated an entire industry, or the conglomerate, which had substantial holdings in several industries. As an example, in 1900 Dale Carnegie sold his steel company for the enormous sum of $419 million to a group of financiers. They merged it with other steel concerns to create a monopoly steel producer employing 200,000 workers and valued at $1.3 billion. This was at a time when the British industry, which had led the world, comprised 100 blast furnaces owned by 95 separate companies.

As might be imagined, the numbers of Americans employed in factories and offices grew rapidly – almost tripling between 1880 and 1910 (Levine, 1967; Zinn, 1980). Such an increase in demand for labour could not be met by the indigenous population alone and was fuelled by successive waves of immigration. Whilst solving one problem, the shortage of labour, this merely created others. The culture shock of industrial work, a foreign language, and problems of housing and integration created enormous pressures in American society. Consequently, most industries found themselves sitting on a pressure cooker which could, and frequently did, explode in unexpected and violent ways. If management-labour relations were poor in Britain, they were far worse in the USA (Pelling, 1960).

Not surprisingly, therefore, there was great pressure and endeavour to find organisational arrangements which would allow employers to control and organise their employees in a manner that reduced conflict and was cost-effective. This is no doubt why one of the earliest and most enduring approaches to organisation theory emerged in the USA, and why the USA continued to dominate the development of organisation theory.

The Classical approach

As can be seen, at the end of the nineteenth century, there was a clear need to replace the rule-of-thumb approach to organisational design with a more consistent and organisation-wide approach. This was not because of an academic interest in the functioning of organisations, though this was present, but in order to improve their performance, enhance their competitiveness and, an increasing concern at the time, to sustain and legitimise managerial authority. This was certainly the case in the USA, where explosive growth and a workforce suffering from culture shock had created dangerous social pressures which questioned the legitimacy of managerial power, and even the capitalist system itself. This was also true in Europe; although Europe industrialised earlier, it was not only having to come to grips with the increase in size and complexity of business life, but it was also facing considerable, and unexpected, competitive pressure from the USA.

Nevertheless, these difficulties could not quench the innate optimism of the age. It was a time, much more than now, when people dealt in certainties and universal truths. There was a feeling of confidence that any goal, whether it be taming nature or discerning the best way to run a business, could be achieved by the twin power of scientific study and practical experience. All over the industrialised world, groups of managers and technical specialists were forming their own learned societies to exchange experiences, to discuss common problems and to seek out in a scientific and rational fashion the solution to all organisational ills; to discover 'the one best way'.

Out of these endeavours emerged what was later termed the Classical approach to organisational design. It was an approach, as the name suggests, which drew heavily on what had gone before; taking from writers such as Adam Smith and practitioners such as Josiah Wedgwood and leavening their ideas with contemporary experience, views and experiments. This approach, reflecting the age in which it emerged, portrays organisations as machines, and those in them as mere parts which respond to the correct stimulus and whose actions are based on scientific principles. The emphasis was on achieving efficiency in internal functions; seeing organisations as closed and changeless entities unaffected by the outside world. Though this approach first originated in the early part of this century, its influence on managerial practices and assumptions is still strong today, but its credibility amongst academics has waned (Kelly, 1982; Rose, 1988; Scott, 1987).

The Classical approach, or the Scientific-Rational approach as it is sometimes called, whilst not being homogeneous, is characterised by three common propositions:

1 *Organisations are rational entities* – collectivities of individuals focused on the achievement of relatively specific goals through their organisation into highly-formalised, differentiated and efficient structures.
2 *The design of organisations is a science* – through experience, observation and experiment, it has been established that there is one best universal organisational form for all bodies. This is based on

the hierarchical and horizontal division of labour and functions, whereby organisations are conceived of as machines which, once set in motion, inexorably and efficiently will pursue and achieve their pre-selected goals.

3 *People are economic beings* – they are solely motivated by money. This instrumental orientation means that they will try to achieve the maximum reward for the minimum work, and will use whatever bargaining power their skills or knowledge allow to this end. Therefore, jobs must be designed and structured in such a way as to minimise an individual's skill and discretion, and to maximise management control.

The key figures in the development of the Classical approach are Frederick Taylor (1856–1915), and his loyal lieutenants Frank and Lillian Gilbreth, in the USA, Henri Fayol (1841–1925) in France and Max Weber (1864–1920) in Germany. All were writing in the first two decades of the twentieth century, though Weber's work was not generally available in English until the 1940s. Below is an outline of their work.

Frederick Taylor's Scientific Management

Taylor was a highly controversial figure during his lifetime and still remains so more than 75 years after his death in 1915. He was an American engineer who, through his experience as a machinist and manager in the engineering industry, made a major contribution to the development of managerial theory and practice in the twentieth century (Locke, 1982; Rose, 1988).

There can be little doubt that the publication of *The Principles of Scientific Management* in 1911 laid the foundation stone for the development of organisation and management theory. Taylor's primary focus was on the design and analysis of individual tasks; this process inevitably led to changes in the overall structure of organisations. Such was the impact of his work that it created a blueprint for, and legitimised, the activities of managers and their support staff. In so doing, he helped to create the plethora of functions and departments which characterise many modern organisations.

Before Taylor, the average manager tended to operate in an idiosyncratic and arbitrary manner with little or no specialist support. Taylor saw this as being at the root of much industrial unrest and workers' mistrust of management. Though criticised for his anti-labour postures, Taylor was also highly critical of management behaviour, which may account for this group's initial lack of enthusiasm for his ideas (Scott, 1987). After Taylor, managers were left with a 'scientific' blueprint for analysing work and applying his 'one best way' principle to each job in order to gain 'a fair day's work for a fair day's pay'.

These last two phrases sum up Taylor's basic beliefs that:

● It is possible and desirable to establish, through methodical study and the application of scientific principles, the one best way of carrying out any job. Once established, the way must be implemented totally and made to operate consistently.
● Human beings are predisposed to seek the maximum reward for the minimum effort, which Taylor referred to as 'soldiering'. To overcome this, managers must lay down in detail what each worker should do, step by step; ensure through close supervision that the instructions are adhered to; and, to give positive motivation, link pay to performance.

Taylor incorporated those beliefs into his precepts for Scientific Management, comprising three core elements: the systematic collection of knowledge about the work process by managers; the removal or reduction of workers' discretion and control over what they do; and the laying down of standard procedures and times for carrying out each job.

The starting point is the gathering of knowledge:

> *The managers assume ... the burden of gathering together all the traditional knowledge which in the past has been possessed by the workman and then of classifying, tabulating and reducing this knowledge to rules, laws and formulae .... (Taylor, 1911b:36)*

This lays the groundwork for the second stage: increased management control. As long as workers possess a monopoly of knowledge about the work process, increased control is impossible. But once the knowledge is also possessed by managers, it becomes possible not only to establish what workers actually do with their time, but also by 'reducing this knowledge to rules, laws and formulae', to decrease the knowledge that workers need to carry out a given task. It also, importantly, paves the way for the division of labour.

The last stage is that 'All possible brain work should be removed from the shop and centred in the planning ... department ....' (Taylor, 1911a:98–9). The divorce of conception from execution removes control from the worker, who no longer has discretion as to how tasks are carried out:

> *Perhaps the most prominent single element in modern scientific management is the task idea. The work of every workman is fully planned out by management ... and each man receives in most cases complete written instructions, describing in detail the task which he is to accomplish, as well as the means to be used in doing the work. This task specifies not only what is to be done but how it is to be done and the exact time allowed for doing it.*
> *(Taylor, 1911b:39)*

This completes the process of gaining control over workers by managers. The workers become 'human machines', told what to do, when to do it and how long to take. But, more than this, it allows new types of work organisation to be developed, and new work processes and equipment introduced. Thus, workers move from having a monopoly of knowledge and control over their work to a position where the knowledge they have of the work process is minimal, and their control vastly reduced. The result is not only a reduction in the skills required and the wages paid, but also the creation of jobs which are so narrow and tightly-specified that the period needed to train someone to do them is greatly reduced. This removes the last bargaining counter of labour: scarcity of skill.

According to Taylor, this transforms not only workers' jobs but also managers' jobs. 'The man at the head of the business under scientific management is governed by rules and laws ... just as the workman is, and the standards which have been developed are equitable' (Taylor, 1911a:189).

Taylor stated that the 'scientific' basis and equal applicability of his methods meant they were neutral between labour and management; therefore they legitimised managerial action to analyse and change work methods, because managers are merely applying science to determine the best method of work. He claimed that his approach benefited both the worker and the company. The worker was enabled and encouraged to work to his maximum performance and be rewarded accordingly, whilst the company benefited from higher output.

Though often claiming that his system was innovative and unique, which in terms of its presentation as scientific and neutral it was, it can be seen that Taylor drew on many of the management practices and attitudes towards labour which were prevalent during the nineteenth century. He was also heavily indebted to many contemporaries and associates who helped develop the work study techniques necessary to implement Scientific Management (Kempner, 1970). However, his greatest debt was to Frank and Lillian Gilbreth, who were not only pioneers of work study but also Taylor's most vigorous promoters, both before and after his death in 1915.

The Gilbreths and work study

Much of modern work study (a central element of the Classical approach) owes its origins to the methods and techniques developed in the first quarter of this century by Frank and Lillian Gilbreth (Gilbreth and Gilbreth, 1914). The work was initiated by Frank Gilbreth who was a contemporary of Taylor's. In many respects their careers were similar. Taylor began his career on the shopfloor and later rose to eminence as a manager and management consultant. Frank Gilbreth rose from being a bricklayer to running his own construction company, as well as being a leading campaigner for Scientific Management. Lillian Gilbreth was a trained psychologist who collaborated closely with her husband (Thickett, 1970).

The Gilbreths developed a number of procedures for breaking work down into its constituent components. Flow process charts were used which split work into five basic elements: operations, transportation, inspection, storage and delay. Arising out of this, they developed a method of minutely analysing tasks which broke handwork into seventeen basic elements. Examples of these are:

Grasp: Begins when hand or body member touches an object. Consists of gaining control of an object.
Release: Begins when hand or body member begins to relax control of object. Consists of letting go of object.
Plan: Begins when hand or body members are idle or making random movements while worker decides on course of action. Consists of determining a course of action. Ends when course of action is determined.

The purpose of this micro-analysis was not only to establish what was done, but also to discover if a better method of performing the task in question could be developed. In this respect, they did much original work in establishing the distinction between necessary and unnecessary movements. The latter were to be eliminated immediately and the former further analysed in more detail to see if they could be improved, combined or replaced by special equipment.

If this sounds remarkably similar to Adam Smith's pin factory, mentioned earlier, this is no accident. The Classical approach is descended from Smith through the nineteenth century pioneers of work organisation. Though remarkable in the level of minute detail to which they reduced tasks, the Gilbreths were only, as they saw it, taking Smith's maxims to their logical conclusion. If in the process they give the impression of dealing more with machines than people, that too is no accident. Like others who propounded the Classical approach, they viewed organisations and workers very much as machines. The work study methods developed by the Gilbreths and their successors are still widely used today, not just in manufacturing industries, but in all areas of life from hospitals to computer programming (Grant, 1983).

The Gilbreths were also concerned that, having established the best way to carry out a task, this should not be undermined by selecting the wrong person to carry it out or by creating the wrong environment. Therefore, they set about analysing employee selection and establishing environmental criteria with the same determination as they had applied to analysing work performance. However, in neither case could they achieve the same micro-analysis that characterised their work study technique. What finally emerged were effectively opinions based on their own 'experience', rather than the product of experiment and observation.

The Gilbreths were devoted to one objective – to discover the best method of doing any job. They were firm supporters of Frederick Taylor and his work and saw their efforts as contributing to the enhancement of Scientific Management. Like Taylor, they saw themselves as creating a neutral system which benefited both labour and management. They felt that any increase in boredom or monotony brought about by their methods would be compensated for by workers' opportunities to earn more money.

While the Gilbreths and Taylor devoted their efforts to improving the productivity of individual workers, there were others who took a wider but complementary perspective.

Henri Fayol and the principles of organisation

Writing in France at the same time as Taylor was propounding his views on Scientific Management in the USA, Fayol based his work on his experience as a practising manager rather than on experimentation. Fayol trained as a mining engineer and spent all of his working life in the French coal mining industry. He rose to the position of Chief Executive, taking over an ailing company and turning it in to a much admired and financially strong enterprise by the time he retired. In his 'retirement' he founded the Centre for Administrative Studies in France which had a profound influence on both the public and private sectors in France. Unlike Taylor and the Gilbreths, his focus was on efficiency at the organisational level rather than the task level: top down rather than bottom up (Cuthbert, 1970; Fayol, 1949).

Given his background, it is not surprising that Fayol was more concerned with general rather than departmental or supervisory management, and with overall organisational control as opposed to the details of tasks. Because of this, his views should be seen as complementing those of Taylor rather than duplicating or contradicting them.

As the following shows, Fayol (like all the Classical school) was concerned to develop a universal approach to management which was applicable to any organisation: 'There is no one doctrine of administration for business and another for affairs of state; administrative doctrine is universal. Principles and general rules which hold good for business hold good for the state too, and the reverse applies' (quoted in Cuthbert, 1970:111). Therefore, in business, public administration, or indeed any form of organisation, the same principles apply.

The principles of organisation which Fayol saw as being universally applicable were (Mullins, 1989:202–3):

1   *Division of work* – the object is to produce more and better work from the same effort, through the advantages of specialisation.
2   *Authority and responsibility* – wherever authority is exercised, responsibility arises. The application of sanctions is needed to encourage useful actions and to discourage their opposite.
3   *Discipline* – is essential for the efficient operation of the organisation. Discipline is in essence the outward mark of respect for agreements between the organisation and its members.
4   *Unity of command* – in any action, any employee should receive orders from one superior only; dual command is a perpetual source of conflicts.
5   *Unity of direction* – in order to co-ordinate and focus effort, there should be one leader and one plan for any group of activities with the same objective.
6   *Subordination of individual or group interests* – the interest of the organisation should take precedence over individual or group interests.

7 *Remuneration of personnel* – methods of payment should be fair, encourage keenness by rewarding well-directed effort, but not lead to over-payment.

8 *Centralisation* – the degree of centralisation is a question of proportion and will vary in particular organisations.

9 *Scalar chain* – is the chain of superiors from the ultimate authority to the lowest ranks. Respect for line authority must be reconciled with activities which require urgent action, and with the need to provide for some measure of initiative at all levels of authority.

10 *Order* – includes material order and social order. The object of material order is avoidance of loss. There should be an appointed place for each thing, and each thing in its appointed place. Social order requires good organisation and good selection.

11 *Equity* – there needs to be fairness in dealing with employees throughout all levels of the scalar chain.

12 *Stability of tenure of personnel* – generally, prosperous organisations have a stable managerial personnel.

13 *Initiative* – represents a source of strength for the organisation and should be encouraged and developed.

14 *Esprit de corps* – should be fostered, as harmony and unity among members of the organisation are a great strength in the organisation.

According to Fayol (1949), it is the prime responsibility of management to enact these principles. Consequently, in order to achieve this, he prescribed the main duties of management as:

- *Planning* – examining the future, deciding what needs to be done and developing a plan of action.
- *Organising* – bringing together the resources, human and material, and developing the structure to carry out the activities of the organisation.
- *Command* – ensuring that all employees perform their jobs well and in the best interests of the organisation.
- *Co-ordination* – verifying that the activities of the organisation work harmoniously together to achieve its goals.
- *Control* – establishing that plans, instructions and commands are correctly carried out.

Fayol was a gifted and highly successful businessman who attributed his success to the application of his principles rather than personal ability. Certainly, he was one of the pioneers of management theory, and many of his principles are still taught and practised today.

However, clearly, part of the success of his work lay in the fact that he was writing for a receptive audience, and at a time when management practice and ideas were becoming international currency. Just as Taylor's system arose at the time when a need for a management theory had grown amongst the business community in the USA, so Fayol's was aimed at a similar demand in France, where the business community was developing rapidly but on an ad hoc basis. A similar approach to management was also being developed in Germany at this time by Max Weber.

Max Weber on bureaucracy

Though Weber's work on bureaucracy is much clearer and more detailed, there is a considerable affinity between it and Fayol's work on the principles of organisation. Both were concerned with the overall structuring of organisations, and the principles which guide senior managers in this task. Though writing in the early part of the century, it is unlikely that Weber's work was known to Fayol, Taylor or the Gilbreths.

Unlike other proponents of the Classical approach, Weber was an academic – a sociologist – rather than a practitioner. Also, his work on administrative structures was only a limited aspect of his major interest in the development of Western civilisation. From this Weber concluded that the rise of civilisation was a story of power and domination. He noted (Weber, 1946) that each social epoch was characterised by a different form of political rule, and that for a ruling elite to sustain its power and dominance, it was essential for them both to gain legitimacy and to develop an administrative apparatus to enforce and support their authority.

Weber identified three types of authority based on the following grounds (Weber, 1947:328):

1 *Rational-legal* – resting on a belief in the 'legality' of patterns of normative rule, and the right of those elevated to authority under such rules to issue commands.
2 *Traditional* – resting on an established belief in the sanctity of immemorial traditions and the legitimacy of those exercising authority under them.
3 *Charismatic* – resting on devotion to the specific and exceptional sanctity, heroism or exemplary character of an individual person, and of the normative patterns or order revealed or ordained by them.

Weber argued that, in the context of the rational-legal authority structures which prevailed in Western societies in the twentieth century, the bureaucratic approach to organisation was the most appropriate and efficient. Under bureaucracy, laws, rules, procedures and pre-defined routines are dominant and not subject to the vagaries and preferences of individuals. They give form to a clearly-defined system of administration – whether it be public administration, such as the Department of Social Security, or private administration, such as the Halifax Building Society – where the execution of routine, pre-programmed procedures is all-important.

Weber considered this approach to be both appropriate, because it was the ideal tool for a centralised administration where the legitimacy of those in power was underpinned by the rule of law; and efficient, because the bureaucratic approach mechanises the process of administration in the same way that machines automate the production process in factories.

Weber frequently asserted that the development of bureaucracy eliminates human fallibility:

> *Its [bureaucracy's] specific nature ... develops the more perfectly the more bureaucracy is 'dehumanised', the more completely its success in eliminating from official business, love, hatred, and purely personal, irrational and emotional elements which escape calculation. (Weber, 1946: 217)*

Bureaucracy is characterised by the division of labour, a clear authority structure, formal selection procedures, detailed rules and regulations and impersonal relationships. How Weber saw these organisational characteristics supporting and reproducing rational-legal authority is best seen by contrasting them with the traditional administrative forms based on patronage (Weber, 1946 and 1947) (see Table 1.1).

Table 1.1

Characteristics of rational-legal authority	Characteristics of traditional authority
Areas of jurisdiction are clearly specified: the regular activities required of personnel are allocated in a fixed way as official duties.	The allocation of labour is not defined, but depends on assignments made by the leader, which can be changed at any time.

Characteristics of rational-legal authority	Characteristics of traditional authority
The organisation of offices follows the principle of hierarchy: each lower office is controlled and supervised by a higher one. However, the scope of authority of superiors over subordinates is circumscribed, and lower offices enjoy a right of appeal.	Authority relations are diffuse, being based on personal loyalty, and are not ordered into clear hierarchies.
An intentionally established system of abstract rules governs official decisions and actions. These rules are relatively stable and exhaustive, and can be learned. Decisions are recorded in permanent files.	General rules of administration either do not exist or are vaguely stated, ill-defined, and subject to change at the whim of the leader. No attempt is made to keep permanent records of transactions.
The 'means of production or administration' – for example, tools and equipment or rights and privileges – belong to the office, not the office-holder, and may not be appropriated. Personal property is clearly separated from official property, and working space from living quarters.	There is no separation of a ruler's personal household business from the larger 'public' business under their direction.
Officials are personally free, selected on the basis of technical qualifications, appointed to office (not elected), and recompensed by salary.	Officials are often selected from among those who are personally dependent on the leader – slaves, serfs, and relatives, for example. Selection is governed by arbitrary criteria, and remuneration often takes the form of benefices – rights granted to individuals which, for instance, allow them access to the ruler's stores, or give them grants of land from which they can appropriate the fees or taxes. Benefices, like fiefs in feudalistic systems, may become hereditary and sometimes are bought and sold.
Employment by the organisation constitutes a career for officials. An official is a full-time employee and looks forward to a lifelong career in the agency. After a trial period, he or she gains tenure of position and is protected against arbitrary dismissal.	Officials serve at the pleasure of the leader, and so lack clear expectations about the future and security of tenure.

For Weber, therefore, bureaucracy provided a rational-legal form of organisation which distinguished itself from, and eradicated the faults and unfairness of previous administrative forms by its mechanical adherence to set rules, procedures and patterns of authority. It removed the system of patronage and eliminated human variability, replacing it by the rule of law. In Weber's view, bureaucracy was universally applicable to all organisations, big or small, public or private, industrial or commercial. The influence of Weber's work, and its application, especially to large organisations, can be seen in the way that bureaucracy is an ever-present and pervasive feature of modern life.

Conclusions

It is not an inevitable fact of life that modern societies are characterised by organisations, of all shapes and sizes; rather that they are the product of a particular combination of circumstances. The rise of capitalism in Britain and other European countries in the seventeenth and eighteenth centuries created new opportunities and new problems which could not be accommodated under the old order. The result was a move away from self-sufficient, autonomous, individual units to collective units of production controlled by an entrepreneur. This trend was gradual, arising as an ad hoc response to new challenges. However, as the nineteenth century progressed, the need for a more coherent approach to organisational design emerged, which crystallised into the Classical approach.

Though writing in different countries and from different perspectives, the proponents of what later came to be known as the Classical approach all adopted a similar perspective to what they saw as one of the main issues for modern societies: how to create organisations that efficiently and effectively pursue their objectives. Taylor, supported by the work study techniques of the Gilbreths and others, concentrated substantially on the operational level, arguing for his 'scientific' method of analysing, designing and managing jobs. Fayol concentrated on the other end of the same problem: the overall administration and control of organisations. Weber set organisations in a wider historical and societal context, bringing together both the detailed tasks to be carried out in organisations and general principles governing them.

Taken together, their views are complementary, and reflect an approach to organisations and people based upon a number of basic assumptions:

- There is a 'one best way' for all organisations to be structured and operate.
- This approach is founded on the rule of law and legitimate managerial authority.
- Organisations are rational entities: collectivities consistently and effectively pursuing rational goals.
- People are motivated to work solely by financial reward.
- Human fallibility and emotions, at all levels in the organisation, should be eliminated because they threaten the consistent application of the rule of law and the efficient pursuit of goals.
- For this reason, the most appropriate form of job design is achieved through the use of the hierarchical and horizontal division of labour to create narrowly-focused jobs encased in tight procedures and rules which remove discretion, dictate what the job-holder does and how they do it, and which allow their work to be closely monitored and controlled by their direct superiors.

Seen from the perspective of the early twentieth century, when there appeared to be a substantial questioning of, and challenge to, managerial authority by workers, the Classical approach had many merits: not least in its attempt to replace arbitrary and capricious management with rules and procedures which apply equally to everyone in the organisation.

Similarly, it is important to see this work in terms of what went before. Weber explicitly drew on history to support his views; the historical debts of the others, though not openly acknowledged in their work, are clearly there. From Smith, through Wedgwood, Boulton and Watt, Babbage and Ure can be traced key elements of the Classical approach: the division of labour, the distrust of human variability, the need for written rules, procedures and records, the need for rational and consistent management and objectives. Parallel to these are key themes that run through other aspects of nineteenth century life: the search for the rational, scientific, universal principles which govern the natural world, the belief in the Protestant work ethic, the emergence of Social Darwinism, the greater democratisation of societies and the gradual reduction of laws favouring one class or group over another.

All these strands coalesced – not always neatly – in the Classical approach, creating the first real and consistent attempt at a theory, a set of guidelines, for constructing and managing organisations. However, given that it grew out of and was designed to meet particular circumstances, so its appropriateness began to be questioned and criticised as these circumstances changed. Taylor and his adherents have been criticised both for their lack of scientific rigour and their one-dimensional view of human motivation (Burnes, 1989; Kelly, 1982). Fayol has been attacked on three fronts: firstly, that his principles are mere truisms; secondly, that they are based on questionable premises; and lastly, that the principles occur in pairs or clusters of contradictory statements (Massie, 1965; Simon, 1957). Likewise, Weber's arguments for bureaucracy have also received criticism. For instance, Udy (1959) questioned Weber's assertion that bureaucracies are necessarily rational, whilst Parsons (1947) suggested that Weber puts forward contradictory arguments for the basis of authority within bureaucracies.

In particular, although the Classical approach sought to eliminate the worst excesses of the arbitrary approach to management which had existed previously, it also incorporated the negative view of human nature which existed alongside, and strongly influenced, past management practices. Consequently one of the main criticisms of the Classical approach as a whole is that its view of people is negative. Bennis (1959:263) called the Classical perspective one of 'organisations without people' because it is founded on the belief that people can be reduced to the level of cogs in a machine. The counter-argument is that not only is it impossible to remove the element of human variability from the running of organisations, but it is also counterproductive to attempt to do so. Rather than making people work more efficiently in pursuit of organisational goals, it alienates them from their work and makes them resentful of it (Mayo, 1933). This was one of the central issues taken up by proponents of the Human Relations approach which emerged in the 1930s as a reaction to the 'de-humanised' Classical approach. This, together with Contingency Theory – the third approach to organisations to emerge in the twentieth century – will be discussed in the next chapter.

2

Developments in organisation theory: *from certainty to contingency*

Introduction

If the nineteenth century laid the foundations for modern organisations, then the twentieth century has seen the structures that they support rise to dizzy heights. The pre-eminent example of this is General Motors, which, with sales in excess of $126 billion, is the largest company in the world (Fortune, 1990). Running General Motors, with its 775,000 employees, is akin to running a small country, not just in terms of size and turnover, but also in terms of the problems it faces. Nor is General Motors alone in this; the twentieth century has seen an enormous increase in the size and complexity of enterprises and, in many cases – such as General Motors and Ford in the USA, and ICI and Lucas Industries in Britain – a move from being purely national companies to becoming genuinely multinational.

It would indeed be surprising if these developments in organisational life had not stimulated academics and practitioners to greater efforts to understand the activities of, and provide guidelines for organisations. This could have led to the development and strengthening of the Classical approach, and clearly this did happen to an extent (*see* the work of Ralph Davis, 1928, on rational planning). However, as this chapter will show, in the main, what emerged were two new approaches to organisations: the Human Relations approach, which originated in the 1930s, and the Contingency approach, which emerged in the 1960s.

The Human Relations approach was a reaction against the mechanistic view of organisations put forward in the Classical approach. It attempted to reintroduce the human element into organisational life, and claim for itself the title of the 'one best way'. Contingency Theory, on the other hand, began by rejecting the idea that there is a 'one best way' for all organisations. In general, it argues that the structures and practices of an organisation are dependent (i.e. contingent) on the circumstances it faces. Therefore, the twentieth century has seen organisation theory move from the certainty of the 'one best way' approach to the variability of the Contingency approach.

The context for the emergence of the Human Relations and Contingency approaches was the rapid and headlong expansion of organisations that has been taking place since the early years of this century. In a classic study, Chandler (1962) charted these developments in the USA. In particular, he noted the move from unitary 'U-Form' structures (the conventional organisational form composed of a central office and several functionally-organised departments) to multi-divisional 'M-Form' structures (each of which contains functionally-differentiated departments). He pointed out that the M-Form company began to make its appearance in the USA shortly after the First World War and was apparently independently developed by a number of major companies: Du Pont; General Motors; Standard Oil of New Jersey; and Sears, Roebuck.

Chandler identified four phases in the development of American companies which led to the move from U-Form to M-Form structures. The first phase, just after the American Civil War, was one of rapid expansion and resource accumulation, mainly through vertical integration. This was the period of the larger-than-life entrepreneurs, such as Rockefeller, Du Pont and Carnegie, who built enormous personal fortunes. The second phase saw a new generation of professional managers emerge, who were akin to Taylor, Fayol and Weber in their rational and methodical approach. In this phase, attention was devoted to the reduction of unit costs and the co-ordination of diverse functional activities. Phase three, from the turn of the century to the First World War, saw firms continuing to expand, but doing so by moving into related fields, which allowed them to capitalise on their technical skills and marketing expertise. In the fourth phase, after the First World War, a few large companies that had diversified and were attempting to manage several related product lines found it necessary to reorganise to gain greater efficiency in the use of their resources. What emerged was the decentralised or M-Form structure, the chief advantage of which was that it brought about a clear separation of strategic from operational decision making. Day-to-day activities became the responsibility of divisional managers, whilst the strategic, long-term development of businesses was located at the head office level.

In the last 50 years, this process has continued apace in all industrialised countries. Though in recent years we have seen moves to 'un-
bundle' some of these very large enterprises, the trend is still towards
agglomeration, as is witnessed by the activities of Rupert Murdoch in
the communications field, GEC and the Hanson Trust in manufacturing industry, Nestlé's takeover of Rowntree Mackintosh in the con-
fectionery industry and Fujitsu's takeover of ICL in the computer
industry. Nor is this growth in size and complexity confined to the
business world. It can be seen in the growth of local and national government departments and agencies, the internationalisation of voluntary bodies such as Oxfam, and even in the activities of political
parties, which have become not only more sophisticated in their approach to publicity, but also more professional in terms of fund-raising.

As the following shows, organisation theory has responded to these
events in the form of the Human Relations approach and Contingency
approach. Both can marshal strong arguments in their favour but
both, like the Classical model, are also the objects of fierce criticism.

The Human Relations approach

Even while the Classical approach was still struggling to establish itself, the seeds of a new approach to organisational design were already being sown. The origins of what later became known as the
Human Relations approach can be traced to studies on work fatigue
carried out in Britain during the First World War and work in the
USA, at the same time, on employee selection which gave new insights into employee motivation (Burnes, 1989). This work was developed and extended in the 1920s by Myers (1934) in Britain and
Mayo (1933) in the USA, providing new perspectives on organisational
life. These studies gave substance to a growing suspicion that the
Classical view of organisations as being peopled by machines motivated by money was badly flawed. Indeed, in 1915, the United States
Congress took a stand against the use of Taylor's techniques in their
establishments; although Scientific Management was becoming more
accepted in private industry and was beginning to cross national
boundaries, not always successfully (Rose, 1988). Similarly, though
the growth of bureaucracy was gathering pace, so too was people's antagonism to faceless, machine-like organisations where employees and
customers alike lost their individuality and became numbers.

Nevertheless, it was not until the 1930s and 1940s that substantial
evidence emerged in print which challenged the Classical view of

organisations and allowed the Human Relations approach to stand alongside, if not quite supersede, it. The main precepts of the Human Relations approach were almost diametrically opposed to those of the Classical approach. In particular, it argued that:

- *Man is an emotional rather than an economic-rational being* – human needs are far more diverse and complex than the one-dimensional image that Taylor and his fellow travellers conceded. People have emotional and social needs which can have more influence on their behaviour at work than financial incentives.
- *Organisations are co-operative, social systems rather than mechanical ones* – people seek to meet their emotional needs through the formation of informal but influential workplace social groups.
- *Organisations are composed of informal structures, rules and norms as well as formal practices and procedures* – these informal rules, patterns of behaviour and communication, status, norms and friendships are created by people to meet their own emotional needs. Because of this they can have more influence on individual behaviour and performance, and ultimately overall organisational performance, than the formal structure and control mechanisms laid down by management.

For these reasons, organisations can never be the predictable, well-oiled machines envisaged by the Classical approach. Therefore, in most respects, the Human Relations approach represents a distinct break from the ideas of the Classical school. However, in two important ways, similarities exist. The first is their shared belief in organisations as closed, changeless entities. Once organisations have structured themselves in accordance with the correct precepts, then, regardless of external or even internal developments, no further changes are necessary or desirable. This leads on to the second similarity: both believed they had discovered the 'one best way'; regardless of the type, nature or size of organisation, their precepts were the correct ones.

With that in mind, we can now begin to examine in detail the case for Human Relations. Despite the work of precursors, no one doubts that the Human Relations approach began in earnest with the famous Hawthorne Experiments.

Elton Mayo and the Hawthorne Experiments

The name of Elton Mayo is inextricably linked with the 'Hawthorne Experiments' which took place in the Western Electric Company's Hawthorne Works in Chicago during the 1920s and 1930s. Though Mayo publicised and took credit for masterminding these, the exact role played by him is unclear even to the most rigorous of investigators (Smith, 1987). Did Mayo design and implement the experiments himself? What was the role of his colleagues at Harvard? How frequently did he visit the Hawthorne Works? The questions are now unanswerable; what is clear is that his writings on the Hawthorne Experiments and his later work have given Mayo the reputation, perhaps undeserved, of being the dominant figure in the Human Relations movement (Rose, 1988). Having stated the difficulty in separating out the myth from the man, we should not let that undermine the significance of the Hawthorne work or what we know of Mayo and his colleagues' contribution, even if we cannot clearly identify who did what.

The Hawthorne programme was originally devised by Western Electric's own industrial engineers in the 1920s to examine the effects of various levels of lighting on workers' productivity. The engineers established control and experimental groups; the latter were subject to different levels of illumination as they carried out their work whilst the lighting of the control group was left unchanged. At the outset this looked like a standard Scientific Management experiment in the mould of Taylor and the Gilbreths. What the engineers were expecting was a set of unambiguous results which would allow them to establish the 'one best' level of illumination. This did not happen and, instead, data began to emerge which challenged the very basis of Scientific Management.

The engineers had expected the performance of the experimental group to vary with increases and decreases in illumination and for an optimum level to be established, but instead as the illumination was varied, so output continued to increase. Indeed, output only decreased in the experimental group when the lighting became so dim that it was difficult to see. More puzzling still, output in the control group, where no changes were made, also increased. In 1927 Western Electric called in Mayo and his colleagues to investigate these apparently contradictory findings. In the years which followed, a series of experiments were carried out in which groups of workers were subjected to changes in hours, payment systems and rest periods. The subsequent changes in output, and the reasons for these, undermined many of the

assumptions regarding organisations and human behaviour previously perceived as sacrosanct (Mayo, 1933; Roethlisberger and Dickson, 1938).

The experiments were monitored continuously and from this work,
Mayo and his colleagues concluded that it was not the changes in
working conditions which affected output, but the fact that those workers involved had been singled out for special attention. This acted to
increase their morale and make them want to perform better. It was
the very fact that they were being studied which produced the increased performance; this later became known as the 'Hawthorne Effect'. This accounted for the improved performance by the original
control group, even with no changes to the lighting in their area: they
also felt 'special' because they were being studied. These findings led
Mayo and his group to move the focus of their work away from the reaction of individual workers to changes in their working conditions.
Instead, they began to investigate the role and behaviour of the 'informal' groups that workers themselves established, and the norms and
attitudes of these groups.

As a result of this work, Mayo and his colleagues put forward two
major propositions which came to form the core of the Human Relations approach. The first related to the importance of informal groups
within the formal structure of organisations. The Western Electric
studies demonstrated the need to see the work process as a collective,
co-operative activity as opposed to an individual, isolated one. The
studies showed in particular the important effect that the informal,
primary work group has on performance. These groups tend to develop their own norms, values and attitudes which enable them to
exert strong social, peer-group pressure on individuals within the
group to conform to group norms, whether this be in relation to the
pace of work or attitudes to other groups and supervisors. Taylor had
also noted the pressure that groups of workers could exert over their
members to make them conform; however, he believed that this was
abnormal behaviour which could be remedied by tight managerial
control. What the Western Electric studies demonstrated was that far
from being abnormal, such behaviour was perfectly normal.

The second proposition put forward by Mayo and his colleagues was
that humans have a deep need for recognition, security and belonging.
Rather than being purely economic beings, the Hawthorne Experiments demonstrated that workers' performance and attitudes could be
influenced more by their need for recognition and security and, also,
the feeling of belonging engendered by informal groups. This latter
point in particular reflected, in Mayo's view, a deep-seated desire by

humans as social beings for intimacy, consistency and predictability. Where these social certainties were lacking, workers would deliberately seek to manufacture them by creating their own informal work groups. Therefore, rather than seeking to eradicate or undermine the workings of these informal groups, as Taylor had advocated, the Western Electric studies showed that management needed to gain the collaboration and co-operation of such groups if they were to get the best performance from workers.

It is generally agreed (Mullins, 1989; Rose, 1988) that the Western Electric studies had a dramatic effect on management and organisation theory. The studies ushered in an era where the Economic Man of the Classical approach was supplanted by Social Man. It was no longer possible for managers to ignore the effects of organisational structures and job design on work groups, employee attitudes and management-worker relations. The crucial issue became one of social relationships – Human Relations – in the workplace. In future, the focus of good management practice would shift to the importance of leadership and communication in order to win over employees. As the 1930s and 1940s progressed, other work began to emerge which both substantiated and broadened these findings.

Chester Barnard and co-operative systems

Barnard was an executive with American Telephone and Telegraph, whose book *The Functions of the Executive* (1938) has a comparable place in the Human Relations literature to that of Fayol's work in the literature of the Classical school. In this work, Barnard put forward the idea of organisations as co-operative systems. In so doing, this gave him a double claim to fame: not only did he draw attention to the co-operative nature of organisational life but he was also one of the first to treat organisations as systems rather than machines. He was in frequent contact with Mayo and his colleagues at Harvard, and closely followed their work at Western Electric. Therefore, although *The Functions of the Executive* was a personal and idiosyncratic work, reflecting Barnard's own distinct views and opinions, it was far from being bereft of academic substance. Indeed, his book was the first systematic attempt in English (Weber's work on bureaucracy was still not translated into English at this time) to outline a theory of organisations as a whole.

In this respect, Barnard can claim both to have made a substantial contribution to the Human Relations approach and to have laid the groundwork for subsequent writers such as Selznick and Simon (Robbins, 1987; Scott, 1987).

An organisation is a co-operative system, he argued, because without the willingness of its members to make contributions to and pursue its goals, it cannot operate effectively. Like others that espoused the Human Relations approach, he believed co-operation could not be achieved solely by monetary incentives. Instead, he advocated a mixture of monetary and non-monetary inducements. Similarly, co-operation by itself would not be effective unless an organisation also possessed a common purpose: clear and realistic goals and objectives which the organisation's members could understand, relate to and pursue. Establishing this common purpose, in Barnard's opinion, had to be the responsibility of those at the top of the organisation, but achieving it required the co-operation of those at the bottom, and all levels in between.

This leads to another of Barnard's assertions: the flow of authority is not from the top down but from the bottom up. He defined authority not as a property of management but as a response by subordinates to superiors. If subordinates did not respond willingly and appropriately, then no authority existed. In this example, as in many others, he is both reflecting the influence of and supporting the findings of the Western Electric studies, which drew attention to the ability of workers through social groupings to facilitate or frustrate the will of management.

In order to avoid a negative response from workers, Barnard advocated systematic and purposeful communication. Indeed, he portrayed organisations as a purposeful, co-ordinated system of communications linking all participants in a manner which not only encouraged the pursuit of the organisation's common purpose, but also legitimised the premises on which it was based. However, he argued that this does not happen automatically or accidentally; it is the product of effective leadership. This is why Barnard stressed the key role of the executive in leading the organisation by facilitating communication and motivating subordinates to high levels of performance; such developments could only come from the top.

Given the emphasis placed by Barnard on the setting and pursuit of clear objectives, and in his approach in general, there is a degree of overlap with the work of the Classical school. However, what significantly distinguishes him from them is his insistence on the non-rational, informal, interpersonal, and indeed, moral basis of organisational life.

Barnard rejected the idea of material incentives being the only ones to make people work purposefully. Indeed, he saw them as being 'weak incentives' which needed to be supported by other psychological and sociological motivators if organisations were to be successful in achieving their common purpose. In so challenging the effectiveness of material incentives, he was to receive substantial support a few years later from a more academic source.

Abraham Maslow's hierarchy of needs

Abraham Maslow, an American psychologist, was one of the first to differentiate between and classify different types of human need. For Taylor and his adherents, there was only one form of need: material/monetary need. Mayo et al. and Barnard took a different view; they drew a distinction between material and non-material needs, but made no distinction within these two categories. Maslow (1943) identified five distinct forms of human need which he placed in a hierarchical order. He argued that, beginning at the lowest level, a person had to satisfy substantially the needs at one level before they could move up the hierarchy and concentrate on 'higher order' needs.

In ascending order, the five levels in Maslow's hierarchy of needs are:

- *Physiological needs* – hunger, thirst, sleep, etc; only when these basic needs have been satisfied do other needs begin to emerge.
- *Safety needs* – the desire for security and protection against danger.
- *Social needs* – the need to belong, gain love and affection; to be in the company of others, especially friends.
- *Esteem needs* – these reflect a person's desire to be respected – esteemed – for their achievements.
- *Self-actualisation needs* – this is the need to achieve one's full potential. According to Maslow, self-actualisation will vary from person to person and, indeed, may differ over time, as a person reaches a level of potential previously considered unattainable and so goes on to strive for new heights. For these reasons, self-actualisation is a continuously-evolving process throughout a person's lifetime.

Though not designed specifically for organisational analysis, but rather in the context of life in general, it can be seen why Maslow's work was so readily accepted by proponents of the Human Relations approach. For them, it explained why in some situations Tayloristic incentives were effective, whilst in other situations, such as the Hawthorne Experiments, other factors proved more important.

Applying Maslow's hierarchy of needs to human behaviour in organisations, it can be seen that people will first of all be motivated by the desire to satisfy physiological needs through monetary rewards. However, once those have been substantially satisfied, workers will seek to satisfy – be motivated by – their safety needs, such as job security and welfare benefits. In a similar fashion, once safety needs are substantially met, these will fade into the background and social needs will come to the fore. People will want to be accepted as part of a group, to share common intents and aspirations with the group, to experience the bonds of friendship and loyalty. Clearly, these social needs played an important role in the Hawthorne Experiments, as did esteem needs. After social and esteem needs are substantially met, finally self-actualisation needs come to the fore. However, as mentioned above, the need for self-actualisation never wanes but tends to act as a continuing spur to further achievements.

Clearly, Maslow's work cannot be transferred fully into the organisational setting, given that most jobs do not allow individuals to approach, let alone attain, self-actualisation. Indeed, even the very basic physiological needs are beyond the reach of many millions of people in the world. Nevertheless, in distinguishing as he does between types of intrinsic (non-material) and extrinsic (material) motivators and arguing that, at any one time, it is the unmet needs which act as positive motivators, Maslow has had an enormous impact on job design and research (Child, 1984; Smith *et al.* 1982). The influence of Maslow's theory of needs can be seen in the work of other exponents of Human Relations, especially Douglas McGregor.

Douglas McGregor and Theory X – Theory Y

One of the most widely-cited Human Relations writers is Douglas McGregor. He developed his views from his personal experience as a manager, consultant and academic rather than from empirical research.

McGregor (1960) argued that there are basically two commonly-held views of human nature: a negative view – Theory X, and a positive view – Theory Y. He believed that managers' behaviour towards their subordinates was based upon one or other of these views, both of which consist of a certain grouping of assumptions about human behaviour.

Theory X consists of the following assumptions:

- The average person dislikes work and will avoid it wherever possible.
- Employees must be coerced, controlled or threatened with punishment if they are to perform as required.
- Most people try to avoid responsibility and will seek formal direction whenever possible.
- Workers place security above other factors relating to employment and will display little ambition.

Theory Y, on the other hand, comprises a group of assumptions which gives a much more positive view of human nature:

- Most people can view work as being as natural as rest or play.
- Workers are capable of exercising self-direction and self-control.
- The average person will accept and even seek responsibility if they are committed to the objectives being pursued.
- Ingenuity, imagination, creativity and the ability to make good decisions are widely dispersed throughout the population and are not peculiar to managers.

Theory X and Theory Y are not statements about what people are actually like, but rather the general assumptions that managers, and the rest of us, hold about what people are like. The fact that such views may not have a base in reality is irrelevant if managers act as though they are true. Managers who adhere to Theory X will use a combination of stick and carrot methods to control their subordinates, and will construct organisations that restrict the individual's ability to exercise skill, discretion and control over their work. Those managers who adhere to Theory Y will adopt a more open and flexible style of management. They will create jobs that encourage workers to contribute towards organisational goals, allow them to exercise skill and responsibility, and where the emphasis will be on non-material incentives.

Obviously, Theory X is akin to the Classical view of human nature and organisational design, whereas Theory Y falls more in the Human Relations tradition. Though McGregor tended to pose his views in neutral terms, it is clear that he favoured Theory Y; however, he argued that there was nothing deterministic about which approach to adopt. The choice lies with managers; those who adopt Theory X will create a situation where workers are only able and willing to pursue material needs (as Maslow observed). Such workers will be neither prepared nor in a position to contribute to the wider aims and objectives of the organisation which employs them. Managers who follow Theory Y precepts are likely to receive an entirely different response from their employees; workers will identify more clearly with the general interests of the organisation and be more able and more willing to contribute to their achievement.

Though stressing the element of choice, McGregor, along with other Human Relations adherents, believed that organisations were moving, and should move, more in the direction of Theory Y.

Warren Bennis and 'The Death of Bureaucracy'

By the 1950s and 1960s, the Human Relations approach and the values it espoused were in the ascendancy. One clear sign of this was the widely-held view in the 1960s that bureaucracy was dying and being replaced by more flexible, people-centred organisations which allowed and encouraged personal growth and development. Warren Bennis (1966) is credited with coining the phrase and making the case for 'The Death of Bureaucracy'. Bennis argued that every age develops an organisational form appropriate to its time. Bureaucracy was, in his view, appropriate for the first two-thirds of the twentieth century but not beyond that. He believed that bureaucracy emerged because its order, precision and impersonal nature was the correct antidote for the personal subjugation, cruelty, nepotism and capriciousness which passed for management during the Industrial Revolution.

Bureaucracy, he stated, emerged as a creative and wholesome response to the needs and values of the Victorian Age. Up to this point, there is little to distinguish Bennis from Weber; however, he then went on to argue that the Victorian Age, and its needs, were dead and that new conditions were emerging to which bureaucracy was no longer suited.

These conditions were:

- *Rapid and unexpected change* – bureaucracy's strength lies in its ability to manage efficiently the routine and predictable; however, its pre-programmed rules and inflexibility make it unsuitable for the rapidly-changing modern world.
- *Growth in size* – as organisations become larger, then bureaucratic structures become more complex and unwieldy, and less efficient.

- *Increasing diversity* – rapid growth, quick change and an increase in specialisation create the need for people with diverse and highly-specialised skills; these specialists cannot easily or effectively be fitted within the standardised, pyramid structure of bureaucratic organisations.
- *Change in managerial behaviour* – the increasing adoption of the Human Relations approach by managers challenges the simplistic view of human nature put forward by the Classical school, which underpins bureaucracy. If coercion and threats administered in a de-personalised, mechanistic fashion are counter-productive as a way of controlling people in organisations, then the case for bureaucracy is severely diminished.

For Bennis and others such as Bell (1974) and Toffler (1970), bureaucracy was rightly dying and being replaced by more diverse, flexible structures which could cope with the needs of the modern world.

The Human Relations approach: conclusions

Though many tend to associate the Human Relations movement exclusively with the work of Mayo, the discussion above shows that it is a much more diverse school of thought. Indeed, some have argued that to call it a school owes more to academic convenience than actual reality (Rose, 1988). Nevertheless, there are continuing and overlapping themes in the work of the writers cited above which strongly link them together. The first, and most obvious, is their almost total rejection of the Classical movement's mechanistic-rational approach to people and organisation structures. The second, and more fundamental feature is that whilst approaching the issues involved from different perspectives and emphasising separate aspects, they create an organisational model which possesses both coherence and plausibility.

The Human Relations model stresses three core elements:

- Leadership and communication.
- Intrinsic job motivation (as well as extrinsic rewards).
- Organisation structures and practices which facilitate flexibility and involvement.

These elements are underpinned by two central propositions:

- Organisations are complex social systems and not mechanical contrivances. Therefore, they cannot effectively be controlled by close supervision, rigid rules and purely economic incentives.

- Human beings have emotional as well as economic needs. Organisation and job structures need to be designed in such a way as to enable workers to meet both their material and non-material needs. Only in this way will workers perform efficiently and effectively in the best interests of the organisation.

It is not difficult to see why the Human Relations approach proved popular. In a period when many people were becoming increasingly worried about the growth of impersonal bureaucracies, it provided an attractive alternative. It is an approach which stresses that human beings are not mere cogs in a machine but that they have emotional needs – humans want to 'belong', achieve recognition, and develop and fulfil their potential. It should also be noted that the Depression of the 1930s and the Second World War and its aftermath created, in Britain, the USA and much of the Western World, a greater sense of collectivism and community than had hitherto been the case; another reason why the Human Relations doctrine found such a ready audience.

However, in the 1950s and 1960s, a substantial and often vitriolic body of opinion came to be ranged against the Human Relations approach. Economists rejected the argument that non-material incentives have a potentially stronger motivating influence than material incentives. The emphasis placed by the proponents of Human Relations on people's need for 'togetherness' and 'belonging' was seen by some as a denial of individualism. Others thought that it belittled workers and portrayed them as irrational beings who, given the chance, would cling to management as a baby clings to its mother. It was also attacked from both a management and a trade union viewpoint. Some of the former felt that its supposedly powerful manipulative techniques were either useless or inoperable; whilst representatives of the latter saw Human Relations as a vehicle for manipulating labour, and undermining – even attempting to eliminate – trade unions. Sociologists criticised it for attempting a sociological analysis of organisations without taking into account the larger society within which each organisation existed (Kerr and Fisher, 1957; Landsberger, 1958; Rose, 1988; Whyte, 1960).

Many of the criticisms were clearly directed at the work of Mayo and his colleagues, including inconsistencies between them. Landsberger (1958), for example, was one of the first to point out the difference between Mayo's (1933) interpretations of the Hawthorne Experiments and his colleagues', Roethlisberger and Dickson (1938), account. However, by no means were all the criticisms levelled at Mayo and his colleagues. Maslow's work, a key theoretical cornerstone of the Human

Relations approach, was found to lack empirical substance when re-searchers attempted to validate it (Hall and Nougaim, 1968; Lawler and Suttle, 1972). Similarly, Bennis's views were attacked. The Aston Studies in the 1960s (Pugh *et al.* 1969a and b) showed that bureau-cracy was growing rather than declining. Also, Miewald (1970) argued that Bennis did not understand the nature of bureaucracy; in his view, far from being rigid, it could and did adapt to changing and dy-namic environments.

There is one further criticism of the Human Relations approach, one which it shares with the Classical approach; it claims for itself the title of the 'one best way'. Yet, the question was posed, how can any approach claim that there is only one method of structuring and man-aging organisations, and that it holds good for all organisations and for all time? Indeed, the kernel of this criticism can be found in Ben-nis's (1966) work, where he argued that organisations in the last third of the twentieth century would experience rapid and unexpected change, continue to increase in size – with the problems of complexity which this brings – and become more diverse and specialised. Clearly, whilst not explicitly advocating it, Bennis was making the case for an approach to organisations which recognised not only that they face different situations but also that these are not stable over time. In the 1960s, and more so in the 1970s and 1980s, such an approach emerged.

The Contingency Theory approach

Contingency Theory emerged in the 1960s out of a number of now classic studies of organisation structure and management (Child, 1984; Mullins, 1989; Scott, 1987). Since the 1970s, it has proved – as a theory at least – to be more influential than either the Classical or Human Relations approach. In essence, Contingency Theory is a rejec-tion of the 'one best way' approach previously sought by managers and propounded by academics. In its place is substituted the view that the structure and operation of an organisation is dependent ('Contingent') on the situational variables it faces – the main ones being environ-ment, technology and size (Burnes, 1989). It follows from this that no two organisations will face exactly the same contingencies; therefore, as their situations are different, so too should their structures and operations be different. Consequently, the 'one best way' for *all* or-ganisations is replaced by the 'one best way' for *each* organisation.

As Scott (1987:23) pointed out, one of the clear distinctions between Contingency Theory and its predecessors is that:

> *The previous definitions tend to view the organisation as a closed system, separate from its environment and comprising a set of stable and easily identified participants. However, organisations are not closed systems, sealed off from their environments but are open to and dependent on flows of personnel and resources from outside.*

Therefore, organisations are not in complete control of their own fate; they can be, and often are, affected by the environment in which they operate, and this can and does vary from organisation to organisation.

One of the earliest writers who pointed Contingency Theorists in this direction was Herbert Simon. Writing in the 1950s (Simon, 1957), he criticised existing approaches as providing managers with nothing more than proverbs or lists of 'good practice' based on scant ideas, many of which contradicted each other. He argued that organisation theory needed to go beyond superficial and over-simplified precepts, and instead study the conditions under which competing principles could be applied.

Nevertheless, it was not until the 1960s that a considered approach emerged, which broke with the Classical and Human Relations movements' attempts to establish a universal approach suitable to all organisations. The former had concentrated on the formal structure and technical requirements of organisations and attempted to establish sets of general principles. The latter focused on the informal aspects of organisations and the psychological and social needs of their employees. As with the Classical approach, this produced lists of good practice and desired objectives but lacked precise guidance on how these should be applied.

Contingency Theorists adopted a different perspective, based on the premise that organisations are open systems whose internal operation and effectiveness is dependent upon the particular situational variables they face at any one time, and that these vary from organisation to organisation. This is consistent with evidence that not all organisations – or even all successful ones – have the same structure, and also that even within organisations, different structural forms can be observed (Mintzberg, 1979). Though many situational variables, such as the age of the organisation and its history, have been put forward as influential in determining structure, it is generally agreed that the three most important contingencies are as follows:

● *Environmental uncertainty and dependence* – it is argued that the management of any organisation is undertaken in circumstances of uncertainty and dependence, both of which change over time.

Uncertainty arises because of our inability ever to understand and control events fully, especially the actions of others, whether outside or inside an organisation. Because of this, forecasting is an inexact and hazardous enterprise. (Recent examples of this are the collapse of the Communist regimes in Eastern Europe, the full consequences of which are still not clear, and the British Government's misreading of the depth and duration of the recession in 1991.) Similarly, the dependence of management upon the goodwill and support of others, whether they be customers, suppliers or employees, makes an organisation vulnerable, and may in some circumstances even threaten its very existence. Levels of uncertainty and dependence will vary, but can never be totally eliminated, and must therefore be taken into account – treated as a contingency – when designing organisational structures and procedures (Burns and Stalker, 1961; Child, 1984; Lawrence and Lorsch, 1967; Pugh, 1984; Robbins, 1987; Thompson, 1967).

- *Technology* – the argument for technology being a key variable follows similar lines to that of environment. Organisations creating and providing different products and services use different technologies. Indeed, even those producing similar products may use differing techniques, for example, the difference between the Japanese approach to car manufacture and that practised by its competitors in the West. Given that these technologies can vary from the large and expensive, such as a nuclear reactor, to the relatively small and cheap, such as an architect's drawing board, the form of organisation necessary to ensure their efficient operation will also vary. If so, there is a need to treat technology as a contingent variable when structuring organisations. Indeed, with the spread of increasingly more powerful and wide-ranging forms of information technology over the last decade, the case for technology being a key variable has, if anything, increased (Wood, 1989).

However, there are distinct variants of the case for technology which reflect different definitions of technology at the organisational level of analysis that theorists and researchers have employed. The two best-developed approaches are found in Woodward's (1965 and 1970) studies of 'operations technology' and Perrow's (1967 and 1970) analysis of 'materials technology'. The former refers to the equipping and sequencing of activities in an organisation's work flow, whilst the latter refers to the characteristics of the physical and informational materials used. Woodward's work tends to relate more to manufacturing organisations, whereas Perrow's is more generally applicable (Hickson *et al.* 1969; Thompson,

1967; Zwerman, 1970).

- *Size* – some would argue that this is not just *a* key variable but *the* key variable. The case for size being a significant variable when designing organisations has a long antecedence within organisation theory, being first cited by Weber in the early part of this century when making the case for bureaucracy (Weber, 1947). The basic case is quite straightforward. It is argued that the structure and practices necessary for the efficient and effective operations of small organisations are not suitable for larger ones. In the former case, centralised and personalised forms of control are claimed to be appropriate but as organisations grow in size, more decentralised and impersonal structures and practices become more appropriate (Blau, 1970; Mullins, 1989; Pugh *et al.* 1969a and b; Scott, 1987).

The main figures in developing and establishing Contingency Theory were academics in Britain and the USA, among whom the pioneers were Burns and Stalker.

Tom Burns and G M Stalker and the importance of environment

The first major study to establish a relationship between organisations' environment and their structure was carried out by Burns and Stalker (1961) in Britain. They examined 20 firms in a variety of industries in order to assess how their structures responded to the environment in which they operated. Their findings were to have a major impact on organisation theory, and provide concrete evidence for rejecting a universal, 'one best way', approach to organisational structure and practice. They identified five different types of environment, based upon the level of uncertainty that was present, ranging from 'stable' to 'least predictable'. They also identified two basic or ideal forms of structure: 'Mechanistic' and 'Organic'. Their data showed that Mechanistic structures were more effective in stable environments, whilst Organic ones were better suited to less stable, less predictable environments.

The Mechanistic structure, which is akin to the Classical approach, is characterised by:

- The specialisation of tasks.
- Closely-defined duties, responsibilities and technical methods.
- A clear hierarchical structure with insistence on loyalty to the organisation and obedience to superiors.

In contrast, the Organic structure, which has some resemblance to the Human Relations approach, is characterised by:

- Much greater flexibility.
- Adjustment and continual redefinition of tasks.
- A network structure of control, authority and communication.
- Lateral consultation based on information and advice rather than instructions and decisions.
- Commitment to the work group and its tasks.
- Importance and prestige being determined by an individual's contribution to the tasks of their work group rather than their position in the hierarchy.

As can be seen, Burns and Stalker neither reject nor accept what went before. Instead, they argued that both the Classical approach and the Human Relations approach can be appropriate, but that this depends on the nature of the environment in which the organisation is operating. In this respect, they not only built on the past rather than rejecting it, but also restored responsibility to managers. Instead of being called on to adopt blindly the orthodoxy with regard to structure, managers would in future have to assess their organisation and its needs, and then adopt the structure and practices suitable to its situation (Child, 1984; Mullins, 1989; Scott, 1987).

Paul Lawrence and Jay Lorsch and the case for environment

Burns and Stalker's findings on the relationship between organisational environment and structure were examined and developed by a number of researchers in Europe and the USA. One of the most significant pieces of work was that carried out by Lawrence and Lorsch (1967) in the USA. Their work went beyond that of Burns and Stalker, in that they were interested not only in the relationship between environment and a company's overall structure, but also how individual departments within companies responded to, and organised themselves to cope with, aspects of the external environment which were of particular significance to them. They undertook a study of six firms in the plastics industry, followed by a further study of two firms in the container industry and two in the consumer foods industry. The structure of each of the firms was analysed in terms of its degree of 'differentiation' and 'integration'.

Differentiation refers to the degree to which managers and staff in their own functional departments see themselves as separate and have distinct practices, proceedings and structures from others in the organisation. Integration refers to the level and form of collaboration that is necessary between departments in order to achieve their individual objectives within the environment in which the firm operates. Therefore, differentiation is the degree to which departments are distinct from each other, whilst integration refers to the degree to which they have common structures, procedures, practices and objectives at the operational level.

Generally, the greater the interdependence among departments, the more integration is needed to co-ordinate their efforts in the best interests of the organisation as a whole; however, this may not always be easy to achieve. In a rapidly-changing environment, the conditions faced by individual departments may differ greatly, and a high degree of differentiation may be necessary. In such a situation, the need for integration is also likely to be great, but the diversity and volatility of the environment are likely to make this difficult to achieve (Cummings and Huse, 1989).

In their study of the plastics industry, Lawrence and Lorsch (1967) found clear differentiation between key departments such as research, production and sales. Research departments were more concerned with long-term issues and were under pressure to produce new ideas and innovations. These departments, in Burns and Stalker's terminology, tended to adopt an Organic form of structure. Production departments on the other hand were, for obvious reasons, concerned with short-term performance targets relating to output, costs, quality and delivery. Such departments tended to operate in a fairly stable environment and had Mechanistic structures. Sales departments tended to fall in between research and production in terms of environment and structure. They operated in a moderately stable environment and were concerned more with getting production to meet deliveries than with long-term issues.

Whilst highlighting the degree of differentiation between key departments, the study also found that the degree of integration was critical to a firm's overall performance. Indeed, the two most successful firms in their sample were not only amongst the most highly differentiated, but also had the highest degree of integration. These findings were confirmed by their studies of the container and consumer foods industries, which showed that differentiation and integration in successful companies varies with the demands of the environment in which they operate. The more diverse and dynamic the environment, the more the successful organisation will be differentiated and highly integrated. In a more stable environment, the pressure for differentiation is less, but the need for integration remains.

Therefore, Lawrence and Lorsch found that the most effective organisations had an appropriate fit between the design and co-ordination of departments and the amount of environmental uncertainty they faced. However, the most successful firms were the ones which, whilst operating in an environment that required a high level of differentiation, also managed to achieve a high level of integration.

Clearly, in a situation where departments have dissimilar structures, practices and procedures, achieving integration is not easy and often leads to conflict. Lawrence and Lorsch found that the effective firms achieved integration by openly confronting conflict, and by working problems through in the context of the overall needs of the organisation. In addition, in firms which dealt successfully with conflict, the success of those responsible for achieving integration was based mainly on their knowledge and competence rather than their formal position. This was because their colleagues in the different departments respected and responded to their perceived understanding of the issues involved. It follows that to achieve high levels of integration and differentiation, an organisation cannot rely solely on the formal managerial hierarchy. This must be supplemented with liaison positions, taskforces and teams, and other integrating mechanisms.

As with Burns and Stalker, Lawrence and Lorsch did not reject the Classical and Human Relations approaches per se but instead, saw them as alternative options dependent on the environment in which an organisation operated. In looking at the internal operations of organisations in this way, Lawrence and Lorsch raised the issue of dependence as well as uncertainty. This was a subject that James Thompson tackled in greater depth.

James Thompson and environmental uncertainty and dependence

Thompson's (1967) influential work took the environmental perspective forward in three important ways. The first was to argue that although organisations are not rational entities, they strive to be so because it is in the interests of those who design and manage the organisation that its work be carried out as effectively and efficiently as possible. In order to achieve this, organisations attempt to seal off their productive core from the uncertainty of the environment.

However, it is not possible to seal off all, or perhaps even any, parts of an organisation, given that it must be open to and interact with its environment if it is to secure resources and sell its products. This leads on to Thompson's second major contribution: different levels of an organisation may exhibit, and need, different structures and operate on a more rational or less rational basis. Thompson's third contribution was to recognise that organisational effectiveness was contingent not only on the level of external environmental uncertainty, but also on the degree of internal dependence present.

This last point echoes Lawrence and Lorsch's argument for integration and differentiation; however, Thompson made this point much more explicitly and related it to different structural forms. He formulated a three-type classification in relation to internal dependence:

- *Pooled interdependence* – this is where each part of an organisation operates in a relatively autonomous manner, but by fulfilling their individual purposes they enable the organisation as a whole to function effectively.
- *Sequential interdependence* – where overall effectiveness requires direct interaction between an organisation's separate parts.
- *Reciprocal interdependence* – where the outputs from one part of an organisation constitute the inputs for other parts of the system.

Thompson went on to argue that the type of interdependence could be related to the degree of complexity present: simple organisations rely on pooled interdependence; more complex organisations demonstrate both pooled and sequential interdependence; and in the most complex organisations all three forms of interdependence may be present. Thompson envisaged that each form of interdependence would require distinct methods for co-ordinating activities. Pooled interdependence would be characterised by standardisation through the use of rules and procedures. Sequential interdependence would require the use of detailed plans and written agreements, whilst reciprocal interdependence would achieve co-ordination by means of personal contact and informal agreements between members of those parts of the organisation involved.

Therefore, in a nutshell, Thompson's main arguments are as follows:

- Different sections of an organisation will be characterised by varying levels of complexity, rationality and formalisation, depending on the extent to which managers can shield them from the level of uncertainty present in the environment.

- The higher both the overall level of uncertainty and that faced by each area of an organisation, the greater will be the dependence of one area on another.
- As this interdependence increases, co-ordination through standardised procedures and planning mechanisms will become less effective, and the need for more personal contact and informal interaction will grow.
- The more that co-ordination is achieved through mutual reciprocity in this manner, the less rational will be the operation of the organisation.

Thompson's work is of seminal importance in the development of organisation theory, not only because of the case he made for linking external uncertainty to internal dependence, but also, as a number of writers have observed (Robbins, 1987; Scott, 1987), because of the attention he drew to technology influencing organisation structures as well as environmental factors. Thompson's contribution in this respect lay in creating a classification scheme for technology, and arguing that technology determines the selection of the specific structural arrangements for reducing the effect of uncertainty on the various functions of an organisation. The issue of technology and structure had been raised earlier in a major study by Joan Woodward published in 1965.

Joan Woodward and the case for technology

In the 1960s, Joan Woodward carried out a major study of 100 manufacturing firms in south-east Essex in order to establish the validity of the claims made by advocates of the Classical approach that the adoption of a bureaucratic-mechanistic structure was essential for organisational success (Woodward, 1965 and 1970).

After much work, Woodward concluded that no such correlation existed; what she found, however, was that the more successful companies adopted an organisational form that varied according to their main production technology. By technology, Woodward meant not only the machinery being used, but also the way it was organised, operated and integrated into a distinct production process. From her sample, she identified three distinct types of production technology, ranging from least to most complex:

- *Small batch (or unit) production* – where customers' requirements were for one-off or small-volume specialist products.

- *Large batch (or mass) production* – where standardised products were made in large numbers to meet a forecast demand.
- *Process production* – where production was in a continuous flow such as an oil refinery.

When the firms were grouped in this manner, a pattern emerged which showed that though they apparently differed considerably in terms of their organisational structure, many of the variations for the more successful firms could be explained by reference to the technology employed. Among firms engaged in small batch production, the most appropriate structure appeared to be one with relatively few hierarchical levels and wide middle management spans of control. Woodward noted that technology became more complex as firms moved from small batch to large batch and finally process production. In turn, structures became taller and more narrowly based, with smaller middle management and larger chief executive spans of control. Within each category of technology, the best performing companies were those closest to the median in the type of structure adopted. Therefore, Woodward's work clearly established a link between technology, structure and success which ran counter to the notion that there was a 'one best way' for all organisations.

Though qualified by later studies (Child, 1984; Handy, 1986; Smith *et al.* 1982), Woodward's research remains a milestone in the development of Contingency Theory. In particular, she demonstrated the need to take into account technological variables in designing organisations, especially in relation to spans of control. Nevertheless, a major drawback of her work was the difficulty of applying it to non-manufacturing companies. This was remedied by the work of Charles Perrow in the USA.

Charles Perrow and the case for technology

In the USA, Charles Perrow (1967 and 1970) extended Joan Woodward's work on technology and organisation structure by drawing attention to two major dimensions of technology:

- The extent to which the work being carried out is variable or predictable.
- The extent to which the technology can be analysed and categorised.

The first, variability, refers to the incidence of exceptional or unpredictable occurrences, and the extent to which these problems are familiar and can be easily dealt with or are unique and difficult to solve. For example, an oil refinery should experience few non-routine occurrences, whilst an advertising agency will encounter many unpredictable and exceptional occurrences. The second major dimension, analysis and categorisation, refers to the extent to which the individual task functions can be broken down and tightly specified, and also whether problems can be solved by recourse to recognised, routine procedures or if non-routine procedures have to be invoked.

Bringing these two major dimensions of technology together, Perrow constructed a technology continuum ranging from routine to non-routine. With the latter, there are a large number of exceptional occurrences requiring difficult and varied problem-solving techniques to overcome them. Routine technology, on the other hand, throws up few problems, which can be dealt with by recourse to standard, simple techniques.

Perrow argued that by classifying organisations according to their technology and predictability (routine to non-routine) of work tasks, it is then possible to identify the most effective form of structure in any given situation or for any activity. Perrow's routine – non-routine continuum can be equated with Burns and Stalker's Mechanistic and Organic dimensions for organisation structures. In routine situations, where few problems arise and those that do are easily dealt with, a Mechanistic structure is more effective because of the stable and predictable nature of the situation. However, in a dynamic and unpredictable situation, a more flexible, Organic form of structure will be more effective in dealing with the non-routine and difficult problems which occur. By formulating his work in this manner, i.e. by combining technology and predictability, it became possible to apply it to non-manufacturing situations.

Therefore, Perrow's work both reinforced and extended Woodward's case for recognising technology as a key situational variable to be taken into account when designing organisations. Nevertheless, whilst Perrow was developing his ideas, a further group of researchers were making the case for yet another 'key' contingency.

The Aston Group and the case for size

Though there are many proponents of the case for organisational size being a key contingency (Child, 1984; Robbins, 1987), perhaps the earliest and most ardent were a group of British researchers based at the University of Aston (who became known as the Aston Group). In the 1960s, they carried out a series of studies to examine and identify the relationship between different forms of organisational structures and their determinants (Pugh *et al.* 1969a and b). The Aston Group began in the early 1960s by examining a sample of 87 companies, and, as the work developed, further samples were added to their – eventually – very impressive database.

In analysing their results, the Aston Group found that size was the most powerful predictor of specialisation, use of procedures and reliance on paperwork. In effect, what they found was that the larger the organisation, the more likely it was to adopt (and need) mechanistic (bureaucratic) structures. The reverse was also found: the smaller the organisation, the more likely it was to adopt (and need) organic (flexible) structures.

This was clearly a major finding. Not only did it support (at least in terms of larger organisations) Weber's earlier work on bureaucracy, but it also struck a blow against those, such as Bennis, who saw bureaucracy as dysfunctional and dying. The work of the Aston Group, along with that of others such as Blau and Schoenherr (1971), who also argued that size is the most important condition affecting the structure of organisations, gave bureaucracy if not a new lease of life then, at least, a new lease of respectability. Bureaucracy, according to the Aston results, was both efficient and effective, at least for larger organisations; and, given the tendency for the average size of private companies and public bodies to increase throughout the twentieth century, its applicability would grow.

There are two explanations for the relationship between size and bureaucracy, both of which have similar implications for organisational efficiency and effectiveness. The first argues that increased size offers greater opportunities for specialisation – the Adam Smith argument, in effect. This will manifest itself in terms of greater structural differentiation and a high degree of uniformity amongst sub-units. In the first instance, this will make managerial co-ordination more difficult, especially with the emergence of functional autonomy. To counter this, senior managers will move to impose a system of impersonal controls through the use of formal procedures, standardised reporting and control systems, the written recording of information, etc. The second argument reaches similar conclusions, by pointing out that the difficulty of directing ever larger numbers of staff makes it highly inefficient to continue to use a personalised, centralised style of management. Instead a more decentralised system, using impersonal control mechanisms, has to be adopted. The introduction of such a system inevitably leads to the expansion of the administrative core (the bureaucracy) in organisations (Child, 1984).

As with all the Contingency Theorists, those who argued for size as the key situational variable were not attempting to reinvent the 'one best way' approach. Rather they were rejecting it in favour of an approach which drew attention to meeting the particular needs and circumstances of each organisation when deciding upon an appropriate structure.

Contingency Theory: conclusions

The Contingency approach can be considered a much more cohesive school of thought than either the Classical or Human Relations approaches. It has three unifying themes as follows:

- Organisations are open systems.
- Structure is dependent upon the particular circumstances, situational variables, faced by each organisation.
- There is no 'one best way' for all organisations.

The attractions of Contingency Theory are obvious. Firstly, it was in tune with the times in which it emerged – the 1960s and 1970s. This was a period of rapid economic and technological change, a tendency towards much larger organisations, and a significant increase in domestic and international competition. In this situation, Contingency Theory explained not only why these events were causing problems for organisations, but also how to resolve them (Burnes, 1989). Secondly, on the surface at least, it was simpler to understand and apply than the Human Relations approach. Lastly, whilst rejecting the Classical approach, it was a rational approach, based on matching known structural options to identifiable contingencies – size, technology and environment.

It follows from the last point that one of the outcomes of Contingency Theory was to reintroduce the notion of organisations, and their members, as rational entities. If the various structural options are known and the key situational variables can be identified, then all managers have to do is to adopt the structural form best suited to their circumstances, and success will follow. However, it is at this point – the attempt to apply this approach rationally and mechanically – that problems and drawbacks emerge which give rise to a number of major criticisms of Contingency Theory. The main ones are as follows:

- The difficulty in relating structure to performance. A number of writers have pointed out that there is no agreed definition of 'good performance'. For example, should performance be measured by short-term or long-term financial criteria? Should it be judged by market share or sales turnover? Without any agreed definition of good performance, it becomes difficult to show that linking structure to situational variables brings the benefits claimed (Hendry, 1979 and 1980; Mansfield, 1984; Terry, 1976).

- Despite the length of time that Contingency Theory has been in circulation, there is still no agreed or unchallenged definition of the three key situational variables – environment, technology and size. The literature gives a wide and conflicting range of definitions of these, making it difficult not only to establish a link between them and structure, but also to apply the theory (Dastmalchian, 1984; Mullins, 1989; Pugh and Hickson, 1976; Robbins, 1987; Warner, 1984; Wood, 1979).

- Whilst, as argued above, a relationship has been established between size and structure, it has proved difficult to show that this relationship has an appreciable impact on performance. Some researchers have suggested that the link between size and structure related to preferred systems of control, which may have more to do with the political and cultural nature of organisations than any attempt to improve performance (Allaire and Firsirotu, 1984; Child, 1984; Mansfield, 1984; Pugh and Hickson, 1976; Salaman, 1979).

- In examining the link between structure and contingencies, researchers use the organisation's formal organisational structure for comparison purposes. Yet, as the Hawthorne Experiments showed, the actual operation of an organisation may depend more on the informal structures created by workers than the formal ones laid down by management. This was a point made by Woodward (1965) in her study of technology and structure. She noted that organisation charts failed to show important relationships which, taken together, can have a significant impact on performance (Argyris, 1973; Burawoy, 1979; Selznick, 1948).

- Rather than managers being the virtual prisoners of organisational contingencies when making decisions regarding structure, the reverse may be the case. Managers may have a significant degree of choice and influence over not only structure but also the situational variables. Whether this is called 'Strategic Choice' (Child, 1972),

'Organisational Choice' (Trist *et al.* 1963) or 'Design Space' (Bessant, 1983), the meaning is the same. Those senior managers responsible for such decisions can exercise a high degree of freedom in selecting and influencing the technology to be used, the environment in which they operate and even the size of the organisation. Indeed, one of the architects of the technology-structure hypothesis, Charles Perrow, now argues that technology is chosen and designed to maintain and reinforce existing structures and power relations within organisations rather than the reverse (Perrow, 1983). Other writers make the case for size and environment being manipulated in similar ways (Abell, 1975; Clegg, 1984; Hendry, 1979; Leifer and Huber, 1977; Lorsch, 1970).

- It is assumed that organisations pursue clear-cut, well-thought-out, stable and compatible objectives which can be fitted into a Contingency perspective. However, researchers and practising managers argue that this is not the case. In reality, objectives are often unclear and organisations may pursue a number of conflicting goals at the same time. Clearly, the objectives of an organisation will impact on its situation and its structure. If these objectives are arbitrary, conflicting or open to managerial whim, it becomes difficult to apply a Contingency approach (Abodaher, 1986; Edwardes, 1983; Hamel and Prahalad, 1989; Mintzberg, 1987; Sloan, 1986).
- The last criticism is that Contingency Theory is too mechanistic and deterministic, and ignores the complexity of organisational life. As argued by the Human Relations school, organisations are by no means the rational entities many would like to believe. There is a need to see organisations as social systems, with all the cultural and political issues which this raises. In this view, structure is the product of clashes between individuals and groups within the organisation, each arguing and fighting for their own perspective and position (Allaire and Firsirotu, 1984; Buchanan, 1984; Hickson and Butler, 1982; Pfeffer, 1981; Salaman, 1979).

Therefore, despite its attractiveness, Contingency Theory, like the Classical and Human Relations approaches, fails to provide a convincing explanation for how organisations do and should operate.

Where next?

For organisations, if not for academics, the key purpose of any organisation theory or approach is to help them analyse and rectify the weaknesses and problems of their current situation, and to assist them in bringing about the changes necessary to achieve their future objectives. Over the past 100 years, the design and management of organisations has moved from an ad hoc process based on, at best, guesswork to one that is highly complex and informed by a host of practical and theoretical considerations. To the uninitiated, it might appear that this has made running organisations an easier and more certain process; yet a close examination of most organisations will reveal that this is far from being the case. Not only are organisations, in general, larger and more complex than in the past, but also the practical and theoretical reference points on which managers can draw are diverse and give conflicting and confusing signals.

Not surprisingly in such a situation, many managers look for simple foolproof solutions: often ones which, as Douglas McGregor noted, appeal to their own basic orientation – whether that be Theory X or Theory Y. This is one of the reasons why the Classical approach, with its deep roots in the Industrial Revolution and its straightforward mechanical approach to organisations and their members, has proved so enduring – despite strong evidence of its lack of suitability in many situations.

This search for simple, often quick-fix solutions, to the problems of organisational life has been manifest in many ways in the last decade, not least in the emergence of a series of 'panaceas' such as new technology, Human Resources Management, cultural change, etc. This is not to deny the benefits these can bring but, taken on their own, at best they encourage a piecemeal approach and at worst they create an atmosphere of resignation within organisations as one 'flavour of the month' is succeeded by yet another, and none is given the time necessary to prove itself. Clearly, in such situations, without an overall, long-term plan, the result of these various 'solutions' is to make the situation worse rather than better (Burnes, 1991; Burnes and Weekes, 1989).

Organisations clearly need to reject a short-term piecemeal approach, and instead see themselves in their totality and adopt a consistent and long-term approach. But which organisation theory should they choose? We have seen in this and the previous chapter that well-thought-out and well-supported cases exist for a number of different approaches, but each has its drawbacks and critics. It may well be that each is capable of assisting organisations to analyse and understand the strengths and weaknesses of their present situation. However, whether they can provide more effective organisational arrangements for the future is more debatable. Similarly, it is not obvious how organisations should actually achieve the process of transformation or that, given the criticisms of these approaches, they would be any better off.

In short, none of the approaches we have discussed hold the solution to all known organisational ills that their proponents seem to claim. They fail to reflect and explain the complexities of day-to-day organisational life which we all experience. In particular, the issue of organisational culture (Allaire and Firsirotu, 1984) gets short shrift; yet over the last decade its importance as both a promoter of, and a barrier to organisational competitiveness has become apparent. Nor do the approaches pay regard to many of the wider societal factors which now impact on our lives, such as the need to show greater social responsibility, whether it be in the area of 'green' issues or equal opportunities. Yet, as we approach the year 2000, it is clear that enormous changes are already taking place in the world, and others may be necessary if some of the worst predictions for the future are to be avoided.

The next chapter describes new perspectives on organisational life which are being put forward by leading management thinkers. Crucially, these perspectives stress the role of culture in shaping and sustaining organisational competitiveness. They also place the onus on the organisation and its members to take control of their own destiny, rather than hoping for someone else to come along with tailor-made solutions.

3

New perspectives in management

Introduction

The term 'paradigm' describes a set of assumptions, theories and models that are commonly accepted and shared within a particular field of activity at any one point in time (Kuhn, 1962). The previous two chapters have discussed the paradigms that have emerged and become common currency in the field of management and organisation theory. Though these paradigms have their adherents as well as critics, increasingly managers and theorists have experienced real difficulties in applying and defending them in today's turbulent business world. It seems as if the changes taking place in the business environment are so enormous and rapid that existing paradigms, whatever their past merits, are breaking down and new ones emerging.

This chapter examines the emerging paradigms from the perspective of key writers from both sides of the Atlantic, namely Peters and Waterman (1982), Kanter (1989) and Handy (1989). The writers are all practising and internationally-recognised management consultants, not just academics. Therefore, though their work is attempting to predict the way firms will need to organise and operate in the future, it is firmly based on what the best companies are doing now or planning to do in the future. These three perspectives form the spearhead of the movement that is simultaneously charting and creating the new organisational forms that have begun to appear. Their work – though both complementary and distinct – is of profound influence in shaping our understanding of what the future holds in the field of management. This work will now be examined in detail, starting with the American perspectives of Peters and Waterman, and Kanter, and concluding with Handy's British perspective.

Tom Peters and Robert Waterman's eight attributes of excellent companies

One of the earliest and most discussed contributions to the emergence of new forms of organisations is that made by Peters and Waterman (1982) in their book, *In Search of Excellence: Lessons from America's Best-Run Companies*. The origins of the book lie in a major study of the determinants of organisational excellence which Peters and Waterman carried out for the management consultants McKinsey and Company. From their study of 62 of America's most successful companies, Peters and Waterman argue that there are eight key attributes which organisations need to manifest if they are to achieve excellence. These attributes are largely opposed to the rational theories of management described in previous chapters. They argue that the rational approach is flawed because it leads to:

- *Wrong-headed analysis* – situation or information analysis that is considered too complex to be useful and too unwieldy to be flexible. This is analysis that strives to be precise about the inherently unknowable.
- *Paralysis through analysis* – this is the application of the rational model to such an extent that action stops and planning runs riot.
- *Irrational rationality* – this is where rational management techniques identify the 'right' answer irrespective of its applicability to the situation in question.

In the light of these criticisms, Peters and Waterman argue that the analytical tools which characterise the rational approach should only be used as an aid to, rather than a substitute for, human judgment. They believe that it is the freedom given to managers and employees to challenge the orthodox and to experiment with different solutions which distinguishes the excellent companies from the less successful. This can clearly be seen by looking at their eight attributes of excellence, which are as follows:

1 A bias for action.
2 Close to the customer.
3 Autonomy and entrepreneurship.
4 Productivity through people.
5 Hands-on, value-driven.
6 Stick to the knitting.
7 Simple form, lean staff.
8 Simultaneous loose-tight properties.

1   A bias for action

One of the main identifiable attributes of excellent companies is their bias for action. Even though they may be analytical in approach, they also favour methods which encourage rapid and appropriate response. One of the methods devised for achieving quick action is what Peters and Waterman term 'Chunking'. Chunking is an approach whereby a problem that arises in the organisation is first made manageable (i.e. broken into 'chunks') and then tackled by a small group of staff brought together specifically for that purpose. The main reason for the use of such groups, variously called project teams, taskforces or quality circles, is to facilitate organisational fluidity and to encourage action. Key characteristics of these groups are that:

- They usually comprise no more than ten members.
- They are voluntarily constituted.
- The life of the group is usually between three to six months.
- The reporting level and seniority of the membership is appropriate to the importance of the problem to be dealt with.
- The documentation of the group's proceedings is scant and very informal.
- These groups take on a limited set of objectives, which are usually determined, monitored, evaluated, and reviewed by themselves.

Chunking is merely one example of the bias for action that exists in excellent companies and reflects their willingness to innovate and experiment. These companies' philosophy for action is simple: 'Do it, fix it, try it.' Therefore, excellent companies are characterised by small, ad hoc teams applied to solving designated problems which have first been reduced to manageable proportions. Achieving smallness is the key, even though the subject or task may be large. Smallness induces manageability and a sense of understanding, and allows a feeling of ownership.

2   Close to the customer

Excellent companies really do get close to the customer, while others merely talk about it. The customer dictates product, quantity, quality and service. The best organisations are alleged to go to extreme lengths to achieve quality, service and reliability. There is no part of the business that is closed to customers. In fact, many of the excellent companies claim to get their best ideas for new products from listening intently and regularly to their customers. The excellent companies are more 'driven by their direct orientation to the customers rather than by technology or by a desire to be the low-cost producer. They seem to focus more on the revenue-generation side of their services' (Peters and Waterman, 1982:197).

3 Autonomy and entrepreneurship

Perhaps the most important element of excellent companies is their 'ability to be big and yet to act small at the same time. A concomitant essential apparently is that they encourage the entrepreneurial spirit among their people, because they push autonomy markedly far down the line' (Peters and Waterman, 1982:201). Product champions are allowed to come forward, grow and flourish. The champion in this case is not a blue-sky dreamer, or an intellectual giant. The champion might even be an ideas thief. But above all, the champion is the pragmatist; the one who latches on to someone else's ideas, and doggedly brings about something concrete and tangible.

In fostering such attitudes, the excellent companies have what they label 'Championing Systems', consisting of:

- *The Product Champion* – a zealot or fanatic who believes in a product.
- *A Successful Executing Champion* – one who has been through the process of championing a product before.
- *The Godfather* – typically, an ageing leader who provides the role model for champions.

The essence of this system is to foster, promote, and sustain the budding entrepreneur. It is claimed that the three elements of the Championing System are essential to its operation and credibility.

Another key part of this system is that in some companies product champions tend to be allocated their own 'suboptional divisions'. These are similar to small, independent businesses and comprise independent new venture teams, run by champions with the full and total support of senior management. The suboptional division is independent in that it is responsible for its own accounting, personnel activities, quality assurance and support for its product in the field. To encourage entrepreneurship further, teams, groups and divisions are highly encouraged by the companies' reward structures to compete amongst themselves for new projects.

Autonomy and entrepreneurship are also encouraged by the type of no-holds-barred communications procedures adopted by excellent companies. These exhibit the following characteristics:

- *They are informal* – even though there are several meetings going on at any one time, most meetings are informal and comprise staff from different disciplines gathering to talk about and solve problems.
- *The communication system is given both physical and material support* – blackboards, flip-charts and small tables that foster informal small-group discussions are everywhere. The aim is to encourage people to talk about the organisation: what needs changing; what is going on; and how to improve things around the place. There are also people, variously described as dreamers, heretics, gadflies, mavericks, or geniuses, whose sole purpose is to spur the system to innovate. Their job is to institutionalise innovation by initiating and encouraging experimentation. They can also call on staff in other divisions of the organisation to assist them in this process, as well as having financial resources at their disposal.
- *Communication is intensive* – given the freedom, the encouragement and the support (financial, moral and physical) in the organisations, it is no wonder that the level of communication between and amongst workers is not only informal and spontaneous but also intense. This is borne out by the common occurrence of meetings without agendas and minutes. Also, when presentations are made in these meetings, questioning of the proposal is unabashed and discussion is free and open. Those present are expected to be fully involved in such meetings and there are no 'sacred cows' that cannot be questioned.

This intense communication system also acts as a remarkably tight control system, in that people are always checking on each other to see how each is faring. This arises out of a genuine desire to keep abreast of developments in the organisation rather than any untoward motive. One result of this is that teams are more prudent in their financial expenditure on projects. Another is that the sea of inquisitors act as 'idea generators', thereby ensuring that teams are not dependent entirely on their own devices to innovate and solve problems. This usually also ensures that all options are considered before a final decision is made. The concomitant result of this fostering of creativity is that senior management is more tolerant of failure; knowing full well that champions have to make many tries, and consequently suffer some failures, in the process of creating successful innovations.

4 Productivity through people

A cherished principle of the excellent companies is that they treat their workers with respect and dignity; they refer to them as partners. This is because people, rather than systems or machines, are seen as the primary source of quality and productivity gains. Therefore, there is 'tough-minded respect for the individual and the willingness to train him, to set reasonable and clear expectations for him, and to grant him practical autonomy to step out and contribute directly to his job' (Peters and Waterman, 1982:239). There is a closeness and family feeling in such companies; indeed many of the 'partners' see the organisation as an extended family. The slogans of such companies tend to reflect this view of people: 'respect the individual', 'make people winners', 'let them stand out', 'treat people as adults'.

5 Hands-on, value-driven

Excellent companies are value-driven; they are clear about what they stand for and take the process of value shaping seriously. There is an implicit belief that everyone in the organisation, from the top to the bottom, should be driven by the values of the organisation; hence the great effort, time and money spent to inspire people by, and inculcate them with these values:

> ... these values are almost always stated in qualitative, rather than quantitative, terms. When financial objectives are mentioned, they are almost always ambitious but never precise. Furthermore, financial and strategic objectives are never stated alone. They are always discussed in the context of the other things the company expects to do well. The idea that profit is a natural by-product of doing something well, and not an end in itself, is almost always universal. (Peters and Waterman, 1982:284)

Implanting these values is a primary responsibility of the individual members of the management team. They set the tone by leading from the front. Coherence and homogeneity must, however, first be created among senior management by regular meetings (both formal and informal). The outcome of this is that management speak with one voice. They are passionate in preaching the organisation's values.

They unleash excitement, not in their offices, but mainly on the shop-floor where the workers are. Inculcating these values, however, is a laborious process and persistence is vital in achieving the desired goal.

6   Stick to the knitting

Acquisition or internal diversification for its own sake is not one of the characteristics of excellent companies. They must stick to the knitting – do what they know best. But when they do acquire, they do it in an experimental fashion; by first dipping a 'toe in the waters'. If the water does not feel good, they get out fast. Acquisitions are always in fields related to their core activities and they never acquire any business that they do not know how to run. As a general rule, they 'move out mainly through internally-generated diversification, one manageable step at a time' (Peters and Waterman, 1982:279).

7   Simple form, lean staff

A guiding principle in excellent companies is to keep things simple and small. Structurally, the most common form is the 'product division'. This form, which is rarely changed, provides the essential touchstone which everybody understands and from which the complexities of day-to-day life can be approached. Since the use of teams, groups and taskforces for specific projects is a common stock-in-trade of these companies, most changes in structure are made at the edges, such as allocating one or two people to an ad hoc team. By this approach, the basic structure is left in place, while all other things revolve and change around it. This gives these organisations great flexibility but still enables them to keep their structures simple, divisionalised and autonomous.

Such simple structures only require a small, lean staff at the corporate and middle management levels. This results in fewer administrators and more doers: 'it is not uncommon to find a corporate staff of fewer than 100 people running a multi-billion-dollar enterprise' (Peters and Waterman, 1982:15). Therefore, in excellent companies, flat structures, with few layers, and slimmed-down bureaucracies – which together allow flexibility and rapid communication – are the order of the day.

8 Simultaneous loose-tight properties

This is the 'firm and free' principle. On the one hand, it allows the excellent companies to control everything tightly, whilst on the other hand, allowing and indeed encouraging individual innovation, autonomy and entrepreneurship. These properties are jointly achieved through the organisation's culture; its shared values and beliefs. By sharing and believing the same values, self-control and self-respect result in each person becoming their own, and everyone else's, supervisor. The individual members of the organisation know they have the freedom, and are encouraged, to experiment and innovate. However, they also know that their actions will be scrutinised and judged, with the utmost attention paid to the impact they have on product quality, targets, and above all, the customer. The focus is on building and expanding the frontiers of the business. The ultimate goal is to be the best company, and in the final analysis, this is the benchmark against which the discipline and flexibility of the individual will be measured.

Therefore, Peters and Waterman maintain that the main attributes of excellent companies are: flat, anti-hierarchical structures; innovation and entrepreneurship; small corporate and middle management staffs; reward systems based on contribution rather than position or length of service; brain power rather than muscle power; and strong, flexible cultures.

Peters and Waterman's vision of the organisation of the future, based on their study of leading American companies, has proved extremely influential, not only in the business world but in academia as well. This is not to say that they are without their critics – far from it (Cummings and Huse, 1989) – however, there is little doubt that they laid the groundwork, especially in highlighting the important role played by culture, for other leading thinkers whose work draws on and gels with theirs.

Rosabeth Moss Kanter's post-entrepreneurial model

Kanter is one of America's leading management thinkers. As well as being a professor at the Harvard Business School, she is also a leading and influential management consultant. Her work complements and develops that of Peters and Waterman by attempting to define what organisations need to be like in the future if they are to be successful. Kanter calls for a revolution in business management to create what she terms post-entrepreneurial organisations. She uses this term:

> *... because it takes entrepreneurship a step further, applying entrepreneurial principles to the traditional corporation, creating a marriage between entrepreneurial creativity and corporate discipline, cooperation, and teamwork. (Kanter, 1989: 9–10)*

Kanter believes that:

> *If the new game of business is indeed like Alice-in-Wonderland croquet, then winning it requires faster action, more creative manoeuvring, more flexibility, and closer partnerships with employees and customers than was typical in the traditional corporate bureaucracy. It requires more agile, limber management that pursues opportunity without being bogged down by cumbersome structures or weighty procedures that impede action. Corporate giants, in short, must learn how to dance. (Kanter, 1989:20)*

In her (1989) book, *When Giants Learn To Dance: Mastering the Challenges of Strategy, Management, and Careers in the 1990s*, she argues that today's corporate elephants need to learn to dance as nimbly and speedily as mice if they are to survive in our increasingly competitive and rapidly-changing world. Companies must constantly be alert and on their guard, and keep abreast of their competitors' intentions. By evaluating the response of modern organisations to the demands placed upon them, Kanter has produced her post-entrepreneurial model of how the organisation of the future should operate. She sees post-entrepreneurial organisations as pursuing three main strategies:

1 Restructuring to find synergies.
2 Opening boundaries to form strategic alliances.
3 Creating new ventures from within – encouraging innovation and entrepreneurship.

1   Restructuring to find synergies

Synergy occurs where the whole adds up to more than the sum of its constituent parts. In an age where resources are scarce, one of the priorities of organisations is to make every part of the business add value to the whole. In practice this means selling-off a company's non-core activities and ensuring that what remains, especially at the corporate and middle management levels, is lean and efficient. Nevertheless, it is not sufficient merely to have a strategy of reducing the size of the organisational bureaucracy. Companies must also ensure that the essential tasks which these people previously carried out are still undertaken. This can be accomplished in a number of ways, such as: the use of computers to carry out monitoring and information gathering; devolving greater responsibility and power down to individual business units; and contracting out services and tasks previously carried out in-house.

The essence of this approach is to identify and concentrate on the core business areas and to remove all obstacles and impediments to their efficient and effective operation. Therefore, all non-core activities are eliminated, and authority is devolved to the appropriate levels of the business: those in the front line. The result is to create flatter, more responsive and less complex organisations which have a greater degree of focus than in the past. However, Kanter argues that such radical changes need to be well-planned, and executed with care and in a way which ensures that employee motivation is increased, not eliminated.

2 Opening boundaries to form strategic alliances

With the slimming down of the organisation and the contracting out of some of its functions, there arises the need to pool resources with other organisations; to band together to exploit opportunities and to share ideas and information. These alliances take three forms: service alliances, opportunistic alliances and stakeholder alliances. The first, a service alliance, is where two or more organisations form a cross-company consortium to undertake a special project with a limited life-span. Such alliances are usually considered when the resources of the various partners are insufficient to allow them to undertake the project by themselves. For this reason, and not surprisingly, many such alliances involve research and development projects. Ford and General Motors collaborating on research into the development of new materials for making cars is an example of this. This approach allows organisations to mobilise resources, often on a large scale, whilst limiting their exposure and protecting their independence. It is the limited purpose of the consortium which makes it possible even for competitors to join together for their mutual benefit.

The second form, an opportunistic alliance, comprises a joint venture whose aim is to take advantage of a particular opportunity which has arisen: 'the two principal advantages behind this kind of alliance are competence-enhancing ones: technology transfer or market access or both' (Kanter, 1989:126). An example of such an alliance is the link-up between the Rover Group and Honda Motors; the former gained access to Japanese know-how, whilst the latter gained greater access to the European market. However, as Kanter (1989:126) has pointed out, such alliances are not always equally beneficial 'once one of the partners has gained experience with the competence of the other, the alliance is vulnerable to dissolution – the opportunity can now be pursued without the partner.'

The third form, a stakeholder alliance, unlike the previous two, is seen as a continuing, almost permanent partnership between an organisation and its key stakeholders, generally considered to be its employees, customers and suppliers. There is a growing awareness among employees, trade unions and management of the need to see each other as partners in the same enterprise rather than rivals. A similar case is made for treating customers and suppliers as partners too. The main reason for the organisation to exist is to serve its customers; therefore, there is a need to keep close to them, not only being aware of their present concerns and future needs, but also in relation to joint product development. In the same way, the organisation relies on its suppliers, who will in any case want to get closer to them as their customers.

Stakeholder alliances have gained a growing band of adherents in Britain in recent years, especially, though not exclusively, amongst Japanese companies such as Nissan Motors (Partnership Sourcing, 1991; Wickens, 1987). As Kanter points out, major innovations in technology and organisational systems require longer-term investments. Companies can only enter into such investments if they are secure in the knowledge that their key stakeholders are themselves committed to the same aims and approach.

The result of these alliances is that structures and positions within organisations will change, sometimes quite dramatically. This is especially the case amongst senior and line managers, but even previously protected groups – such as R&D specialists – will also see their roles and responsibilities change. They will have to work more closely not only with colleagues internally, but also with external groupings. An example of this is the car industry, where manufacturers are involving suppliers in the design and development of new models. In some cases this merely involves greater co-ordination, but in others it involves the establishment of joint design teams, or even making the suppliers responsible for most of the design work.

3   Creating new ventures from within – encouraging innovation and entrepreneurship

Traditional organisations face a difficult balancing act between gaining the full benefits from existing mainstream business, and, at the same time, creating new activities which will become the mainstream business of the future. Kanter argues that there is a feeling in many traditional companies that opportunities are being missed due to their inability to give staff the flexibility to pursue new ideas and develop new products. The job of creating new products or ventures used to be the sole domain of the strategic planners or the R&D departments. However, this will no longer be the case; innovation will move from these specialised domains to the centre stage. This can already be seen in some organisations which are deliberately forming new, independent units to nurture innovation and entrepreneurship. New cultures are being created which encourage and aid innovation, and old barriers and restrictions are being eradicated. As a result of such changes, the innovative potential of employees can be tapped, and a proliferation of new ideas, products and ways of working is emerging.

The consequences of the post-entrepreneurial model

There is no doubt that the post-entrepreneurial model carries profound implications for both organisations and their employees. However, Kanter, unlike Peters and Waterman, does not see these new developments as being an unalloyed blessing, especially in the case of employees. In particular, she draws attention to three areas where the changes will have a major impact on employees: reward systems; career paths and job security; and lifestyle.

Reward systems

Employers and employees will more and more come to look for new and more appropriate ways of rewarding and being rewarded. Indeed, with the advent of performance-related pay, in both the private and public sectors, there is already a gradual change from determining pay on the basis of a person's position and seniority to basing it on their contribution to the organisation. These changes are being driven by four main concerns. The first is cost – the concern is that the present system is too expensive for companies that must conserve resources to be competitive. The second is equity – organisations are concerned that the present system does not reward employees fairly for their efforts. The third concern is with productivity – the worry here is that the present system is inadequate to motivate high performance from employees. The last concern is with entrepreneurial pressure – companies are aware that the present system does not always adequately reward entrepreneurs for their efforts.

These concerns are being approached through the application of three different, though not necessarily mutually exclusive, payment methods. The first is profit sharing, whereby the pay of the employee is pegged to a company's performance. This means that salaries are not fixed but instead are related, by the use of a predetermined formula, to the profit of the organisation over a given period of time, usually the previous financial year.

The second method is the use of performance bonuses, which are paid on top of basic salary and are related to a predetermined performance target. This method has the advantage of enabling individuals to establish a direct correlation between their personal effort and the bonus payment they receive. Though this method is not new, the sums involved are, sometimes, as much as twice basic salary.

The third payment method is the venture returns method, which is perhaps the most radical break with the past. This is a scheme whereby entrepreneurs and inventors within an organisation are given the opportunity to earn returns based on the performance, in the marketplace, of the particular products or services they are responsible for. Through this mechanism, the entrepreneur or inventor remains within the corporate fold but is paid on a similar basis to the owner of a small, independent business. The advantage is that they get the personal satisfaction and reward of running their 'own' business, whilst the larger organisation benefits from having highly-motivated and innovative people in charge of part of its operations.

The picture in terms of new reward systems is not, of course, totally rosy. Where there are winners, there may also be losers; not everyone will have the opportunity or drive to be an entrepreneur, or to be in a position that lends itself to some form of bonus system. Also, many people who presently benefit from reward systems based on seniority and position may find they lose out. Older workers, established in organisations and well down their chosen career path, could be particularly adversely affected by such changes. In addition, such payment systems may be divisive and create conflict. Kanter stresses the need for teamwork, yet a situation where some members of the team are receiving high bonuses is bound to create tensions which undermine cooperation and collaboration. It may be that profit sharing schemes, which encompass everyone in the organisation, overcome this threat to teamworking, but if everyone receives the same share of the profits irrespective of their individual contribution, the motivating effect is likely to be diminished. The result of these various approaches to pay could either be minimal in terms of motivation, or even be demotivating and indeed drive out the most experienced people in the organisation.

Careers and job security

As organisations become slimmer and more tasks are contracted out, organisation structures will become flatter as entire layers of hierarchy are dispensed with. The resultant effect may well be the demise of traditional forms of career path. Kanter argues that the idea of staying with one organisation and climbing the corporate career ladder is being replaced by hopping from job to job, not necessarily in the same organisation. Therefore, instead of people relying on organisations to give shape to their career, in future the onus will be on individuals to identify and pursue their own chosen route.

This change will also affect skill development in organisations. It will no longer be sufficient just to be skilled in a particular job or specialism, because these will certainly change over time or even entirely disappear. In future, individuals may find that the concept of job security is replaced by 'employability security' – the ability to adapt and enhance one's skills so as to be able to perform well in different types of jobs and organisations. Careers, therefore, will be shaped by professional and entrepreneurial principles; the ability to develop and market one's own skills and ideas, rather than by the sequence of jobs provided by one company. People will join organisations or accept particular jobs not, as in the past, because of job security or career progression, but in order to develop their skills, add to their knowledge and enhance their future employability.

Kanter argues that:

> ... what people are increasingly working to acquire is the capital of their own individual reputation instead of the organisational capital that comes from learning one system well and meeting its idiosyncratic requirements. For many managers, it might be more important, for example, to acquire or demonstrate a talent that a future employer or financial investor might value than to get to know the right people several layers above in the corporation where they currently work. (Kanter, 1989:324)

Having painted this picture, it must also be acknowledged that there are contradictions and dilemmas which need to be resolved. What is being created are organisations and cultures which facilitate innovation and entrepreneurship, and change and flexibility. These will be organisations where employability and loyalty are transient concepts and what matters, almost exclusively, is the individual's present performance rather than their past or potential future contribution. The two main dilemmas from the organisational perspective are, therefore, how to reconcile the above with their stated objective of treating employees as long-term partners, and how to motivate employees to work in the organisation's interest rather than their own interest. This is an especially pointed dilemma in the case of the champions and entrepreneurs on whom it is argued the future of organisations depends. This is because it is this group of highly marketable individuals who are most likely to see their careers in terms of many different jobs and organisations.

Workers' lifestyle

The future type of organisation is likely to be one where people will be given greater freedom to innovate and experiment, where there will be strong financial rewards for increased performance levels and where people will be given greater control over their area of the business. There is little doubt that in such situations people will be expected, and indeed wish, to work longer hours and centre what social life they have around their work. Nevertheless, where there are benefits, there may also be disbenefits:

> *The workplace as a centre for social life and the workmate as a candidate for marriage mate is, on one level, a convenience for overloaded people who have absorbing work that leaves little time to pursue a personal life outside. It is also an inevitable consequence of the new workforce demographics. But on another level, the idea is profoundly disturbing. What about the large number of people whose personal lives are not contained within the corridors of the corporation? What about the people with family commitments outside the workplace? (Kanter, 1989:285)*

We already know the adverse cost that such work patterns can have on people's physical and mental health and on their family life. In the case of the latter, one might expect to see an increase in our already high divorce rate. Indeed, Kanter believes unmarried or divorced executives are already thought to be preferred to their married counterparts by some companies because it is assumed they can focus more on their job given their lack of home life. Therefore, the line between motivation and exploitation may be a narrow one, and crossing it may benefit neither the individual nor the organisation.

To summarise, much of Kanter's work supports the view of Peters and Waterman in terms of the need for and direction of organisational change. Certainly, on the issues of innovation and entrepreneurship, culture and flexibility, and structure and jobs, there is much common ground. To an extent we might expect this, given that they are both writing from an American perspective, and basing their views on the experience and plans of leading American companies. Where they differ, however, is that Kanter takes a much more critical view of these developments. In particular, she draws attention to the contradiction that lies at the heart of the post-entrepreneurial model: are people – their skills, motivation and loyalty – central to the success of the organisation of the future, or are they just another commodity to be obtained and dispensed with as circumstances and their performance require?

The next and last section will examine the emergence of new organisational forms from the perspective of a leading British theorist: Charles Handy.

Charles Handy's emerging future organisations

Handy is a professor at the London Business School and a consultant to a wide range of organisations in business, government, the voluntary sector, education and health. He is also one of Britain's leading management thinkers. In his (1989) book *The Age of Unreason*, Handy argues that profound changes are taking place in organisational life:

> *The world of work is changing because the organisations of work are changing their ways. At the same time, however, the organisations are having to adapt to a changing world of work. It's a chicken and egg situation. One thing, at least, is clear – organisations in both private and public sectors face a tougher world – one in which they are judged more harshly than before on their effectiveness and in which there are fewer protective hedges behind which to shelter. (Handy, 1989:70)*

He asserts that British companies are fast moving away from the labour-intensive organisations of yesteryear. In future, new knowledge-based structures, run by a few smart people at their core who control a host of equally smart computerised machines, will be the order of the day. Already, he notes, leading British organisations are increasingly becoming entities which receive their added value from the knowledge and the creativity they put in, rather than from the application of muscle power. He contends that fewer, better-motivated people, helped by clever machines, can create much more added value than large groups of unthinking, demotivated ones ever could.

As with the two perspectives we have already examined, Handy believes that the emerging future organisations will be smaller, more flexible and less hierarchical. Similarly, he also believes that the new organisations will need to treat people as assets to be developed and motivated, rather than just industrial cannon-fodder. However, he does not assume that the future will be without diversity in relation to the organisational forms that emerge. Unlike Peters and Waterman, and to a lesser extent Kanter, he recognises that companies will continue to face differing circumstances and will need to respond in different manners. Therefore, instead of trying to re-establish a new 'one best way' for all organisations, with all the contradictions that arise from such attempts, Handy identifies three generic types of organisation which he argues will dominate in the future:

1 The Shamrock organisation.
2 The Federal organisation.
3 The Triple I organisation.

1   The Shamrock organisation

This form of organisation, like the plant of the same name which has three interlocking leaves, is composed of three distinct groups of workers who are treated differently and have different expectations – a small group of specialist 'core' workers, a contractual fringe, and a flexible labour force.

The core workers are the first leaf, and the main distinguishing feature of the Shamrock form of organisation. These are a group of specialists, professional workers who form the brain, the hub or what we might call the 'nerve centre' of the organisation. These are people who are seen as being essential to the organisation. It is these few intelligent and articulate personnel in whose hands and heads reside the secrets of the organisation. They are both specialists and generalists, in that they run the organisation and control the smart machines and computers that have replaced, to a large extent, much of the labour force. This 'all puts pressure on the core, a pressure which could be summed up by the new equation of half the people, paid twice as much, working three times as effectively' (Handy, 1989:118–19).

For their well-rewarded jobs, they are expected to be extremely loyal to the organisation, and to live and breathe their work. It is their responsibility to drive the organisation forward to ever greater success; to be flexible enough to meet the constantly-changing challenge of competitors and the equally changing and sophisticated needs of customers. Core workers operate as colleagues and partners in the organisation, as opposed to superiors and subordinates. In a very real sense, it is their company, and as such they expect to be recognised and rewarded for their roles and achievements, rather than for the position they occupy on the organisation's ladder. It follows that they are managed differently – by consent – they are asked and not told what to do.

The contractual fringe is the second leaf of the Shamrock. A central feature of such organisations is their smallness in relation to their productive capacity. This is achieved by two methods: firstly, as mentioned above, the use of machines to replace people; and secondly, the contracting out to individuals and other organisations of services and tasks previously done in-house. This leads to the creation of a contractual fringe, who may or may not work exclusively for the company in question. They are contracted to carry out certain tasks, for which they are paid a fee based on results, rather than a wage based on time taken. The arguments put forward in favour of such arrangements are numerous, but tend to boil down to three main ones: it is cheaper – companies only pay for what they get; it makes management easier – why keep the people on the payroll with all the attendant human management problems if it is not necessary?; and, when business is slack, it is the contractor who bears the impact of the reduced workload.

The flexible labour force is the third and fastest-growing leaf of the Shamrock and comprises a pool of part-time workers available for use by organisations. These are people with relevant skills who are not in need of, or who cannot obtain, full-time employment, but who are prepared to work on a part-time basis.

Increasingly, among this group of flexible workers are skilled housewives who left their jobs to raise families, but who are willing to return to work on a part-time basis, while still maintaining their child-rearing commitments. Included in this also is the growing army of young and retired executives, who prefer to hop from one job to the other, doing bits and pieces of work on a part-time basis. These workers are sometimes referred to as temps (temporaries) or casuals. The growth of this group can be measured by the proliferation of employment agencies, catering solely for these groups, which have been established in the UK since the early 1980s. However, the flexible workforce never:

> ... *have the commitment or ambition of the core. Decent pay and decent conditions are what they want ... They have jobs not careers and cannot be expected to rejoice in the organisation's triumphs any more than they can expect to share in the proceeds, nor will they put themselves out for the love of it; more work, in their culture, deserves and demands more money. (Handy, 1989: 80–81)*

The picture, therefore, of the Shamrock organisation is one where structure and employment practices allow it to be big in terms of output, whilst being small in terms of the number of direct employees. For the latter reason, it is lean with few hierarchical layers and even less bureaucracy. It achieves this by the application of smart machines and a combination of part-time staff and sub-contractors, whose work can be turned on and off as circumstances dictate. However, in a departure from past practice, the people and organisations involved may be highly skilled and competent. This also has the advantage of requiring much less office and factory accommodation than more traditionally-organised companies. Other than the core staff, the rest are all scattered in different organisations or their own homes, often linked through sophisticated communication systems.

Such organisations, with their flexibility and skills, are well-suited to the provision of high-performance products and services to demanding and rapidly-changing markets. The beauty of it all, as Handy argues, is that they do not have to employ all of the people all of the time or even in the same place to get the work done. According to Handy, small is not only beautiful but also increasingly preferable.

2   The Federal organisation

This is the second type of generic organisation which Handy sees as becoming dominant in the future. He defines this type of organisation as a variety of individual groups of organisations allied together under a common flag with some shaped identity. Federations arise for two reasons. The first is that as Shamrock organisations grow bigger, the core workers begin to find the volume of information available to them to make decisions increasingly difficult to handle. The second reason is in response to the constantly-changing and competitive environment of the business world. Modern organisations need not only to achieve the flexibility that comes from smallness, but also to be able to command the resources and power of big corporations.

As Handy (1989:110) puts it:

> *It [Federalism] allows individuals to work in organisation villages with the advantages of big city facilities. Organisational cities no longer work unless they are broken down into villages. In their big city mode they cannot cope with the variety needed in their products, their processes, and their people. On the other hand, the villages on their own have not the resources nor the imagination to grow. Some villages, of course, will be content to survive, happy in their niche, but global markets need global products and large confederations to make them or do them.*

Federalism, therefore, implies the granting of autonomy to Shamrocks. Autonomy requires that Shamrocks are headed by their own separate chief executives, supported by a team of core workers, who take full responsibility for running the company. In such situations the Shamrocks become separate, but related entities, under the umbrella of the Federal Centre. With the devolving of power to the Shamrocks, who still remain in the Federal portfolio, the Federal Centre is left to pursue the business of providing a common platform for the integration of the activities of the Shamrocks. The Federal Centre has the role of generating and collating ideas from the different Shamrocks and making them into concrete, achievable strategic objectives. Therefore, the Federal Centre is concerned mainly with the future; with looking forward, generating ideas, and creating scenarios and options of what the future will look like. All this is done with the ultimate aim of moving the organisation forward and keeping it ahead not only of its rivals, but also of its time.

Another feature of the Federal organisation is what Handy refers to as the 'Inverted Do'nut':

> *The do'nut is an American doughnut. It is round with a hole in the middle rather than the jam in its British equivalent ... This, however, is an inverted American do'nut, in that it has the hole in the middle filled in and the space on the outside ... The point of the analogy begins to emerge if you think of your job, or any job. There will be a part of the job which will be clearly defined, and which, if you do not do, you will be seen to have failed. That is the heart, the core, the centre of the do'nut ... [but] ... In any job of any*

significance the person holding the job is expected not only to do all that is required but in some way to improve on that ... to move into the empty space of the do'nut and begin to fill it up. (Handy, 1989:102)

Through this approach the Federal organisation seeks to maximise the innovative and creative potential of staff members. It does this by specifying the core job, the target and the quality standard expected of a given product or service. Outside of this specified domain – within the do'nut's empty space, however, staff members are given enough room and latitude to challenge and question existing ideas, to experiment and to come up with new methods of doing things, and new products or services. The aim is to encourage enquiry and experimentation that leads to higher standards.

It follows from this that the essence of leadership under a Federal system is to provide a shared vision for the organisation; one which allows room for those whose lives will be affected by it – either directly or indirectly – to modify it, ponder over it, expand it, accept it and then make it a reality. Leadership in such situations is about providing opportunities for staff to grow and test their potential to the limit.

3   The Triple I organisation

This is the third of Handy's new organisational forms. From the above, it is clear that both Shamrock and Federal organisation types introduce new dimensions into the world of work. Traditional perspectives are being transformed and the established criteria for judging organisational effectiveness are being re-evaluated. Issues such as the definition of a productive contribution to work, reward systems, managerial skills and many more issues are being examined in the light of new management ideas. Indeed, we appear to be on the verge of a revolution in management thought and practice.

An examination of the attributes of the core workers in both Shamrock and Federal organisations gives an indication of what will constitute the new formula for success and effectiveness in tomorrow's companies. The core workers, as seen by Handy, use their Intelligence to analyse the available Information to generate Ideas for new products and services. Thus we find that Handy's first two organisational forms contain the seeds to grow into his third form, the Triple I – organisations based on Intelligence, Information and Ideas. Since the three Is constitute the prime intellectual capital of the new organisations, clearly the core group of workers who possess these attributes are their most important asset.

In future, it is argued, the equation for organisational success will be Triple I=AV, where Triple I = Intelligence, Information and Ideas, and AV = Added Value, either in cash or kind. This will not depend solely on human ability but will be a combination of smart people and smart machines. Therefore, organisations of the future will increasingly have to: invest in smart machines to remain competitive and effective; recruit skilled and smart people to control the machines; and ensure that this group of skilled people are rewarded equitably.

For the Triple I organisation to emerge and remain successful, it must keep the skills, knowledge and abilities of its staff up to date. This means that it must become a learning organisation; one that provides a conducive environment for the development of its intellectual capital. Time and effort must be consciously and officially devoted to learning and study, at all levels of the organisation. The core, especially, must spend more time than their equivalents in more traditional companies on thinking and study. They must regularly meet with other external professionals and experts, go on study tours and listen more to 'partners' within the organisation, all with the objective of improving the organisation's human capital. The new organisations will be dynamic, interactive societies where information is open to all, freely given and freely received. In the Triple I organisation, everyone will be expected to think and learn as well as to do. Nevertheless, it is the core worker from whom most will be demanded. Such people will be increasingly :

> ... expected to have not only the expertise appropriate to his or her particular role, but will also be required to know and understand business, to have the technical skills of analysis and the human skills and the conceptual skills and to keep them up to date. (Handy, 1989:124)

This is one of the key features which makes the Triple I organisation unique; it is a hotbed of intellectual discourse, where the prevailing culture is one of consent rather than instruction. Staff are unsupervised in the traditional sense, and instead are trusted to do what is right and given room to experiment with new ideas and concepts. Finally, the flexibility of such organisations, and the unpredictability of the environments in which they operate, mean that careers will become more variegated and less permanent.

As can be seen, therefore, Handy's view of the future shape of organisations does not appear dissimilar to those of Kanter, and Peters and Waterman. However, he does depart from their views in at least two crucial respects. Firstly, he explicitly acknowledges that not all organisations will adopt the same form or move at the same pace. His three generic forms indicate that organisations will have to exercise choice and judgment in order to match their particular circumstances to the most suitable form. Also, it is clear that he views this as an evolutionary as well as a revolutionary process – companies cannot immediately become a Triple I type of organisation, they have to develop into one over time. Secondly, he explicitly states what is only hinted at by the other writers, namely that in the new organisations where everyone is to be treated as an equal 'partner', some will be more equal than others – i.e. the core workers will be treated and rewarded in a more preferential manner than the contractual fringe or the flexible labour force.

Conclusions

Organisations are becoming increasingly aware that in the last 10 to 15 years, the world has turned on its axis. The days of the mass production of standardised products are over. As Perez (1983) and Freeman (1988) have argued, a new techno-economic rationale is emerging. This new rationale has three main features. Firstly, owing to more expensive energy and relatively cheaper information inputs, there is a shift towards information-intensive rather than energy- or materials-intensive products. Secondly, this leads to a change from dedicated mass production systems towards more flexible systems that can accommodate a wider range of products, smaller batches and more frequent design changes. The pre-eminent example of this is the Japanese car industry which, through the use of Just-in-Time production techniques and the adoption of Total Quality Management approaches, has moved away from mass production and in so doing, gained an enormous advantage over Western car companies who are still stuck in the traditional mould (Womack et al. 1990). Therefore, 'economies of scale' are being replaced by 'economies of scope'. The third feature of this new rationale is the move towards the greater integration of functions and systems within companies and between suppliers and customers. This integration permits a more rapid response to market and customer requirements, whether this be in relation to volume, product characteristics or new market opportunities.

It is the emergence of this new rationale which is driving organisations to a fundamental reassessment of their objectives and operations, rather than a mere change in fashion or managerial whim. This is also the reason why the new organisational forms are so radically different from what has gone before; although we might note in passing that the new forms, especially Handy's Shamrock type, bear an interesting resemblance to the first budding of organisational life during the Industrial Revolution. The entrepreneurial style of management, the stress on a privileged core of skilled workers, and the contracting out of whole areas of organisational activities are all hallmarks of the early industrial organisations. However, the big differences between then and now relate to the level of sophistication and complexity of the new organisations which are emerging, the degree of integration of both internal functions and external relationships, and the grade of intelligence and skill required of all staff, whether they be core or periphery. Watson (1986) argues that for the Culture-Excellence school, as he terms the proponents of this approach, there is one further and crucial difference. In these new organisations, 'What brings the activities of the organisational members to focus upon those purposes which lead to effective performance is the existence of a strong and clearly articulated culture' (Watson, 1986:66).

It is clear, therefore, that the new organisational paradigms that are emerging are remarkably different from most of the theory and practice that has grown up in the last 100 years. Organisations are entering a new age, where familiar themes are taking on different meanings and are being expressed in a new language.

New organisational paradigms: changes

Contrasting the old with the new, we find that what is important in the new is not muscle power, but brain power; the ability to make intelligent use of information to create ideas that add value and sustain competitiveness. The new is flatter in structure, though it might be more accurate to say that structure is decreasing in importance and that its role as a directing and controlling mechanism is being taken over by cultures that stress the need for, and facilitate, flexibility and adaptation. This sounds the death knell of hierarchical organisations and the concept of promotion through the ranks. Careers and skills are taking on new meanings, as are established ideas of reward.

Careers, in future, it is argued, are likely to depend on the individual and his/her ability to remain employable. This in turn means that the skills needed for 'employability' will, in the future, tend to be generic and broad-based rather than organisation- or function-specific.

Likewise, career paths and promotion will no longer be shaped by the particular employing organisation and its structures and criteria, but will be driven more by individuals creating their own opportunities by taking on new roles and responsibilities, either in one organisation or, more likely, by moving from company to company. As for pay, it seems that this will take the form not so much of a wage related to the particular post occupied, but more that of a fee paid for actual performance.

On human relations, the message being transmitted is that the new forms of organisations will treat their employees in a more responsible and humane fashion than has been the norm. Employees will be seen and treated as 'partners', capable of making a substantial contribution to the growth of the organisation. This approach, it is argued, will manifest itself in a tough-minded respect for the individual, who will receive training, be set reasonable and clear objectives, and be given the autonomy to make his/her own contribution to the work of the organisation. The new organisations will seek to develop open, flexible and pragmatic cultures, which help to maintain a learning environment that promotes creativity and entrepreneurship amongst all employees.

Another feature of the new organisational forms, it is claimed, will be their ability to grant autonomy and encourage flexibility and initiative, whilst at the same time keeping a tight control of their operations. Like so much else, this is to be achieved through culture rather than structure, and values rather than rules. Everything is to be monitored closely, not by the watching eye of superiors, but by the creation of a homogenous environment in which all take an equal responsibility for, and legitimate interest in, the work of their colleagues.

New organisational paradigms: potential problems

Clearly, the new organisation forms which are being promoted offer much that is admirable and worth supporting. Equally clearly, their adherents and promoters raise more questions than they answer. To an extent this is inevitable, given that we are dealing with something that is emerging rather than an existing and concrete reality. Nevertheless, it would be remiss to ignore or gloss over the questions and dilemmas that seem apparent, in particular where these relate to areas that are crucial to the operation of organisations: structure, politics and people.

In terms of structure, whilst there are attempts to identify more than one new form, especially by Handy, the organisations of the future all have the same or similar characteristics. They all are at the organic end of the Mechanistic-Organic continuum, to use Burns and Stalker's (1961) classification of organisation types. Whilst this is understandable given the rapid pace of change, it does rather beg the question: will all organisations face exactly the same contingencies? Is the correct approach for them all to respond in the same manner? This appears to be a classic case of what Peters and Waterman call Irrational rationality – attempting to prescribe the 'right' answer irrespective of the particular circumstances.

Therefore, regardless of the general trend, some organisations may still find that Mechanistic structures are more applicable to their circumstances. Examples of this may well be organisations which need to process large amounts of standardised information, such as certain government departments. After all, this is not the first time the death of bureaucracy has been prematurely announced. Nor is it good enough to assume that the real issue is culture rather than structure – i.e. that if one creates the type of cultures that the proponents of the new order advocate, then, irrespective of the official structure, staff will configure themselves to achieve the organisation's objectives. What this line of reasoning ignores, but which Handy (1986) has forcefully argued in the past, is that the cultures which are appropriate for Organic organisations can be disastrous if applied to Mechanistic ones.

In terms of organisational politics, it was argued in previous chapters that the two main areas that existing organisation theories found difficult to accommodate were culture and politics. Clearly, the new approaches cannot be accused of ignoring the issue of culture; indeed it is given a central role. However, as far as organisational politics and conflict are concerned, little is said. The assumption appears to be that employees working in smaller business units, having greater autonomy and more satisfying jobs, will work with each other, pursuing a common purpose. Yet how realistic is this? We know that politics and conflict between individuals and groups are endemic to organisational life (Robbins, 1986). We are told that the new organisations will encourage and reward individual effort and entrepreneurship, though teamwork is to be encouraged. It is also asserted that the new, independent groupings that large organisations will create will compete for resources, and that success will depend, in a situation where there is supposed to be an open exchange of information, on who comes up with the best ideas. On the surface of it, this hardly seems to create the conditions for the elimination of politics and conflict. Nevertheless, the underlying argument appears to be that the apparent incompatibility of these features will be resolved through the creation of strong, flexible, pragmatic cultures which promote the values of trust, co-operation and teamwork. No wonder culture is given such a prominent role by those promoting the new paradigms; without it, it would be difficult to see how key obstacles would be overcome.

The other major area where there are potential problems and dilemmas is that of the role and behaviour of people in the new organisations. On the one hand, they are proclaimed as the chief asset of the new organisations. They are to be treated humanely, trained and developed, given autonomy, well rewarded, all treated as equal partners in the business, etc. On the other hand, there are clearly different grades of employee, from core to periphery, and these different grades will be treated and rewarded in a markedly dissimilar manner.

Nor will life be all roses for the privileged core workers; these will be expected to devote themselves body and soul to the company, regardless of family commitments or health considerations. It is not clear either whether the loyalty such people are expected to give to their employers will be reciprocated. We are told that employers will establish long-term relationships with their employees, but we are also reminded that employability and current performance will be the criteria for the continuation of such relationships. It could be that many workers will find their usefulness is less permanent than the literature indicates; this may well be the case with older workers and women who take career breaks to raise children. Both groups, for different reasons, may find that their skill/commitment levels are judged not to make them suitable as core workers.

There is one final aspect of people and the new organisations which should be touched on, though some might argue it goes beyond the remit of organisation theorists. If the new organisations are going to be radically 'downsized', there could be serious implications for levels of unemployment. We already know that a new army of part-time workers will be created, but even taking these into account, organisations are expected to be markedly smaller in future. Either the new, entrepreneurial organisations will create such an upsurge in economic activity that unemployment will not be a major problem, or mass unemployment, above and beyond what we see at present, will become an established and unavoidable fact of modern life. If the latter does become the reality, then not only will we have major differences between those in work, but also between the employed and the unemployed. This may only mean that the future resembles the present, but it does indicate a potentially large and important gap between the rhetoric and reality of the emerging organisational forms.

Japan: a different approach

It should, of course, be pointed out that, whilst these emerging paradigms are becoming increasingly influential in the USA and Europe, the Japanese have developed a different approach to structuring and managing organisations. As a number of writers have observed (Lu, 1987; Morgan, 1986; Ohmae, 1990), Japanese companies tend to be characterised by:

- A strong, almost family, loyalty to the company by employees.
- Slow promotion and on-the-job training.
- Pay related to length of service.
- Lifetime employment for core workers.
- Authority relationships which are paternalistic, highly traditional and deferential.
- Collective decision making through slow and exhaustive consultation.
- Long-term strategic planning and the consistent pursuit of strategic objectives.

Many of the above characteristics, such as pay related to length of service, do not sit easily with the emerging paradigms we have been discussing. This does not mean the two approaches cannot be reconciled or learn from each other. Indeed, proponents of the new paradigms do claim to draw on the Japanese experience, though perhaps there is yet more to learn.

Nevertheless, it must be restated that emerging paradigms, by their very nature, will contain dilemmas and contradictions which can only be resolved with the passage of time. However, this is not a case for ignoring them; rather the reverse. The future is not, hopefully, immutable. We can and should attempt to influence it by promoting the good and avoiding the bad. The challenge, therefore, is for organisations to ensure that the new paradigms they will create and adopt improve on the past, rather than merely reproducing its worst aspects in another guise. This will entail each organisation undertaking a root and branch reappraisal of its purpose and operation.

In many cases, if not all, this will lead to major changes in form and function. Such developments cannot be accomplished overnight or on a piecemeal basis. What will be required to achieve such radical trans-formations are strategic, long-term plans complemented by well-thought-out and carefully-executed change programmes. This type of approach is alien to many Western companies; even amongst those who have attempted it, the failure rate is high. Yet, the Japanese claim that strategic management has been one of the major factors in the transformation of their companies into world leaders (Ohmae, 1990). In the following sections of this book, we will examine the areas of strategic management (especially comparing the Western and Japanese experiences), and change management, in order to identify how these can be utilised to bring about organisational transformation.

Part Two

Strategic management –
Theory and practice

4

Strategic management:
approaches and perspectives

Introduction

In Part One, we examined the development of organisation practice and theory in the 200 years since the Industrial Revolution. What can be seen most clearly is the way that approaches to the management of organisations have evolved over this period.

In the beginning, management was almost exclusively concerned with labour discipline and working hours. The methods used to pursue these were ad hoc, erratic, short-term and usually harsh and unfair. As the period progressed, more structured and consistent approaches came to the fore. In addition, the emphasis moved to the effectiveness and efficiency of the entire organisation, rather than focusing purely on discipline and hours of work. This can be seen both in the work of the Classical school and the Human Relations movement. Nevertheless, organisation theorists still tended to dwell on identifying the 'one best way' to structure all organisations. In the 1960s, a third approach, Contingency Theory, emerged which stressed the need to take into account external and internal variables when designing organisations.

Now new paradigms are being promoted which, it is argued, make past practice and theories irrelevant in the face of changed economic and social conditions. To an extent, a new 'one best way' is being promoted, but one which is radically different from the old. It is an approach which accepts that organisations must think long-term, whilst operating in the here and now. It is one which recognises the benefits (and shortcomings) of quantitativity, replicability and discipline. However, it does not allow these to overshadow the fact that organisations are basically social systems, whose productivity and success depend on human creativity, flexibility and entrepreneurship. The implications of this approach are enormous in terms of organisational change and upheaval. Not only are organisations being called upon to change their structures and practices, but also their very cultures, with all the implications this carries for conflict and misunderstanding (Allaire and Firsirotu, 1984). Clearly, this cannot be accomplished on either a short-term or an ad hoc basis. In effect, organisations are being asked to embark on an organisation-wide, consistent and long-term programme of development and renewal.

Though few of the major writers we have examined in the last three chapters have used the term, almost all would accept that a strategic approach is required for achieving the radical and long-term change programmes that are necessary if their particular paradigm is to be achieved. This is as true for Taylor and Fayol as it is for Mayo and Barnard, and certainly holds good for Burns and Stalker as well as for Kanter and Handy.

However, though most might agree that, for the scale of change advocated, an overall and forward-looking strategy is essential, not all provide a definition of strategy, nor are they in agreement about its purpose. This chapter will examine the concept and application of organisational strategy. This will be done, firstly, by mapping its development and various definitions. Then the different types of strategy will be discussed, followed by an examination of the main strategic planning tools. Throughout it will be argued that as the concept of strategy has been developed it has become less quantitatively- (mathematically-) orientated and increasingly influenced by more qualitative approaches.

The chapter concludes by examining a radically different approach to strategy, advocated by a new generation of strategists, much influenced by the Japanese. This approach relies much less on quantitative and rational concepts than previous approaches. It is a view of strategy which, perhaps not totally coincidentally, sits much easier with the emergent organisational paradigms than earlier ones would have done.

The origins of strategic management

It is most commonly argued that our concept of strategy has been passed down to us from the ancient Greeks. Bracker (1980:219) argues that the word strategy comes from the Greek *stratego* meaning 'to plan the destruction of one's enemies through the effective use of resources'. However, the Greeks developed the concept purely in relation to the successful pursuit of victory in war. The concept remained a military one until the Industrial Revolution when it began to permeate the business world (Bracker, 1980; Chandler, 1962). Chandler (1962), argued that the emergence of strategy in civilian organisational life resulted from an awareness of the opportunities and needs – created by changing population, income and technology – to employ existing or expanding resources more profitably.

Hoskin (1990) largely agrees with Chandler's view of the development of modern business strategy since the Industrial Revolution. However, he does take issue with both Chandler and Bracker on two crucial points. Firstly, he argues that the modern concept of organisational strategy bears little resemblance to military strategy, at least as it existed up to the First World War.

Secondly, he challenges the view that its origins are untraceable. When investigating the origins of modern strategy he did find a link with the military world, though it was not quite the link that others have proposed. He argues – like Chandler – that one of the most significant developments in business management in the nineteenth century occurred in the running of the US railways. Hoskin gives the credit for initiating business strategy to one of the Pennsylvania Railway's executives, Herman Haupt. He states that Haupt:

> ... *changes the rules of business discourse: the image in which he reconstructs business, on the Pennsylvania Railroad, is that of the proactive, future-oriented organization, which is managed by the numbers...How does he do so? By importing the practices of writing, examination and grading ... .On the Pennsylvania Railroad we find for the first time the full interactive play of grammatocentrism [writing and recording] and calculability [mathematical analysis of the recorded data]. (Hoskin, 1990:20)*

This approach created the bedrock on which strategic management grew in the USA, especially after the Second World War. It also ensured that strategic management became a quantitatively-orientated discipline. A discipline whose focus was on using numerical analysis to forecast market trends in order to plan for the future. Hoskin also points out that Haupt was a graduate of the US military academy at West Point, which pioneered the techniques of 'writing, examination and grading' in the military world. From there its graduates, particularly Haupt, took the techniques out into the business world – hence the link between military and civilian management techniques.

Therefore, it is possible to see why strategic management developed in the way it has – as a quantitative, mathematical approach. We can also see that there are links between the military and business world, but they are not as some have argued. Management strategy has not developed from the approach to military campaigns of the ancient Greeks; instead it has adopted and made its own the techniques of record-keeping and analysis that were developed at West Point in order to measure the performance and suitability for military life, of the US army's future officer class.

In the intervening years these techniques and approaches have become more widely disseminated and used. However, it was only after the Second World War, with increased competition and rapid organisational and technological change, that strategic management began to be taken up on a wider basis, and then only in the USA initially (Bracker, 1980).

Having examined the origins of modern strategic management, we can now look to achieving a more precise definition of what it means today.

Development and definition of strategy

As mentioned above, though the origins of strategic management can be identified in the middle years of the nineteenth century, it was not until after the Second World War that it began to be more widely used, and then only in the USA. Initially, organisations tried to cope with the new and rapidly-changing technological, economic and organisational developments through a form of long-range planning. This necessitated: firstly defining the firm's objectives, then establishing plans in order to achieve those objectives, and finally, allocating resources, through capital budgeting, in line with the plans. A key objective of this process was to reduce the gap that often occurred between a firm's aspirations and plans and the extrapolation of existing trends (Fox, 1975).

The use of long-range planning, in this manner, to formulate strategy, ran into problems when it became increasingly evident that forecasting past trends into the future could not produce accurate results or achieve the firm's desired objectives. Growth was not steady; it could slow down, increase or be interrupted in an unpredictable and violent manner. Also, new opportunities and threats, which nobody had envisaged, could and did emerge. Furthermore, it became evident that closing the planning gap was not necessarily the most critical aspect of strategy formulation. Volatile markets, over-capacity, and resource constraints have taken over as dominant management considerations since the early 1970s.

Consequently, long-range planning has been replaced by strategic management, which incorporates the possibility that changes in trends can and do take place, and is not based on the assumption that adequate growth can be assured (Elliot and Lawrence, 1985). In addition, strategic management focuses more closely on winning market share from competitors, rather than assuming that organisations can rely solely on the expansion of markets for their own growth.

Therefore, long-range planning was essentially concerned with plotting trends and planning the actions required to achieve the identified growth targets, all of which were heavily biased towards financial goals and budgetary controls. The focus of strategic management, on the other hand, is more on the environmental assumptions that underlie market trends (Mintzberg and Quinn, 1991).

Bearing these developments in mind, it is now possible to achieve a clearer definition of what is meant by strategic management. Like many other concepts in the field of management, there is no agreed, all-embracing definition of strategic management. But this must be expected when dealing with an area that is constantly developing. Nor should this inhibit the search for a definition, because in doing so we can see how strategic management is developing and where the main areas of dispute lie.

Ansoff (1965), in his early work, regarded strategic management as primarily concerned with external, rather than internal problems of the firm and especially with the selection of the product-mix which the firm will produce and the markets to which it sells. Chandler (1962) defined it as the determination of the basic long-term goals and objectives of an enterprise and the adoption of courses of action and the allocation of resources necessary for carrying out these goals. Hofer and Schendel (1978) defined strategy as the basic characteristics of the match an organisation achieves with its environment.

The crucial difference between Ansoff, Hofer and Schendel on the one hand and Chandler on the other, is that the former three regard strategy as almost exclusively concerned with the relationships between the firm and its environment, whilst Chandler takes a broader view. His definition includes internal as well as external factors. In particular, he sees issues such as organisational structures, production processes and technology as being essentially strategic. The point he makes is that the external and internal cannot be separated, as the open systems theorists would be the first to point out (Scott, 1987).

The external affects the internal, and vice versa. Therefore, strategic management must encompass the totality of the organisational domain and must not be restricted to one aspect, such as determining the product-market mix (Andrews, 1980).

Another distinction which needs to be made is between the various terms used to describe strategic management activities. Many writers seem to treat corporate planning, long-range planning, strategic planning and formal planning as synonymous. However, not all would agree. Naylor (1979), for example, defines strategic planning as long-range planning with a time horizon of three to five years. Litschert and Nicholson (1974) disagree: they state that strategic and long-term planning are not synonymous. They argue that strategic planning is a process which involves making a sequence of interrelated decisions aimed at achieving a desirable future environment for an organisation. Andrews (1980), similarly, defines strategy as a:

> ... *pattern of decisions in a company that determines and reveals its objectives, purposes, or goals, produces the principal policies and plans for achieving those goals, and defines the range of business the company is to pursue, the kind of economic and human organisation it is, or intends to be, and the nature of the economic and non-economic contribution it intends to make to its shareholders, employees, customers and communities. (Quoted in Smith 1985:10)*

In the use of all these various terms, certain basic features regarding strategic management stand out. These are that strategic management is primarily concerned with:

1 The full scope of an organisation's activities, including corporate objectives and organisational boundaries.
2 Matching the activities of an organisation to the environment in which it operates.
3 Ensuring that the internal structures, practices and procedures enable the organisation to achieve its objectives.
4 Matching the activities of an organisation to its resource capability; assessing the extent to which sufficient resources can be provided to take advantage of opportunities or avoid threats in the organisation's environment.
5 The acquisition, divestment and reallocation of resources.
6 Translating the complex and dynamic set of external and internal variables which an organisation faces, into a structured set of clear future objectives which can then be implemented on a day-to-day basis.

In defining strategic management, there are two further questions which need to be considered:

- Is strategy a process or the outcome of a process?
- Is strategy an economic/rational phenomenon or is it an organisational/social phenomenon?

Taking these two questions together, it can be seen that there is a body of opinion which sees strategy as an intentional, prescriptive process, based on a rational model of decision making (Ansoff, 1965; Argenti, 1974; Steiner, 1969). However, there is an equally insistent body which argues that it is the outcome of the complex social and political processes involved in organisational decision making (Hamel and Prahalad, 1989; Miles and Snow, 1978; Mintzberg, 1987; Pettigrew, 1980; Quinn, 1980).

The former group represents the early work in the field of strategic management. They not only see strategy as an economic/rational process, but also consider its options and usefulness as primarily restricted to issues relating to market share and profit maximisation (Porter, 1980). The latter group, which represents the new face of strategic management, increasingly views strategy not as a process, but as an outcome of a process. Their emphasis is not on the construction of detailed and preformed plans, which in any case they believe is an unworkable approach, but on the organisational/social aspects of strategy formation. The argument here is that the capability of an organisation in terms of its structure, systems and management style can be seen as constituting a strategic solution, which may or may not be successful, depending on external factors, such as the nature of industry competition. In other words, they see strategy as the outcome of the decisions a firm takes in terms of deploying and constructing its organisational capability, rather than the cause (Miles and Snow, 1978).

One of the often-cited examples for this view is that of Japanese management. Pascale and Athos (1982) and Hamel and Prahalad (1989) argue that Japanese business success is not based on well-thought-out strategies per se, but on the commitment of Japanese managers to create and pursue a vision of their desired future. The vision is then used to bind an organisation together and give it a common purpose which all can contribute to. This is made possible by the organisation's inherent capability in terms of its structure and culture. Mintzberg (1987) has come to a similar perspective based on the many Western companies he has studied. He argues that successful companies do not start out with detailed strategic plans. Instead, they have an explicit view of where it is they want the organisation to go. The strategy to get them there 'emerges' from the pattern of decisions they take in order to move towards their desired objective.

It is clear, then, that in the attempt to define strategy, the weight of the argument is shifting from seeing it as a rational, mathematical process, to seeing it as the outcome of the ability of an organisation's management to utilise its strengths and competencies in the competitive pursuit of success. In this respect, the development of our perspective on strategy very much parallels the development of organisation theory. In the first instance organisations were seen very much as mechanical/rational entities; however, as time has progressed, and our understanding developed, the social perspective has come to the fore, and so it is with strategy. The emphasis is, therefore, changing.

Strategy is no longer seen purely in relation to product-market mix. Attention is now becoming concentrated on attaining the appropriate internal arrangements which allow a company to pursue success effectively. The argument, as discussed in Chapter 3, is that it is innovation, flexibility and entrepreneurship which create competitive organisations. This certainly does not invalidate market-place issues, but does emphasise the conditions necessary to tackle these correctly. Nevertheless, because of the origins of strategic management, the types of strategy are still, though no longer exclusively, market- and quantitatively-orientated, as the next section will show.

Types of strategies

There is a wide, and often confusing, variety of types of strategy that organisations can adopt. One important way of categorising these, and thus reducing the confusion, is to recognise that there are three levels of strategic decision making in organisations:

1 *Corporate level* – strategy at this level concerns the direction, composition and co-ordination of the various businesses and activities that comprise a large and diversified organisation, such as ICI.
2 *Business level* – strategy at this level relates to the operation and direction of each of the individual businesses within a group of companies, such as Nissan's car assembly plant at Sunderland.
3 *Functional level* – strategy at this level concerns individual business functions such as marketing or personnel.

Each of these levels, though they are interrelated, has its own distinct strategic concerns and each can draw on a different battery of strategic weapons, or types, to aid them; although there are strategies at the Corporate level which have their counterparts at the Business level, and likewise at the Functional level.

At the Corporate level, strategy deals with the 'game plan' for managing diversified enterprises whose activities cut across several lines of business. It concerns itself with questions such as:

• What is the mission of the organisation?
• How should the business portfolio be managed?
• What existing businesses should be divested and which new ones acquired ?
• What priority and role should be given to each of the businesses in the current portfolio?

According to Thompson and Strickland (1983), the central strategic concerns at the individual Business level are:

• How should the firm position itself to compete in distinct, identifiable and strategically-relevant markets?
• Which types of products should it offer to which groups of customers ?
• How should the firm structure and manage the internal aspects of the business in support of its chosen competitive approach?

Functional- (or Operational-) level strategy concerns itself with the following questions:

• How can the strategies formulated at the Corporate and Business levels be translated into concrete operational terms in such a way that the individual organisational functions (marketing, finance, R&D, manufacturing, personnel, finance, etc.) can pursue and achieve them?
• How should the individual functions of the business organise themselves in order not only to achieve their own aims, but also to ensure that they integrate with the other functions to create synergy?

Given the different concerns of these three levels, it becomes possible to appreciate why there are so many types of strategy available and at which level they are most appropriate. The need to integrate the strategies and structures of these three levels also becomes clear.

Otherwise, for example, the Corporate level may pursue a strategy of diversification whilst the individual businesses are busy concentrating their efforts on fewer products and markets. Nevertheless, it would be wrong to see this as a mechanical process which begins at the Corporate level and moves in a linear fashion through to the Functional level. Strategy formation is inherently iterative and aims to optimise the operation of the organisation in its entirety rather than maximising the product of any one particular part.

These issues, and the main differences in scope and focus of the individual levels, can clearly be seen by a brief examination of the types of strategy that are pursued at the Corporate and Business levels. Functional-level strategies will not be examined because these flow from and facilitate the other two levels.

Corporate-level strategy

A review of the literature broadly reveals six basic types of strategy at this level:

1 *Stability strategy* – as its name implies, strategies under this heading are designed to keep organisations quiet and stable. They are most frequently found in successful organisations, operating in medium-attractiveness industries, who are faced with unpredictable circumstances outside the range of their normal business experience. Because of their markets and products, such organisations believe they have no need to make sudden changes and have the time and position to allow events to unfold before making any response (Wheelen and Hunger, 1989).

2 *Growth strategy* – this is possibly the most common form of all corporate strategies, and involves either concentrating on dominating one industry or growing by diversification across a number of industries. As a number of writers have suggested (Argenti, 1974; Byars, 1984), its basic attraction is twofold. Firstly, there is a strong correlation between increased turnover and increased profit. Secondly, the performance of senior managers tends to be measured in terms of the annual increase in turnover and profit. However, there are those who point out that increases in turnover are not necessarily matched by increases in profits and that, given the need to invest to achieve growth in turnover, growth may actually weaken companies' financial health (Byars, 1984; Drucker, 1974).

3 *Portfolio extension* – this is another variant of the growth strategy but is achieved through mergers, joint ventures or acquisitions, rather than organic growth. The first two of these allow growth or development to take place, without the organisations involved having to invest the level of resources that would be necessary if they were operating in isolation. The latter, acquisition, is usually resource-intensive but brings immediate gains in the form of an established and, hopefully, profitable business (Byars, 1984; Leontiades, 1986; Little, 1984).

4 *Retrenchment strategy* – this strategy is usually only embarked upon when an organisation is in trouble or, because of adverse market conditions, sees trouble ahead. It usually involves a process of cutting back on numbers employed and activities undertaken – to use Peters and Waterman's phrase: 'downsizing'. In some situations this may lead to selling-off the entire enterprise. However, the general aim is to cut back in order to match expenditure to projected income, and refocus the organisation so as to be able once again to attain prosperity in the future (Bowman and Asch, 1985; Thompson and Strickland, 1983).

5 *Harvesting strategy* – this involves reducing investment in a business or area of activity in order to reduce costs, improve cash flow and capitalise on whatever residual competencies or areas of advantage still remain. This approach can be implemented at different rates depending on the urgency of the situation. Slow harvesting consists of reducing financial support at such a slow rate that it almost appears to be a maintenance strategy; at the other extreme, fast harvesting can result in budgets being cut at such a rate that it seems almost indistinguishable from liquidation (Harrigan, 1980; Kotler, 1978; Porter, 1980).

6 *Combination strategy* – the above strategies are not mutually exclusive, and can be linked together in whatever combination seems appropriate given the circumstances of the organisation in question. However, combination strategies are clearly more appropriate, or at least more necessary, in large multi-divisional organisations where the circumstances faced by the various activities are likely to be different. Therefore, in such situations, organisations may appear in a constant flurry of change where some parts are being run down and/or divested, whilst new units are being acquired and other areas of the business rapidly expanded (Glueck, 1978; Pearson, 1977).

The above list is not exhaustive, nor can it be, given that each organisation is free to develop its own strategic variant in relation to its own circumstances. It is the circumstances of the particular organisation in question which should dictate the type of strategy adopted, rather than any attempt to copy what has been successful elsewhere. However, it should be noted that all except the first, maintenance strategy, imply fundamental restructuring of the internal operations of the organisation.

Business-level strategy

Whilst Corporate-level strategies are mainly concerned with managing diversified enterprises whose activities span a number of different areas, Business-level strategies relate to the different ways that an individual business unit can compete in its chosen market(s). However, it must be remembered that they are chosen and deployed within the framework of an overall Corporate strategy and not in isolation from it. Just as at the Corporate level, the available Business-level strategies are many and varied. To attempt to describe them all would be time-consuming, confusing and unnecessary. Instead, we shall examine the main variants through the work of one of the leading authorities on Business level strategies, Michael Porter.

Porter (1980) argues that there are only three basic Business-level strategies:

1 *Cost leadership* – the aim of this strategy is to achieve overall lower costs than one's competitors, without reducing comparable product quality. To do this requires a high volume of sales in order to allow organisations to structure themselves in such a way that they can achieve economies of scale. This strategy, to quote Porter, requires the:

> ... *aggressive construction of efficient scale facilities, vigorous pursuit of cost reductions from experience, tight cost and overhead control, avoidance of marginal customer accounts, and cost minimisation in areas like R&D, services, sales force and so on. (1980:15)*

2 *Product differentiation* – this is based on achieving industry-wide recognition of different and superior products and services compared to those of other suppliers. This recognition can be accomplished through the design of special brand images, technology features, customer service or higher quality, all of which have

implications for the structure and operation of companies. Achieving differentiation is likely to result in insulation against competitive rivalry due to securing customer loyalty. The resultant competitive advantage also leads to increased returns, sometimes through making customers less sensitive to high product price.

3 *Specialisation by focus* – in this case the strategy is concerned with selecting (focusing upon) only certain markets, products or geographic areas in which to compete. Porter argues that by focusing in this way, it becomes feasible for a firm to dominate its chosen area(s). The method of achieving domination could either be through cost advantage or product differentiation. According to Porter, however, such niche markets must have certain characteristics which separate them out from the market in general: 'the target segment must either have buyers with unusual needs or else the production and delivery system that best serves the target must differ from that of the other industry segments' (1980:15).

If the niche market grows, or is incorporated, into a large market, then market dominance is unlikely to be retained. In such a situation, the previously dominant organisation will find itself having to compete for market share with others. In effect, the rules of the game have changed and a different strategy is required – either attempting to gain cost leadership across the entire market, or adopting a product-differentiation policy which neutralises other competitors' cost advantage.

Porter's assertion concerning these three strategies is that they are distinct and cannot be mixed. That is to say, it is not possible to pursue successfully a cost-leadership strategy and a product-differentiation strategy at the same time because each requires different organisational arrangements to be successful. Also, if a firm does not achieve cost leadership, product differentiation or specialisation in its products, services or markets, it is bound to produce low profitability and have below average performance. He refers to these sort of firms as 'stuck in the middle'. Many others share Porter's view (White, 1986).

A study by Dess and Davis (1984) also broadly supported Porter but, contrary to Porter's assertion, they found that there is some evidence to show that businesses with both a low cost and a high differentiation position can be very successful.

Whilst there are, then, certain generic strategies that can be adopted at the Corporate and Business levels, the appropriateness of any of them for a particular firm is dependent on a number of factors. These include the stage of product-market evolution, the competitive position the firm has, the competitive position it seeks, the business strategies being used by rival firms, the internal resources and distinctive competencies at a firm's disposal, the prevailing market threats and opportunities, the type and vigour of competition, and customer needs, to mention only the more important considerations (Thompson and Strickland, 1983). In addition, it must be acknowledged that generic strategies will always give rise to a host of variants and, therefore, at any one time the choice of the most suitable strategy will be a highly complex task. Indeed, this is what one would expect. If choosing and implementing strategy was easy, then all firms would be successful. But, by definition of success, not everyone can be successful; therefore, strategy formulation will and must remain fraught with danger and complexity.

A major point to note, though, is that almost without exception, all these forms of strategy require organisations to adopt appropriate structures, practices and cultures. Contrary to the views of earlier writers on strategy, it is the internal arrangements that need to be changed, often radically, in order to achieve the desired market-place objectives. This clearly raises the issue of Functional-level strategies; but once again, these do not stand in isolation from the other levels of strategy. However, there is no need to discuss these here, because, by and large, the main ones are either products of Corporate- and Business-level strategies, such as market and product strategies; or, like personnel and structural strategies, received ample exposure in earlier chapters. Therefore, having outlined the various strategies that are available to organisations, we can now move on to examine the strategic tools that they have at their disposal.

Strategic planning tools

Having indicated above that there are a wide variety of strategies which organisations can adopt, we can now, briefly, review the main tools that organisations use to select and construct their strategies. In the main, though not exclusively, these tend to be mathematical models. This is partly, as explained earlier, due to the origins and development of strategic management. It is also the product of the preference for quantification, especially in the financial arena, which permeates the culture of most Western organisations. Nevertheless, though there is a preference for such techniques, there has been some movement away from sole reliance on them, as the discussion below on scenario building will show. This follows the move away from quantification and towards the use of more qualitative techniques, both in the area of strategy and in terms of organisation theory in general.

Three of the main tools being used are:

1 The PIMS (Profit Impact on Marketing Strategy) model.
2 The Growth-Share Matrix.
3 The Scenario construction approach.

The first two tools focus on Corporate- and Business-level strategies, but the latter can be applied to the Functional level as well.

PIMS

This technique originated in 1960 as a research project at General Electric (GE) of America. General Electric began by analysing their operations with the aim of identifying those factors responsible for business success. In 1975, the work was moved to the Harvard Business School, where it was located in the Strategic Planning Institute (SPI), which was specifically set up to manage it. By the early 1980s, the project had grown to encompass some 200 corporations, covering more than 2,000 individual business units (McNamee, 1985).

The rationale underlying the PIMS model is that certain characteristics of a business and its markets determine profitability. Consequently, understanding these characteristics and acting upon them will aid a company to become more profitable. Using company and industry data, the PIMS model seeks to provide individual companies with answers to questions such as:

- What profit rate is 'normal' for a given business?
- What strategic changes are likely to improve performance?
- Given a specific contemplated future strategy, what are its effects on matters such as profitability and cash flow, both in the short and long term?

There has been much discussion as to the success of the PIMS model. Certainly some of its users, as well as academic observers, regard it as having only a limited use (Ford, 1981; Mitroff and Mason, 1981). The main criticisms levelled against PIMS are that:

- It is flawed because it uses historic data, without consideration for future changes. The argument is that, as organisations operate in a dynamic environment, to use the past to explain the future can be a dangerous exercise. Indeed, PIMS seems to be useful only in a stable environment, where companies stick to doing what they know best. It is even questioned whether PIMS can be regarded as a tool for policy in a strategic sense, since it can be argued that the 'variables' it so relies on, such as market share, are performance variables, not strategic ones (Abell, 1977).

- It is highly analytical but very limited in solving problems. In addition, because PIMS has to use a very large database for its analysis, it is argued that this creates a major problem for managers in terms of absorbing all the data generated. In turn, since the statistical errors in its output are rarely openly discussed, there is a tendency for managers not to question its findings because 'the computer is always right' (Andrews, 1980).

- Its assertion that profitability is closely linked to market share, and that an improvement in market share can be associated with a comparable increase in return on investment, is of dubious validity. It could equally be argued that both are due to common factors, such as low costs and good management (Smith, 1985).

- Most of the factors which govern the forecasts of the model are beyond the control of individual companies. Therefore, since PIMS relies heavily on this data, whatever conclusions it reaches about the fate of a company are final. It is not comforting, or even particularly useful, to be told you cannot do anything to turn a negative forecast around, because the factors responsible are beyond your control (Anderson and Paine, 1978).

- It assumes that a rather large set of quantitative variables, primarily of a financial nature, are sufficient to capture the state of a business and from this determine a realistic strategy (Naylor, 1981).

- It is based on the premise that business problems are orderly or well-structured. PIMS thus assumes that the determination or classification of the level of the organisation or business unit, the customer group, the competition, the market and the product line to which the analysis applies are all either well-known or well-specified. It is, therefore, not equipped to handle imprecise, let alone conflicting, definitions of business problems (Naylor, 1981).

To summarise, the main criticisms of PIMS are that it is too mechanistic, overly complex, based on unreliable data, and cannot cope adequately with dynamic and unpredictable environments. Nevertheless, despite the criticisms levelled against it, many researchers still believe that PIMS is a useful tool. The PIMS method has also been praised for the insight it has given into the true nature of the relationships between strategic variables. Obviously, managers must deal with these variables and their relationships on a daily basis, but attempts at conceptualising these relationships had been lacking until the advent of the PIMS research programme (Anderson and Paine, 1978; Ford, 1981; Mitroff and Mason, 1981).

The Growth-Share Matrix

This is the brainchild of the Boston Consulting Group (BCG) in the USA. It is based on the assumption that all except the smallest and simplest organisations are composed of more than one business. The collection of businesses within an organisation is termed its business portfolio. Using pictorial analogies, it posits that businesses in an organisation's portfolio can be classified into Stars, Cash Cows, Dogs and Problem Children (Smith, 1985) as follows:

- *Stars* are business units, industries or products with high growth and high market share. Because of this, Stars are assumed to use and generate large amounts of cash. It is argued that as they, generally, represent the best profit and investment opportunities, then the best strategy for Stars, usually, is to make the necessary investments to maintain or improve their competitive position.
- *Cash Cows* are defined as former Stars whose market growth is in decline. They were once market leaders, during the early days when the market was rapidly growing, and have maintained that position as the growth tapered off. They are regarded as businesses with low growth but high market share. Because they are entrenched in the market, they have lower costs and make higher profits than their competitors. These businesses are cash rich; therefore the appropriate strategy for such businesses is to 'milk' them in order to develop the rest of the organisation's portfolio.
- *Dogs* are businesses that have low market share and which operate in markets with low growth potential. Low market share normally implies poor profit, and because the market growth is low, investment to increase market share is frequently prohibitive. Also, in such situations, the cash required to maintain a competitive position often exceeds the cash generated. Thus, Dogs often become cash traps. It follows from this that, generally, the best strategy is for Dogs to be sold off.
- *Problem Children* or *Question Marks*, as they are sometimes labelled, are regarded as having a high growth rate and low market share. They have high cash requirements to keep them on course,

but their profitability is low because of their low market share. They are so named because, most of the time, the appropriate strategy to adopt is not clear. With their high growth rate, it might be possible to turn them into Stars, by further investment. On the other hand, because of the uncertainty that surrounds these types of businesses, the best strategy might be to sell them off altogether.

The originators of the Growth-Share Matrix see it as a dynamic tool. As growth in their industries slows down, the original Stars are expected to move into the position of Cash Cows, as long as they keep maintaining their high market share; otherwise they will become Dogs, and so on with changes in the other characteristics. This means the Growth-Share Matrix can be used to forecast the development of a business portfolio over a period of time.

There are two basic assumptions underlying the Matrix: firstly, that those industries, products or businesses that have a high growth rate can be differentiated from those that have a low growth rate; secondly, that those that have a high competitive position/market share can be differentiated from those that have a low competitive position/market share. Based on these assumptions, the matrix classifies business units or activities according to the growth rate of the industry of which they are part and by their market share.

Over the years, the Growth-Share Matrix has attracted its fair share of criticism as well as praise. One of the glaring objections to the Matrix is the labels it employs for the classification of businesses. Andrews (1980) described these labels as a 'vulgar and destructive vocabulary'. There are, however, other more serious criticisms concerning the assumptions underlying, and the operation of, the BCG model. The main one is that the uniqueness of an organisation and its problems may not be adequately captured by this, or any other tight classification scheme. This is reflected in the views of Mitroff and Mason (1981), who argue that the critical assumptions underlying the Matrix are tautologous and simplistic. They summarise these assumptions as follows:

- That the classification scheme applies to all businesses, because all businesses can be classified as one of the four basic types.
- That the classification scheme is relevant to all businesses, meaning that all businesses ought to be classified as one of the four types.
- That the model and its recommendations for action are universally applicable to all businesses, no matter what the characteristics of a particular business may be.

In addition, a wide range of researchers have drawn attention to the difficulty in defining and measuring the major variables on which the Matrix relies. In this respect, the criticisms are similar to those raised against PIMS. As examples, Hax and Majluf (1982) argue that the definition of market share used in the Matrix is unrealistic. Similarly, Hax and Nicholson (1983) point out that a product/market segment can be defined in a variety of ways, and that, in reality, there is a whole hierarchy of product/market segments. Another reservation, expressed by Fawn and Cox (1985), is that the concept of what constitutes a single business is difficult to operationalise.

There is also some concern as to the validity of the indicators of profitability used: market share and industry growth. Hax and Nicholson (1983) pose two interesting and vital questions in this respect: 'Is market share really the major factor determining profitability?', and, 'Is industry growth really the only variable that fully explains growth opportunities?' These reservations are echoed by Smith (1985). A further concern is that the Matrix assumes that a good portfolio analysis should identify the competitive strengths and the industry attractiveness of each business unit. Alternatives to the Growth-Share Matrix, however, reject this assertion. Instead they start by assuming that these two dimensions cannot be revealed by a single measurement, but require a wider set of critical factors for reliable positioning of the business units (Hax and Majluf, 1982; Hofer and Schendel, 1978).

In the face of such criticisms, a number of modifications have been made to the original Growth-Share Matrix. General Electric, for example, in association with McKinsey and Company in the USA, have developed a 9-way matrix instead of the original 4-way classification (Hax and Nicholson, 1983). A similar system called the Directional Policy Matrix (DPM) has also been developed by Shell Chemicals in the UK (Hussey, 1978). Many other organisations have, in their turn, developed or employed similar schemes to meet their organisational needs (Patel and Younger, 1978).

Regardless of the merits of these criticisms, few would dispute that, like PIMS, the Matrix is primarily suited to well-structured planning problems in which the basic definition of a business unit, product or competition is not an issue (Bowman and Asch, 1985). Unfortunately, because of the uncertain and rapidly-changing nature of business today, such situations are becoming less and less common. This, to an extent, may account for the increase in the popularity of the next approach.

The Scenario construction approach

As a way of overcoming some of the criticisms of the above two (quantitative) approaches, the use of Scenario-building techniques emerged in the 1970s. The aim of the Scenario approach is to enable an organisation to picture and make various assumptions about future events and trends which might affect the operations of the organisation. Organisations, like individuals, are unique and complex. As argued above, this can undermine the effectiveness of models or general principles as tools for strategic planning. If this is the case, rather than the application of standard, but inappropriate, tools, each organisation must be considered on its own individual merits. This process should be based on an intensive examination of its unique features and needs by a personally concerned, involved and experienced analyst. It is this that Scenario building attempts to do (Linneman and Klein, 1979).

The Scenario approach has been defined in a number of ways. McNulty (1977) defined it as a quantitative or qualitative picture of a given organisation or group developed within the framework of a set of specified assumptions. Kahn and Weiner (1978) defined it as a hypothetical sequence of events constructed for the purpose of focusing attention on causal processes and decision points. To Kahn and Weiner, the purpose of scenarios is to display, in as dramatic and persuasive a fashion as possible, a number of possibilities for the future. To Norse (1979), scenarios are a means of improving our understanding of the long-term global, regional or national consequences of existing or potential trends or policies and their interaction. All these definitions are useful in the sense that they portray the different uses (national, international, corporate level, business level) to which scenarios can be put.

Essentially, therefore, building scenarios can be regarded as making different pictures of the future (business or otherwise) through the construction of case studies, either quantitatively or qualitatively. The quantitative method, sometimes called the hard method, uses mathematics, models and computers to make pictures of the future, through the production of a vast array of numbers and figures. The qualitative, or soft, method is essentially intuitive and descriptive; it is based on the resources of the human mind and derived from the methods of psychology and sociology. The two main Scenario-building approaches which have been established are the Delphi method and the Cross Impact method. However, in recent years another approach has become increasingly influential: Vision building. Though this bears some relation to other Scenario-building techniques, it comes from a different tradition and is qualitatively orientated.

The Delphi method

This uses a panel of experts who are interrogated about a number of future issues within their area of expertise. In the Classical application, the interrogation is conducted under conditions whereby each respondent is unknown to the others, in order to avoid effects of authority and the development of a consensual bandwagon. After the initial round of interrogations, the results are reported to the panel and another round of interrogations is conducted. Several rounds may be carried out in this manner.

Results produced from these interrogations may be amenable to statistical treatment with a view to yielding numbers, dates and ranges from them. At the end of the process, depending on whether a quantitative or qualitative approach is taken, either a detailed numerical forecast of the future is obtained, or a more descriptive and richer picture. In both cases, the central tendencies of majority opinion and the range of minority disagreements will also be presented (McNulty, 1977; Zentner, 1982).

The Cross Impact method

This is a variation of the Delphi method. It uses essentially the same interrogation method as the Delphi, i.e. a panel of experts; the difference, however, lies in what they are asked to do. The Delphi method requires the experts to identify a number of future issues that they think will affect the organisation or business within their area of expertise. The Cross Impact method, on the other hand, asks its panel of experts to assign subjective probabilities and time priorities to a list of potential future events and developments supplied by the organisation. The emphasis is on identifying, reinforcing or inhibiting events and trends, to uncover relationships and to indicate the importance of specific events. The accruing data from this exercise is processed to yield curves of the probabilities for each event as a function of time (Lanford, 1972).

Like all approaches to strategic planning, the Scenario-building approach has attracted criticism. One criticism is its reliance on subjectivity. The fact that any five management specialists can interpret the same situation in two totally different ways is an oft-quoted example of this type of criticism. Also, this approach is prone to retrospection. People's ideas of the future are informed by their knowledge and experience of the past. Since experience is not always the best teacher, scenarios may be based on false assumptions.

Another claimed drawback is that scenario development cannot be carried out by novices. It requires experts in the field concerned to be able to look into the future and make judgments about the likelihood of what might happen. In a survey of US industrial companies using scenarios in 1979, a senior vice-president claimed that 'The major problem is the amount of time and quality of personnel required to prepare meaningful scenarios'. Others in the same survey complained that 'multiple anything is more work than single anything, especially if the need for the multiple is questionable'. A further respondent said, 'As no one is clairvoyant, to develop more than a most probable scenario is counter-productive and an exercise of mental gymnastics'. Most concluded that 'it is a waste of time and effort, since it mostly deals with the improbable' (Keshavan and Rakesh, 1979: 57–61).

Nevertheless, in a study conducted in 1984 to review the extent of the use of multiple scenarios in Europe, the researchers discovered that 46 per cent (of a sample of 100 companies) said they would increase their use of the method in the future and only 12 per cent stated that they would make less use of the method. Companies in the same report stated that scenario construction was useful in controlling the 'uncertainty and unpredictability of the corporate environment'. It also helped them to 'organise co-operation between different levels of management and participation in creating the company's future, and thus improved not only planning, but the whole strategic management' (Malaska *et al.* 1984:48). Finally, Shell, a company which pioneered the use of scenarios in corporate strategy and has, since 1973, adopted it as a permanent strategy tool, regards the use of scenarios as a way out of the ills associated with predicting the future. Shell asserts that the use of scenarios in planning has provoked better strategic thinking throughout the company and has increased flexibility (Leemhuis, 1990; Smith, 1985).

Vision building

This approach has gained in popularity in recent years, especially in the USA. Whilst it certainly bears a resemblance to the other Scenario building techniques, and therefore is open to the same criticisms, it is influenced more by Japanese management practices than those in the West (Cummings and Huse, 1989; Hamel and Prahalad, 1989). It is a much less structured approach than the other two Scenario-building techniques, and relies more on a company's own management. The major elements of Vision building are:

- The creation by a company's senior management team of an 'ideal' future state for their organisation.
- The identification of the organisation's mission, its rationale for existence.
- A clear statement of desired outcomes and the desired conditions needed to achieve these.

This is an iterative process which is designed to move from the general (the vision) to the specific (desired outcomes and conditions), and back again. By going round the loop in this manner it is argued by Cummings and Huse (1989), that an ambitious yet attainable future can be constructed and pursued. This owes much to the Japanese, who pioneered the concept of Strategic Intent on which Vision building is based.

The work of Hamel and Prahalad (1989) is of particular importance in this respect. They have argued that the strategic approach of Japanese companies is markedly different to that of their Western counterparts. Rather than attempting to lay down a detailed plan in advance, Japanese companies operate within a long-term framework of Strategic Intent. They create a vision of their desired future – their 'intent' – which they then pursue in a relentless but flexible manner. They quote examples of leading Japanese companies who, in the 1960s, when they were insignificant in world terms, set out to dominate their markets. Honda's strategic intent was to be the 'Second Ford', Komatsu's to 'Encircle Caterpillar' and Canon's to 'Beat Xerox'. These companies then mobilised their resources to achieving their individual strategic intent. In this, the prime resource they deployed was the commitment, ingenuity and flexibility of their workforces.

To summarise, therefore, in the case of strategic planning tools, as with other aspects of strategy we have examined, we find that a trend appears to be emerging. The trend is away from the use of mathematical models and techniques towards attempts to draw on human mental creativity. This trend is by no means fully accepted or established, but the case for a substantial re-evaluation of how strategy is determined appears overdue.

Conclusions

As can be seen from this chapter, the concept of strategic management has developed considerably since it began to be widely used in the USA in the 1950s. No longer is strategy purely about the external world, no longer is it solely seen as a rational, quantitative process. Indeed, writers and practitioners from different backgrounds and countries, such as Hamel and Prahalad (1989), Johnson and Scholes (1988), Mintzberg (1987), Mintzberg and Quinn (1991), Pettigrew (1988), Ohmae (1986) and Turner (1989) have argued that it is not a process at all, but the outcome of a process: an outcome that is shaped not by mathematical models but by human creativity.

The move towards this new approach has been brought about by the mounting criticisms against the old, as practised in the West. These criticisms are that it is mechanistic, prescriptive, inflexible, and reliant on quantitative variables of dubious validity. The result of this is that when organisations attempt to construct strategies in this manner, they fall foul of what Peters and Waterman (1982) describe as 'Paralysis through analysis' and 'Irrational rationality'. In effect, organisations contort themselves in a vain attempt to make the real world fit the constraints and limitations of their mathematical models, rather than vice versa.

The alternative view, and one that is clearly gaining ground, is that organisations should move away from exclusive reliance on mathematical models. Instead, human creativity should be brought into play. Senior managers should create a vision of the organisation's future – establish its Strategic Intent. This should then be pursued relentlessly by the organisation. In the process of doing so, the strategy emerges from the decisions that are taken with regard to resource allocation, organisation structure and the other key areas of operation. Mintzberg (1987) uses the analogy of the potter to describe this process. When she sits down at her wheel, the potter has a vision (a mental image) of what she wants to create, but no detailed plan of how she will do it. What she does have is her skill and experience, and she draws on these to turn the heap of wet clay into what she sees in her mind. The resultant pot emerges from this combination of past experience, present competence and vision.

In Mintzberg's view, senior managers in successful companies adopt exactly the same approach. Like the potter, they establish objectives for their organisation (create a vision of a desired future state), and through a combination of experience and resources (human and physical) they pursue their objectives. Organisations operate in a dynamic environment, and it is not possible to lay out a strategy in advance to achieve the desired objectives. The actual strategy to achieve the objectives only emerges and becomes evident over time. In Mintzberg's view, it is only possible to see the strategy with hindsight, because the strategy comprises a stream of actions taken over a period of time to achieve the desired objectives.

Therefore, from different perspectives, a number of writers have come to the same conclusion. For successful companies, strategy is not a preconceived and detailed set of steps for achieving a coherent package of concrete goals within a given timescale. Neither is it a rational process which is amenable to mathematical modelling. Rather, it is the outcome of a process of decision making and resource allocation that is embarked upon in pursuit of a vision. Such an approach is inherently irrational, inherently unplannable – it cannot be modelled or quantified, though it can and must be pursued with rigour and determination.

Though the creation of the vision (the intent) is crucial to what follows, the actual strategy to achieve it emerges from the actions of the entire organisation. Not only does this mean that the successful development of a strategy is an organisation-wide responsibility but, also, there is no real separation between strategy formulation and execution. This means that, for an organisation to be successful, it must structure its internal operations in order to promote the achievement of the vision and ensure that its culture reinforces this direction. It follows that the key to success lies not in the boardroom, but on the shopfloors and in the offices where staff are, on a day-to-day basis, taking and implementing decisions which reshape their organisations and transform them into the vision. It is the process of change that takes the organisation forward, which shapes the strategy.

The next chapter will examine the experience of four organisations who have attempted to construct and implement their own strategic plans, with varying degrees of success. It will show not only the difficulty of embarking on the process but also the necessity to see it as essentially a process of continuous development. Nevertheless, regardless of the advantages of, and necessity for, strategic management, the creation of plans and objectives by themselves change nothing. It is only when these are implemented and change occurs that organisations move forward. Therefore, Part Three of the book will examine the theory and practice of managing change.

5

Case studies in strategic management

Introduction

The previous chapter examined approaches to strategic management by leading theorists. It described its origins and development, showing how strategic management has moved from being an approach solely concerned with product-market issues, to one that recognises that organisations are social systems which need to be considered in their entirety – including internal as well as external factors.

This chapter will present four case studies of organisations which have undertaken strategic management. It will examine whether and how the developments discussed in the previous chapter are reflected in the experience of these four companies. The case studies cover a range of situations, from attempts to develop strategic plans, both successfully and unsuccessfully, to the implementation and continuing development of strategy over a number of years, in one case over a number of decades.

The chapter begins with the case of Process Control Inc., which examines the difficulties it experiences in constructing business and functional level strategies. It highlights the importance of senior management commitment, understanding and stability. It shows how, in its case, the absence of these undermined the company's attempts to restructure and renew itself.

Case study two, International News Gatherers, presents an entirely different picture of strategic management. Not only has the company been successful in developing strategic plans but, over a period of 20 to 30 years, it has implemented and recreated them as objectives have been met and situations have progressed. This study covers corporate-level strategy, encompassing the shaping and direction of a network of companies separated by function and geography but united by a common strategic intent. The case study also shows the need to buttress corporate strategy with appropriate and well-thought-out functional strategies, such as, in this case, management and staff training and development.

The situation in FFT International, case study three, has strong similarities with case study two, given that both deal with corporate strategy and its long-term implementation. However, what distinguishes this company from International News Gatherers is that it illustrates what can happen to a company when its management becomes complacent and the organisation loses drive and direction. To rekindle FFT's fortunes required both a change of senior management, and the development of a strategy, aiming not only to restructure the company's operations, but also to create a culture which encouraged innovation and ambition, replacing one which discouraged them.

The concluding case study, Seaside Biscuits, like case study one, is concerned with business and functional strategies. However, unlike Process Control Inc., its decision to embark on strategic planning was taken at a time when its performance was satisfactory. Nevertheless, it was not a company without problems, and it had already experienced one unsuccessful attempt to develop a strategic plan. However, it learnt from this experience, and decided to use outside consultants as facilitators to assist in the development of its strategic plan, and also to weld its senior management into a co-operative team which shared a common vision of Seaside's future.

The chapter concludes by arguing that, judging from the experience of the above companies, strategic management is a messier and less transparent process than many theorists appear willing to admit. In particular, the assumption that senior managers work co-operatively and are necessarily always willing participants in this process, not to mention capable of carrying it out, is severely dented by the case studies.

To assist the reader in identifying the key issues involved, the conclusion is followed by a list of discussion topics.

Case study one: Process Control Inc.

Background

Process Control Inc. (PCI) is the European manufacturing arm of an American conglomerate and is located in the Midlands. Although this plant shares the same site as the European Marketing and Technology (product development) divisions of its parent company, the three concerns are operationally separate with very little liaison. PCI's present operation came into being in 1979, through a merger with a subsidiary of a British-owned electronics company. PCI specialises in the production of printed circuit boards (PCBs) and process control equipment. In 1988, PCI's PCB business was significantly expanded when its parent company centred most of its PCB manufacture there, by transferring work from its US base. At present, PCI produces over 95 per cent of the conglomerate's total PCB needs. PCI employs a staff of 395.

With the rapid expansion of PCB assembly in 1988, the company began to experience major operational problems relating to quality and delivery. This in turn caused increasing difficulties for the parent company in the USA, who found its own deliveries and quality suffering as a consequence.

Alongside the increase in workload for PCI came a greater dependence on the other two functions on the PCI site, Marketing and Technology. Indeed, it was alleged by PCI that many of its problems were caused by staff in both the Marketing and Technology divisions making erratic and unrealistic demands on them. Managers claimed that volumes and product-mix forecasts were rarely accurate, and that PCB designs were often changed by the Technology division during manufacture. The cumulative effect of all these factors was that manufacturing performance was worsening rather than improving, so that a large proportion of its target completion dates could not be met. There were also concomitant quality problems.

When this situation failed to improve, the parent company sacked the plant's British Chief Executive Officer (CEO) and replaced him with an American who was to be seconded to PCI for a one- to two-year period. This came as a shock not only to the CEO but also to the entire workforce. There was widespread feeling, at all levels in the company, that he had been treated shabbily, especially given that he had been with the company, in its various forms, for 25 years. This shock was compounded by the character of the new CEO. He was a colourful and flamboyant person who wore a Mickey Mouse watch, dressed as Father Christmas and the Easter Bunny at the appropriate time of the year, and was given to public soul-searching.

His remit was two-fold: (1) to turn the plant around to a position where it could meet its obligations; and (2) to identify an in-house replacement for when his secondment came to an end. The assumption underlying this remit was that PCI's difficulties were all of their own making and that a combination of a new CEO and some relatively minor managerial changes – to improve the CEO's position and communication within the management structure – would shake the company up enough to remedy the situation.

In his first three months, the Chief Executive flattened the management hierarchy. The previous CEO had only three managers reporting directly to him, with a further tier of eight managers reporting to them. The new CEO combined these two layers and created a new 11-person management team responsible to him. This levelling-up created some resentment amongst the original three team members, which was compounded when two of them were told to switch jobs with their former subordinates. Indeed, at one point there was talk that these managers might resign.

Overall, because of these changes, the newly-created management team was anything but a team. The CEO, nevertheless, stuck to his decision. When justifying his action, the CEO said: 'If you've got a business that you expect to change, because the technology and customers are changing rapidly, which is the business we are in, then you have to have a flatter, more flexible organisation'. Another reason advanced for flattening the senior management structure was that the CEO envisaged a team of senior managers who could work together co-operatively. He wanted to, in his own words, 'change the mind set' of the managers so that 'they can know the strength that can come through working in a team'.

In addition, the CEO foresaw the need to broaden his managers' work experience in order to identify and develop a potential successor. This was the rationale behind the moving of some of the managers to 'unfamiliar grounds' and the swopping of roles with their former subordinates.

Developing strategy

By March 1989, the new CEO had come to the conclusion that the problems of PCI were much greater than had been assumed, and that more radical solutions than 'administering a shock to the system' were required. He identified the underlying causes as follows:

- The organisation structure and the attitudes and skills of both management and employees prevented the company from achieving the high levels of performance and flexibility required of it.
- There was a lack of appropriate liaison between PCI, Technology and Marketing – in effect, he claimed that the latter two were

acting in such an erratic manner that the company's task was made doubly difficult.

In a bid to bring the management team closer together and to begin to tackle the underlying problems of ᵤhe plant, the CEO organised a weekend, off-site management seminar. This was led by an outside organisation development specialist and was, the CEO said, about soul-searching and team-building. His aim was to deliberate on the state of the organisation and to develop a vision for a 'high performance organisation' and a strategy for achieving this.

At the end of this, he felt that the weekend was a turning-point in the organisation's fortunes. Not only did they emerge as a more coherent and committed team, but they also came up with the bones of a strategic plan which they saw as the solution necessary to pull the organisation out of its predicament. According to the CEO, who introduced the concept and continued to be its main champion, the initial reaction of the management team to the idea of developing a manufacturing strategy was: 'Yes, we need to do planning but Jesus!, we are in a deep mess, we don't have time to do it'. The CEO said that, 'in the end, I had to force the idea of strategic planning on the organisation'. The vision produced by the management team aimed to 'empower the organisation to be a world-class manufacturing unit and thereby achieve customer delight'.

The strategic plan to achieve the vision had five elements which were to be developed by small sub-groups of the management team:

1 People involvement
2 Supplier partnering
3 Just-in-Time
4 Total Quality
5 Social responsibility.

The middle three of these are, in principle, recognisable. The first, seen by the CEO as the most important, but also the most difficult and contentious, aimed to restructure the company into high performance, semi-autonomous work groups on both the shop-floor and in the offices, along the lines advocated by writers such as Peters and Waterman (1982). However, in so doing, this plan threatened not only the conventional supervisors, but also, because of its emphasis on breaking down functional barriers, the core skills of managers. It was also the least understood of the five elements. The fifth element, social responsibility, was a declaration that the company wished to do well not only by its employees but also by the community at large – especially in relation to environmental issues.

Throughout the summer of 1989, the management team and its sub-groups met to develop and approve the strategies. However, whilst some maintained their original enthusiasm, others became more sceptical. Some managers felt the process was being rushed, and that as a consequence the time available for thinking through and discussing the proposals was limited. One example of this was that the sub-groups responsible for developing the five elements of the plan did not have the time to meet, and the chairman of each group mainly wrote these with little input from others. Notwithstanding this, by September 1989, the complete strategy was agreed by the management team, along with the priorities and timetables for the next 12 months.

Implementing strategy

The CEO then organised a meeting of all supervisory/middle management staff to brief them on the strategy and to attempt to involve them. This initial meeting was not judged to be particularly successful by the participants. The main reason for this was the sheer volume of information presented. Therefore, a second meeting was organised. The problem, however, with both meetings was that because the organisation was under pressure for quick results to turn its fortunes around, much of the time was spent on the action required to achieve the plan, rather than taking enough time to explain its 'whys' and 'wherefores' and what the outcomes would mean for the workforce. It was left to the members of the management team to explain these to their own subordinates. This would have been acceptable in a situation where the management team was fully conversant with and committed to the plan. In this case, though, some of the managers themselves were unclear or in need of convincing of the merits of the proposed changes. Consequently, rather than giving reassurance, these briefings had the opposite effect – especially when staff compared what different managers were saying.

As is common in such situations, rumours and counter-rumours abounded; complaints focused on attempts by 'some people' to 'Americanise' the plant, the unpreparedness of the workforce for the strategic plan, and the short timescale for the implementation of some aspects of the plan. Also, members of the trade union, usually very supportive of the company, complained about 'the looming prospects of redundancy', whilst others voiced scepticism about the real motives of the CEO and the tactics being employed to implement the changes. Above all, there were real fears among the supervisors and middle managers about their future in the plant, because the plans involved structural changes which would result in the removal of some of these posts.

The management team's response to this 'uneasiness' amongst the workforce was to introduce a series of weekend and lunch-break meetings aimed at educating the workforce. These meetings, to an extent, were able to calm the fears of the workforce on the reasons for the strategic plan and some of the structural adjustments taking place. But, overall, they could not fully come to grips with people's worries, because most of the meetings (especially the plant-wide monthly lunch-break meetings) were too large, and so intimate and sensitive questions were not even asked, let alone discussed in the open.

Despite the many unanswered questions about the strategic plan, by December 1989 elements of the strategy were being implemented. However, there was still much to do both in implementing what had been decided and in clarifying what the new organisational structure should look like. Indeed, the question of structure emerged as the main issue of uncertainty and contention in the management team. It became clear that the plan would require a new organisation structure – if only to make sense of the many apparently isolated structural changes taking place. But though the CEO said he was clear what was required, the rest of his team were not. Despite this, the CEO held to the belief that agreement had been reached to move to a system of 'mini' factories within a new matrix-type structure. This clearly demonstrated the growing gap between the CEO and his team – even those who supported him. The gap was particularly obvious amongst those managers who controlled support functions such as Quality, Purchasing and Production Control, because they felt their specialism would be dismembered and career prospects threatened.

The outcome

In the week before Christmas 1989, all this was thrown into confusion when the CEO announced he was leaving. He had been offered, and had accepted the chance to take over a more important plant in the company's portfolio in the USA and he felt the opportunity was too good to be missed. At this point, it was not clear who would take over – though there had been an undercurrent of fighting for succession in the management team all along. Before long, it was announced that another 'interim' CEO would be appointed until the time was right for someone in PCI to take the post. However, there was a delay before the new person could take up his appointment and, in the early months of 1990, he could only make intermittent visits to PCI. This delay, as well as the change in CEO, inevitably led to uncertainty regarding the strategy.

Most of the management team were content to await the arrival of the new CEO rather than continuing with the more controversial elements of the strategy. However, one manager who had been won over by the Chief Executive's ideas, and who saw himself as a potential successor, began to push the strategy very strongly. This was quickly put down by the rest of the team through non-co-operation. It did, though, have the unexpected side effect of encouraging other managers to come out openly and express their doubts and misgivings about the strategy. Nevertheless, most managers reverted to their former state of dealing with the day-to-day running of the plant, and the manufacturing strategy, which was of top priority a few weeks previously, now came to play a secondary role.

In March 1990, the new CEO assumed office on a full-time basis in the plant. He met a situation completely different from that which faced his predecessor. When the former came in he met a plant that was behind in its output and with severe quality problems. The new CEO inherited a plant making profit, meeting its completion dates and which had considerably reduced defects in its finished products; although how much of this was due to PCI's own efforts and how much to a reduced demand for its product was difficult to say. However, a number of managers feared that a resurgence of demand would once again lead to delivery and quality problems. As far as people were concerned, however, according to the new CEO, the management team had lapsed both in its commitment to working as a team and in its enthusiasm for the manufacturing strategy. Given that he saw his role as an interim one, he was content to maintain the status quo. He was dubious about the strategy and its implementation and simply worked to keep the plant running efficiently, until he was recalled back to the USA.

However, there was an upsurge in demand for PCBs and, as some feared, the plant began to lag behind in its performance. By the end of June 1990, barely six months after the departure of the prime mover of the manufacturing strategy, many of the original difficulties re-emerged. The plant and its managers were once again back to square one; fire-fighting the day-to-day problems of the plant in order to keep the order book on schedule. The combination of this and the new CEO's reluctance to become involved in the strategic plan led to a decision to 'suspend' it until the operating difficulties had been sorted out. Nevertheless, there was a feeling that this particular exercise had come to an end and that the suspension would be permanent.

Case study two: International News Gatherers (ING)

Background

Founded in 1851, International News Gatherers (ING) became a public company in 1984. With its headquarters in Fleet Street, the company is organised into four geographical areas: Europe (generating 56 per cent of revenue), Asia (21 per cent), North America (21 per cent) and 'overseas' (4 per cent). It is a transnational organisation, both by location (it maintains offices in 171 cities in 80 countries), and by philosophy (its share structure has been designed to guarantee that it should never pass into the hands of any single interest group or faction, and that its traditional commitment to integrity, independence and freedom from bias should be preserved).

ING is the world's leading news organisation and supplier of information services, serving business clients in around 115 countries, and media clients in nearly 160. It obtains its business data from over 150 exchanges and over-the-counter markets, from data contributed by some 3,500 subscribers in 79 countries, and other news from a worldwide network of almost 1200 journalists. It distributes the information via over 160,000 video terminals and around 4,600 teleprinters, and directly into clients' own computers.

While ING may be associated in the public's perception with journalism and media services (including general and economic news and news pictures), in fact sales to the media market account for a diminishing share of its revenue: 7 per cent, as against 55 per cent earned by money-market information services transmitted through a computer-based network.

Most business subscribers, in around 24,000 locations throughout the world, receive its services through the ING Monitor System, based on the world's largest privately-leased communications network. Using a keyboard and a video screen, subscribers can access real-time news and price information covering markets for money, commodities, equities, bonds, shipping and energy. Historical databases on money are also available, together with products which enable subscribers to analyse, summarise and reformat information.

The same network provides facilities for dealing in currencies, bonds and bullion between subscribers. Shares can also be traded electronically through a system operated by Instinet, an ING subsidiary. Finally, ING offers a range of interface systems for individually-designed dealing rooms, mostly built by a US subsidiary company.

ING information packages thus unite real-time news and prices with high-speed dealing communications, data processing facilities, graphic displays and archival information. While the company has significant competitors in many of these individual markets, its unique strength lies in its ability to generate and deliver a total information package. Clearly, computing and communications technology are at the heart of ING information services.

Ten years ago, ING employed less than 2,900 people worldwide. Now it employs almost 10,000, of whom 2,800 work in the UK, including headquarters staff. Only about one in every eight is employed as a journalist. ING employs almost as many computer operators, programmers and analysts as journalists, and nearly twice as many engineers and technicians.

Having made such significant changes, the question for ING is whether the culture which helped make it so successful is still appropriate in its changed circumstances. ING sees the answer as dependent on three factors:

- It is not yet a large company in employment terms, but it is fast becoming one.
- It has developed significantly away from its base as a news media service, though this traditional base remains important as the origin of the company's culture, and as a vital marketing aid to the sale of other computer-based services.
- It is not a culturally British but a non-aligned, supranational company. As they say, 'when you join ING, you leave your nationality behind'.

Developing strategy

Many studies of strategy are about corporate rescues. They focus on how organisations have introduced specific policy initiatives in response to the emergence of a threat to their ability to remain competitive in their traditional business activity, often in declining markets. The typical study has an identifiable beginning (the threat), a middle (the management process), and a quantifiably successful ending. The

ING situation is almost completely different. It is one of strategy and change as a continuous response to a variety of opportunities (in markets, products and technology) for developing different business activities, in order to sustain continuing growth and profitability. Like the management of change, it is a continuing story with no obvious beginning or end. Throughout the 1980s, the story was one of successfully managing rapid growth. The goal for the 1990s is to sustain that growth.

The previous section has outlined ING's present situation; the following sections will trace how it got there, taking as its starting point the mid-1960s. At that time, ING was a markedly different organisation. For more than a century it had been a highly-respected member of the international wire-service news fraternity, producing up-to-the-minute dispatches on business and general news for the media markets (primarily newspapers) worldwide. Although it maintained a worldwide network in order to provide this service, it was financially not a very successful organisation. In 1964, ING made an after tax loss of £53,000 on a turnover of £3.5 million. It was still a small company, employing only 1,350 people worldwide. Of these over 400 were journalists.

The contrast with today, in technology used, in product range, in markets served, in levels of profitability and in manpower levels is probably more stark for ING than for most other companies. A great deal of change has clearly taken place. But this has been consciously embarked upon, rather than brought about by force of circumstance. However, certain key strengths of the 'old' ING Agency – the international network, the ING journalistic culture (based on such values as accuracy, objectivity and independence), and the associated rejection of nationalism – remain alive in the 'new'.

The main elements of the company's strategy are as follows:

1 Expand global databases of real-time and historical news and information, through internal development and acquisitions.
2 Maintain a worldwide network of quality, by research and development and investment in the network infrastructure.
3 Expand the communications, dealing and automated trading facilities offered to subscribers, on both a worldwide and a market basis.
4 Broaden the flow of new products and product enhancements, particularly for the purpose of data manipulation.
5 Provide integrated packages of information and communications products and services.

In 1964, ING made a technological breakthrough in pioneering the use of computers to transmit financial data internationally. They developed and marketed a stock market price quotation system, 'Stockmaster', capable of replacing ticker-tape machines. Stockmaster has been ING's most significant technical innovation. The then Head of ING's small new computer bureau (now its Managing Director) recognised that electronics provided a major opportunity. The technology could be used to transform the existing news wire networks into international networks for the instantaneous transmission of financial data. The success of this product created a more general awareness that the company's future could be based on, and revolutionised by, the computerisation of its services. Computerisation also offered an opportunity to apply the technology to the development of a wide range of new products for new markets.

An important opportunity presented itself in 1971, with the ending of fixed-rate currency exchange controls (the Bretton Woods Agreement). ING recognised that banks and company finance managers would need instant information on rapidly-changing prices of currencies. The ING Monitor, launched in 1973 for that purpose, was its major product innovation, a computer-based information network which provided for the first time a real-time data service on currency rates. It effectively created a market-place for foreign exchange: an electronic information system giving currency dealers access, via ING-leased terminals, to foreign exchange quotations, recommendations and other information. The data was entered directly by other dealers and by ING's own financial journalists, and was distributed over high-speed satellite and cable links. By the end of 1987, ING money services were being received in more than 110 countries.

The coverage of Monitor has subsequently been expanded to carry news as well as prices, and to cover securities, commodities and energy as well as money. Before computerisation, to quote one observer, 'as far as markets were concerned, ING didn't exist'. But since Monitor, a new phrase has come into circulation: 'if you're not on the system, you're not in the market'. There are competitors, but ING has retained the leading-edge position it gained by identifying a market need and moving quickly to satisfy it.

In 1981, the creation of a new product, the ING Monitor Dealing Service, marked a further important development of the company's networking services. In place of traditional trading by telephone and telex, perhaps on the basis of Monitor information, dealers were enabled to use the existing network to establish direct private trading contact with their international counterparts. By the late 1980s, the service was handling 735,000 conversations a week between around 6,000 dealers with possibly 30 per cent to 40 per cent of worldwide currency transactions going through the system. The new service signalled a move, not untypical of information companies, from providing information to providing transaction handling. It actually created a formal exchange for foreign currency, since previously none had existed.

The significance of these two applications of new technology for the present and future management of change is considerable. Together, they now account for over half of ING's revenue. By their success, in less than a decade, they effectively made ING into a different company. While it still offers a worldwide news wire service, and actually employs twice as many journalists as in 1981, the company has principally become a real-time transactions processing centre for world currency trading.

By enabling the network to attract the critical mass of traders necessary to make electronic trading feasible, ING has created a basis for many possible options for future product development. The ING Monitor Dealing System itself is being upgraded to provide fully-automated trading. ING is co-operating with the Chicago Mercantile Exchange to provide an electronic out-of-market-hours dealing system for future traders. Volume on the Instinet share trading system has risen to new records.

Between 1980 and 1984, the number of installed terminals and total company revenue grew fast (by about 350 per cent). Employment grew by 35 per cent and profits by 2,000 per cent. The growth made possible the flotation of ING as a public company in mid-1984, which in turn generated £52 million of new capital to finance future growth in order to strengthen its leading position in integrated information services.

Over the next three years, ING acquired ten related companies in Canada, the USA and the UK in order to enhance its technological, product and market strengths in all three of its major product areas: media services, financial services and client systems. Together with organic growth, these acquisitions increased earnings, pre-tax profit and employment, all by roughly 250 per cent.

Implementing strategy

Despite the ups and downs of the stock market in recent years (which have been tracked by thousands of ING screens), ING's strategy remains one of transforming the company into a 'one-stop shopping' global information supermarket for the financial services industry. It recognises that the potential for long-term growth remains enormous, given that the financial world has barely begun to conduct business electronically. The components will be more new markets, new products, new services to existing clients, including the extension of the dealing system to everything from Government securities to futures. ING's internal annual growth rate target for management purposes remains 25 per cent for pre-tax profits and for revenue over the longer term.

As one commentator noted: 'The ability to balance, co-ordinate and control that kind of growth is a very unique feat'. In support of its strategy, ING recognises that it has to continue to invest heavily in research and development, particularly in the network infrastructure. To that end, it has doubled spending on technical development to £47.8 million, and established a new Technical Centre.

Delivering the strategy successfully calls for a wide range of solutions to hardware, software and communications challenges. These will include such developments as:

- Continuing the expansion of the network, simply to accommodate the rising numbers of subscribers and increased traffic loading for existing services.
- Upgrading and expanding the network in the longer term, to cope with new products and services.
- Expanding the recently-introduced Integrated Data Network, which permits the fast packaging of a wide variety of products without the need for separate communications circuits, terminals and software developments.
- Rationalising the products and technologies of the diverse technological groups which have recently been acquired by ING.
- Continuing to make the presentation of data on terminals easier for the user, for example by split screens, and by providing search for information facilities by using key words.

Success in tackling these technical challenges will place more demands on the other key infrastructure investment: human resources. What ING managers are clear about is that the ability to meet strategic goals will not simply be a function of how successfully they manage the technology. The business is not technology-led, but market-led. It is not concerned to advance technology but to apply it; albeit to state-of-the-art levels of sophistication.

As ING have found throughout the 1980s, bottlenecks to growth are more likely to arise from manpower problems than from problems with the technology. As systems become more complicated, their development time grows longer and the window of opportunity gets smaller. In this situation, it is crucial to get things right first time. That puts the priority on managing the associated manpower changes.

As ING's experience since 1980 has demonstrated, there will be many such adjustments as the company grows and changes shape in line with its business strategy. While much of the recent employment growth has been through acquisition, growth has been significant in the 'core' organisation. In the four years before ING became a public company (1980–84), employment increased by more than 30 per cent. While ING has not experienced major recruitment difficulties, such fast growth does pose management problems.

But the organisation is also changing its occupational shape, under the impact of its technology. In 1980, it still had only 400 staff worldwide classed as 'technicians' (14 per cent of the total); this group now exceeds 4,000 (44 per cent). In 1980, there were fewer than 100 'sales executives' (3 per cent of employees); now there are almost 700 (7 per cent).

Similar changes have taken place within the UK section of ING since the end of the 1970s. In addition, the tasks which people have to perform within apparently unchanged functional titles have changed dramatically, as process technology has changed. As well as changes to the jobs of technical and sales staff, the jobs of other grades have changed no less, with editing journalists being a key example. London is the editorial heart of the company, where about 60 per cent of all editorial staff are still employed. Until 1980, their work was on a traditional hard-copy basis. Then, editing on VDU screens was introduced, involving some retraining. This was later followed by the advent of a new, highly-sophisticated video editing system, requiring a major retraining effort. The job today bears no relation to the editorial job of 1980.

ING expects these technology-driven trends to continue into the foreseeable future. Therefore, new skills will be required, such as staff who understand both computing and communications technologies, and, conversely, some old skills will become obsolete as certain products decline. Some groups will increase relatively and often absolutely; for example, those with marketing and software skills, and experts in handling databases. Skills which will decline include hardware skills, as the technology makes installation more customer-friendly, and routine clerical skills. Other standard occupational labels will conceal very different skills; for example, sales staff will increasingly need both a sound technical background and wider understanding of products and markets.

Many of the above job changes arise on a day-to-day basis. Responding to operational needs and solving problems are major (and challenging) tasks for ING managers. As one noted, 'coping with fast growth is one of the more attractive management challenges. But that doesn't make it any easier'. It would be possible to report many specific examples of successful responses, not least in the industrial relations field. (ING is one of the few 'Fleet Street' organisations still operating in Fleet Street, apparently with excellent relations with trade unions.)

However, ING is aware that it cannot merely respond to these changes on a day-to-day basis, and is, therefore, developing a strategy for enhancing the skills and competence of its workforce at all levels. The main element of this emerging strategy is a strong commitment to management and employee development and training.

ING's fast UK growth from the late 1970s exposed some middle management shortcomings. In the words of one senior manager, 'Like many companies, we didn't always pay enough attention to our management strengths in the past. The consequence was, we lost some market opportunities'. To minimise the chance of future lost opportunities, several initiatives have been taken. These are broadly designed to meet two needs: bringing good people into the organisation and developing existing employees.

The main mechanism to achieve the former of these objectives is through MBA and graduate recruitment on an annual basis. The latter, the development of existing managers, or potential managers, is primarily driven by a newly-introduced annual appraisal scheme designed to identify development and training requirements.

In addition, particular attention is now given to the needs of top managers. Ten years ago, top management training was virtually non-existent. Now it has become a board-level agenda item. One outcome has been the introduction of a unique two-week senior management course. While not ignoring theory, it is clearly designed to enable participants to tackle practical problems. That intent is reinforced by the requirement that candidates should clearly establish their objectives before attending, have a debriefing session with their manager upon completion, and submit a report six months after the course on how they have been able to use their new knowledge.

This is neither a cheap nor fast method of training staff (each course, for up to 35 people, costs £100,000 in tuition fees alone, and over 200 managers are expected to attend the course), but it is considered essential if ING is to achieve its long-term objectives. Before the introduction of management development, much of ING's training was done 'sitting next to Nellie'. ING's explanation of why there is no option but to train is like that of many companies: 'we didn't do enough training in the past; we simply can't not do it now'. In particular, the spate of recent acquisitions has revealed training needs. However, their response has been strategic rather than simply reactive. ING has set itself a long-term target of allocating 1.5 per cent of revenue to formal, off-the-job training.

The outcome

ING is a company which regards its culture as important, though it tends to use the term 'values' instead of culture. Values such as accuracy, honesty, objectivity and independence have traditionally been so important to the success of the organisation that, while nobody has formulated them into a 'mission statement', everybody knows and uses them. They constitute a major asset of the company.

ING hardly needs to be told of the contribution which such a 'culture' can make to the coherence of the organisation and to its ability to manage change. Three principal changes have put the culture to the test in recent years. The first was when ING became an electronic information company rather than a news agency in the 1970s. This raised questions about the journalistic culture's continuing relevance.

The second test came when ING became a public limited company in 1984. This prospect raised questions about the culture's continuing existence, and in particular whether the integrity of the news service might be jeopardised. So fundamental was this that the most senior executives had doubts about proceeding with the flotation. A solution was found in the protective device of the ING Founders Share Company Limited, which has duties (inter alia) to ensure that the integrity, independence and freedom from bias of ING shall at all times be fully preserved.

More recently, the acquisition of non-journalist companies has caused questions to be raised again about the appropriateness of the traditional values to the ability to weld disparate organisations into a single, integrated body with a shared purpose. It is feared that the ING culture could be diluted by growth. The company is aware of, and is attempting to protect itself against this threat. It recognises the importance of a strong, shared culture to the effectiveness of the organisation, and the importance of aligning management structures with culture in order to maximise that effectiveness.

It also recognises that, in the dynamic environment in which it operates, its strategy will be a continually developing activity. This means that change is an ever-present aspect of life at ING. This requires flexibility, awareness and the ability to respond quickly to opportunities and threats. In such a situation, without strong and accepted values, it is easy for a company to lose its direction. So far, despite the changes that have taken place over the last 20 to 30 years, there is no sign that this is occurring at ING. The lesson that ING draws from this is that strategy development and implementation is a long-term and continuous process, of which the achievement and maintenance of the right culture is a crucial aspect.

Case study three: FFT International

Background

FFT is an import-export company in the tradition of the seventeenth and eighteenth century merchant traders. It does not manufacture anything; rather, it buys goods in one part of the world and sells them in another. Until the 1960s, this mainly involved exporting from and importing to the UK. Since then, with the gradual decline of the UK's manufacturing base, FFT has become more involved in trade between other areas of the world – noticeably the Far East and North America. By the late 1970s, FFT International had become known as the 'sleeping giant' of the import-export industry, but in the 1980s this changed radically.

FFT International is the core business arm of the FFT Group. Although this case study is mainly concerned with change in the former, it is inextricably linked with the redevelopment of the whole Group. The FFT Group now has a turnover of £500 million, some 3,500 employees and 150 offices worldwide, most of which are connected with the Group's import-export operations.

Import-export companies operate on the age-old principle of buying in the cheqpest market and selling in the dearest. However, this does not just involve buying and selling; it also includes arranging the necessary transport, international documentation and customs clearance of products exported to and imported from around the world. This can involve 24 hours per day real-time monitoring of the progress of an export order, and the electronic interchange of information around the world. Inevitably, the fortunes of import-exporters are linked to the fluctuations in the international economy.

FFT International dates back to 1870. Over the years, a number of offices were opened around the world, but particularly in North America and the Far East, where other firms were also acquired. The company was very successful and innovative, being one of the earliest import-exporters to use air freight.

The FFT Group was built up by one family which controlled the company until the early 1980s, when six of the ten Group directors were family members. Therefore, for over a century, the same family had dominated the company. However, though the first two generations were seen as dynamic and innovative, their descendants were less so. They were accused, not unjustly, of caring more about the golf course than the board room, and knowing more about international jet-setting than international trade. The result was that a complacent and unadventurous Board of Directors presided over a large but stagnating organisation. Such a situation could not and did not persist for ever.

During the late 1970s and early 1980s, the group suffered from the downturn in international trade which resulted in substantial losses. By the early 1980s, after several years of increasingly heavy losses, FFT's bankers insisted upon changes in senior management, and a new Chairman, a former Managing Director of a major engineering firm, was appointed to run the Group.

Therefore, there was an urgent need to reverse the declining financial performance of the Group. There were also a number of external opportunities which were beginning to create pressure for change. Among these was the globalisation of world markets. This was leading to rapidly-increasing levels of international trade, especially between the Far East and North America. Manufacturing industry was rationalising, moving back to core businesses and cutting down on capital tied up in stocks and work in progress. In addition, many companies which were used to carrying out their own import-exports contracted these out in the interests of economy. They looked to specialist firms, such as FFT, to handle their export and import activities instead. In return, an efficient and cost-effective operation was required.

Allied to these developments was the increasing use of information technology for the rapid and efficient exchange of export and import information and documentation for transport, customs and payment purposes. For the import-export industry, these were welcome developments. They provided not only a growing market, but also a means to reduce the cost and time involved in organising international trans-actions. All of these developments had to be adopted, and FFT was not responding as quickly, or as effectively as its competitors. Market share was lost. The import-export industry had never been concen-trated in the hands of a few major companies and even FFT's share was probably not much more than a few per cent of the markets in which they traded. Also, the more rapid take-up of computer technol-ogy among its competitors enabled them to increase their presence in these markets.

During this period, FFT had no business strategy and tended to operate on a reactive rather than pro-active basis. The capability to get an order from one side of the world to another did not amount to a policy to ensure survival at a time when margins were under pressure and competition was increasing. In short, though FFT was one of the oldest and most experienced companies in the import-export business, it had lost its sense of purpose and lacked a clear view of where it was going and how it intended to get there. Therefore, the FFT Group was in need of fundamental change, and was not just suffering short-term financial problems due to the world recession.

The central issue was the morale, attitudes and commitment of em-ployees. These were at a very low ebb by the early 1980s. FFT had a reputation as a good employer. The Group had many long-service em-ployees and these, to a great extent, helped to carry the business. However, by the early 1980s, many of its younger employees had reached the conclusion that their career progression and the ability to develop their talents was being blocked by the 'old hands'. This re-sulted in FFT failing to retain, and even attract able, young staff.

Developing and implementing strategy

The change of leadership in the FFT Group represented a consider-able break with the past century of family control and the start of an era of radical change. The new Chairman saw that there were two basic possibilities for the Group: 'close it down or build it up'.

No strategy was ever set out on paper. There was no 'mission state-ment' sent out from the board or chairman's office. The new Chairman said: 'The strategy was in my head'. He saw his first task as one of 'developing a concept and a strategy and keeping quiet about it'. He realised that the Group had to fulfil people's needs for success, but he also realised that some of the things which needed to be done could well require two steps forward and one backwards. The step backward could too easily be interpreted as failure. In addition, personal experience showed that the time involved in negotiating acquisitions could run to several years in some instances. It was recognised that patience had to be an essential part of the process of change.

The Chairman acknowledged that his style of leadership was 'a bit mysterious', with 'an absence of big statements', but said that it was built on a need for, and a deep belief in, a respect for people. Objectives included 'changing attitudes from negative to positive', 'removing fear' and 'being supportive of people'.

The new style of leadership was open and communicative, with the Chairman getting around the branches. The Chairman believed that 'management owes it to people; they have a contribution to make'. As he had said, 'so far as I am concerned, if people have ability they will be given a chance'. Employees perceived this to be the case: 'the challenge has been getting people to understand it doesn't matter who they are but what they are capable of doing'.

The process of bringing people on has been done with care, with able people being promoted slowly: 'promote when people have a chance of succeeding rather than failing'. Challenges were provided for employees, so as to develop them for jobs they could be doing two years hence. At the top level, FFT International Management, which now provides global co-ordination for all FFT Group trading activities, was established as a natural progression 'when people were sufficiently developed to take a policy-forming role'.

Giving priority to people development resulted in the Group promoting from within, in the main. This helped reinforce the expectations of employees: 'there is nothing worse than people being ignored'. The process of 'putting people first' enabled new structures to be put in place without too much apparent upheaval. The approach sought to incorporate the considerable experience of the Group's many long-serving employees.

The new leadership style and attitudinal changes have underpinned a number of structural changes in the FFT Group and, in particular, FFT International. The changes are complex and interwoven, but fall roughly under the following headings: decentralisation, rationalisation, diversification, integration, technological integration, training and development, and consultation and communications.

Decentralisation

Until recently, the FFT Group and FFT International headquarters occupied a large site in the centre of Bristol, where the Group had been located since 1870. Now the company has vacated these premises, partly to redevelop the site but also to enable the board to decentralise operations, reduce headquarters' overheads and 'flatten' the management structure. The company's headquarters, its accounting services and its personnel and training divisions were all relocated to local offices in the UK. In the process, staff numbers were reduced over a six-year period from 1,250 to 926.

Rationalisation

The 1979–81 economic downturn put profit margins under considerable pressure during a period of increased competition for business. The import-export business is, in any case, a high volume/low margin operation, a real 'nickel and dime' business which requires careful monitoring and tight controls. In such a situation it is very easy to lose considerable amounts of money. To cope with this, the accounting function has been continuously refined, with major changes in cash-management control being introduced. These involved more effective branch budgeting procedures to enable operating effectiveness to be properly monitored, which in turn gives the individual operating units a greater control over their own affairs.

Diversification

The move of the company's headquarters from Bristol enabled it to sell its former base. This provided a significant improvement in the company's financial standing and not only reduced its debt burden but also enabled FFT to fund its restructuring programme. Diversifications have been made by the Group outside its mainstream activities into related fields: in, for example, warehouse security protection, with an interest (now a 49 per cent holding) acquired in an Italian firm; in insurance broking operations; and in property. All of these operations have natural connections with FFT's traditional core business.

FFT makes the point that these diversifications are easy to conceptualise but take considerable time to negotiate to a satisfactory conclusion. For example, acquiring one company took three years from start to finish.

Integration

The last six years have seen a number of steps taken, aimed at making FFT a more unified force in the import-export trade, both at home and abroad. Branches, in the UK and internationally, tended in the past to operate as autonomous units, in competition with one another. In an increasingly globalised business, this was thought to be self-defeating. Speed is the essence of profitability for import-export companies. In such a high volume/low margin business, it is the quantity of transactions and the speed with which they are completed that determines overall profitability, rather than the products involved in any particular transaction. Therefore, integrated global services are now required where international transactions are concerned.

Therefore, FFT embarked on a number of measures designed to ensure that its existing branches were more closely integrated, and geographic and functional gaps were plugged. In this latter respect, FFT acquired a number of well-known import-export companies in North America and the Far East. These, together with other related acquisitions, greatly strengthened FFT's international trading operations, especially in its two most important markets.

The greater integration of FFT also helped to focus strategic attention on extending the Group's activities in fields related to its core business. An important aspect of the import-export business is the role played by certain specialist financial service organisations, especially in the areas of insurance, export credit guarantees and credit rating. For over 20 years FFT had dabbled, increasingly unsuccessfully, in the insurance market on its own behalf. Nevertheless, with the opening-up of the financial service sector due to deregulation, the new management at FFT saw an area where their expertise could be exploited profitably. However, after considerable market research, they realised that entry into the financial service side of the business would only be viable if (a) they offered the service to the industry rather than providing it merely as an in-house function, and (b) they linked up with an established financial service company. After much searching, they entered into a joint venture with a Japanese company which was looking to move into the North American and European markets. This has subsequently proved a wise and profitable relationship.

Another interesting step was the introduction of portfolio responsibilities for directors, so that they cover both functional line management and market responsibilities. In this way, directors hold line responsibility for different regions of the UK, and functional responsibility for areas of overseas development. The Sales and Marketing Director also provides line responsibility for special services, such as the transportation of racehorses around the country. There are no finance, information technology or personnel directors, although managers for the first two of these functions, together with the directors, form the management team.

Technological integration

The modern world of international trade is wholly dependent on electronic data interchange. It is said that 'FFT would be dead without information technology'. FFT has 300 terminals on-line connecting its branch structure, providing control over its purchasing, selling and transport operations, and providing accounting, marketing and management information.

This system, called FFTnet, was first introduced a decade ago but has been significantly developed since then. It helps provide coverage of all aspects of the international trade: demand for and supply of goods, air freight, overland, short and deep sea transport. The globalisation of FFT's services has put this system under increasing pressure. Installations around the world have tended to take place on a local basis, without having to pay too much regard to communication protocols with other software and hardware systems. This is an approach adopted by many multinational concerns, and it is one that has resulted in a proliferation of different types of installation. In FFT's case there are some dozen different systems worldwide.

FFT has taken steps to rationalise and integrate its IT capability, and appointed an IT Manager to provide support for this. Trials with a new system have been running for more than a year in the Far East and North America. Wherever necessary, FFT has upgraded its old system to cope with increasing volumes of business until the new one is fully operational. The purpose of these technological changes is to provide an integrated international service, but with fewer employees. In addition, tighter operational monitoring of branch performance will become possible, while at the same time branch performance is being improved through more effective interchange of information about market opportunities.

Training and development

Training has also been subjected to rigorous review in recent years, although the company was said to have been a noted exception among import-export companies in that it did carry out some training. However, as a consequence of the review, a National Training Manager was appointed to provide a central support to the branches. Each branch has its training budget, with local discretion as to how and where this should be spent.

Training courses are run on the practical aspects of international trade, especially in growing areas such as barter and counter trade. However, the emphasis has been steadily moved towards the broader development of people, rather than just the improvement of their effectiveness in their own jobs. This is said to be partly a reflection of the directors' support for training, and partly a response to improved attitudes among employees, who are keener to develop themselves. Whatever the reasons, the training team has been strengthened and now has four staff, two of whom specialise in training for computer skills.

Even before these developments, FFT was among the first companies in the industry to introduce a management training programme. One of the joint managing directors appointed to run FFT International when the new Chairman took up his post was a product of the programme. The old scheme was based on the recruitment of graduates who were then taken through a fast-track programme. The system had come to be regarded as divisive: 'the graduates were treated as gods'. A new scheme has now been developed to provide management training for anyone judged capable of being a manager, as well as for graduate recruits. The company considers that it 'has a remarkable number of above average performers'. The new scheme is designed to give all employees, most of whom were early school leavers, a chance to develop. Those who continued their education and came into the company having gained their formal qualifications are treated equally.

Consultation and communications

The change process in FFT has been facilitated by the use of a consultant reporting to the Chairman. The consultant has been used, from time to time, to ascertain the views of particular groups of employees or individuals and advise the chairman on courses of action, appointments, problems and opportunities. Forwarding, in FFT, is regarded as a network business with branches providing regular customer contact, supported by a small headquarters staff. It is said to be a simple business and the motto is 'keep it bloody simple'. Consequently, the change process has been kept as straightforward as possible, with the separation of the activities of policy formation from the day-to-day operations. However, the daily round of intensive communication between branches and headquarters, which is a necessary feature of international trade, makes for a considerable informal network of communication and contact. In this way, a good deal of feedback is provided on virtually all aspects of the business. This process of exchange is reinforced by regular visits to branches by the Chairman, the managing director and the directors with regional responsibilities.

Because of the volume of information communication, there has been some ambivalence about formal structures, such as briefing meetings. These were introduced in the mid-1980s but then faded away. Some branch managers continue to hold meetings, and a new company-wide system is to be introduced. FFT International also started to bring all its managers together for regular meetings. The exact form of these, how many and down to what level managers should be involved, is under review.

Customer communications are also being reviewed and, amongst other developments, a regular newsletter is being issued to all clients.

The outcome

The effect of all the changes that have taken place has been to make FFT International more profitable and more competitive. In the early 1980s, the company made a loss of £500,000. Gradually, profits have been restored, and are now in the region of £8 million. Clearly, this turnaround has not been an easy task to achieve. It has meant quite radical changes in the operation of the company. Overall the changes can be summed up as: new leadership, a new decentralised and diversified structure, an integrated international service, new attitudes, improved morale – it is said that 'we want people to come to work whistling' – and increased collective commitment to succeed. The crucial point to note about this list is that it is predominantly concerned with changing the way people think and act and providing them with the appropriate skills, methods, structures and environment in which to give of their best. The result is not only better financial performance but also a greater sense of purpose and a certainty that the company will continue to make considerable progress. Clearly, the 'sleeping giant' has been well and truly woken.

Case study four: Seaside Biscuits

Background

Seaside Biscuits is a wholly-owned subsidiary of a major food and drinks conglomerate, but operates as an independent company. It is a successful business, concentrating on the sale of 'own label' products to the major supermarket chains. In the past five years, it has experienced considerable growth, increasing its workforce from 600 to 900 employees.

The company's Board of Directors, in reviewing Seaside's performance, concluded that, despite its considerable success, the business and its prospects should be evaluated from a strategic perspective. They felt the business was possibly over-dependent upon a single customer and that its products were too traditional, low value-added and insufficiently directed at the higher-value end of the market. The company also had problems because it occupied a cramped, old factory and suffered a chronic shortage of production capacity. Subcontracting was not favoured because contractors would be likely to seek the business for themselves. The Managing Director believed that demand for new products appeared to require a quick £3 million investment programme which, because of shortage of space, would probably have resulted in an unsatisfactory new operation.

In view of this, the Board had recently worked with an academic institute to produce a mission statement and business objectives but, due to urgent day-to-day operational issues, had found it difficult to move from the statement of intent to actual implementation. It therefore decided to approach a firm of consultants who had a reputation for using Action Learning techniques to help companies to develop achievable strategic plans.

The consultants discussed the project with the company's Personnel Director and Managing Director, and agreed to work with Seaside Biscuits to achieve the following:

- Produce a strategic plan and determine how it should be implemented.
- Identify growth areas in the market and plan for the production of appropriate products.
- Produce a manufacturing strategy which provided for short-term efficiency improvements as well as meeting the longer-term market needs to be identified in the strategic plan.
- Produce a management development programme and mechanisms for effectively implementing decisions.
- Decide how issues should be discussed with and communicated to the trade unions and the workforce.
- Encourage wide consultation and involvement with trade union representatives, employees and all levels of management.

During these preliminary discussions, Seaside emphasised that they were essentially a selling organisation and would need assistance in producing a marketing strategy. It followed that an important aspect of the consultants' involvement would be to help the company explore market opportunities. However, though a marketing specialist was co-opted onto the consultants' team, they made it clear to the company that his role would be to facilitate the development of a marketing strategy rather than to produce one for the company. Indeed, it was stated from the outset, in line with Action Learning principles, that the project's success or failure would depend on the extent to which the directors themselves worked at their own perceived problems, drew their own conclusions and undertook actions based upon ownership of the learning process.

Developing and implementing strategy

It was agreed that the work would be based upon six, one-day meetings of Seaside's 'Executive Committee' of ten directors and senior managers. These were split into two project groups, one concerned with manufacturing and the other with marketing. The methodology was for the groups to meet separately and, from time to time, convene in plenary session to report to each other. Four meetings were held at roughly monthly intervals with the final two meetings consisting of a weekend from Friday to Monday. Between meetings each project group undertook separate responsibilities, which were divided up between particular managers and directors. At the start of each meeting, these reported on the work they had undertaken since the previous meeting.

The first meeting consisted mainly of a plenary session at which the consultants' team interrogated the Seaside executives on the mission statement and the company objectives which had been drafted during the work with the academic institute. Seaside also produced detailed information on customer relations, and an analysis of product development describing production and marketing trends over a six-year period.

The first meeting was, occasionally, tense as the Managing Director in particular was asked to justify various policy decisions, including a strong inclination to build a new factory on a greenfield site to supplement existing capacity. As the day progressed, senior managers and directors were gradually persuaded to voice concerns which they had previously either suppressed or raised in a questioning, rather than critical, fashion. The process tended to reduce somewhat the influence of the power relationships within the Executive Committee, and persuade junior members to be more articulate than they would have been at a normal meeting.

At this stage, the Executive Committee showed ready acceptance of the need to examine the marketing opportunities, but some reluctance to concede the possibility of short-term, immediate, improvements in manufacturing performance. They accepted that there were production problems, but explained that these were due to the need to accept shorter runs, the acute difficulties of operating in a small, outdated factory, and technical problems preventing the introduction of efficient production flexibility, scheduling and packaging. Restraints imposed by technical problems of wrapping and packaging were to be a theme throughout the whole exercise.

At this early stage, the Executive Committee was inclined to argue that there was little that could be done to alleviate these problems. They also had difficulty in completing assigned tasks between the meetings because of time constraints and, in the case of the Marketing Group, through inexperience. Nevertheless, these obstacles were gradually overcome by the two groups.

The Manufacturing Group

During its first three meetings, this Group focused attention on problems such as scheduling production, improving the performance of particular production lines and the feasibility of discontinuing certain products. At the start, there was some reluctance to accept that improvements were feasible. However, by the third meeting, the Group had begun a systematic approach to both long- and short-term capacity requirements, and agreed that it would do the following:

- Produce a report on plant utilisation, including proposals for new working patterns and shift systems.
- Consider the manufacturing case for product rationalisation.
- Consider in the long term the case for flexible manufacturing systems; this to be done in the light of marketing proposals. It was accepted that the practical applications of this were uncertain, and, if they proved feasible, were likely to involve higher unit costs.
- Accept that a long-term plan for the factory was desirable, and that it was therefore necessary for incremental changes – where possible – to contribute to overall objectives. This could not be undertaken in advance of the marketing strategy.
- On a particular line, recommend investment expenditure.

- Study operating procedures in order to identify training needs. It was decided to begin this process with one production line, possibly using the equipment suppliers to provide technical and other information.

A study was also initiated to evaluate the use of computerised scheduling. Manufacturing scheduling was at that time carried out manually, which was inefficient in terms of capacity utilisation. But the Works Manager maintained that, because of the complexity of production requirements, computerised scheduling was not applicable in their situation. However, a visit was arranged by the consultants to a paper mill, so that directors and managers could study computerised scheduling in action (for competitive reasons it was not possible to visit a UK biscuit plant). This was deemed applicable because, strangely enough, paper- and biscuit-making processes share many similarities. Later, Seaside employed someone from their parent company to tackle this issue; and as a result extended their enquiries to possible computerisation of other activities.

During meetings two and three, various products were identified by the Manufacturing Group as being possibly unprofitable and apparently offering few prospects of successful development. Their recommendation that these should be discontinued received a positive response from the Marketing Group. Eventually several lines were discontinued, and a procedure introduced for reviewing production so that such decisions could be made routinely. This was a particularly important decision, because it not only discontinued unprofitable lines, but also released capacity for more urgent work. A second important decision concerned a relatively small investment project which would improve performance on a particular line. This decision was to produce significant improvements in manufacturing performance in 1989.

Another important proposal was the move to negotiate a new shift system. Seaside knew that their short-term capacity problems could partly be met by more hours of work. The Manufacturing Group therefore decided to seek to negotiate a four-day-week shift system for the whole factory, thereby reducing shift overlap, to be supplemented by a three-day-weekend shift running from Friday to Sunday. The three-day-weekend shift would initially operate where production demands were high and be extended if and when justified by manufacturing requirements.

Throughout the meetings of the Manufacturing Group, the need to operate equipment more efficiently was inevitably an important issue.

The Group decided that new investment would improve matters, but eventually also accepted that plant down-time was a problem; it was agreed, with the approval of the operatives concerned, to video down-time procedures. As a result, improvements were agreed, including better equipment availability and training to improve team performance.

The discussion on manufacturing flexibility never reached a satisfactory conclusion, partly because computerised scheduling of work was still at the study stage, and partly because packaging methods were unsatisfactory and acted as a brake on improvements down the line.

As the Action Learning programme proceeded beyond the third meeting, the Manufacturing Group found their activity increasingly concerned with routine management decision making. One consequence was realisation of the need to improve supervision, so that effective responsibility for plant performance could be assigned. It was decided that discussions should start with supervisors about giving them product line responsibility, which would gradually provide for a move to a teamwork system. Training, improved systems and management development could therefore be co-ordinated.

The Marketing Group

The first step in generating a marketing strategy was for the Marketing Group to define the company's strengths and weaknesses in preparation for evaluating possible options. With little previous experience of strategic planning, this proved difficult. The Group was therefore asked to take its customer base as a starting point and define what they believed their customers wanted now and in the future, and the implications for Seaside. As primarily an 'own label' supplier, the company tended to be driven by its customers. This approach helped focus attention on key marketing issues.

By the end of the third meeting, the Marketing Group had completed its systematic assessment of its customer base and had evaluated the implications for each product type currently produced or of future interest to the business. Export, extended distribution and brand development opportunities had also been evaluated. In terms of the latter, it was evident that the company's concentration on own label production greatly simplified the tasks of marketing, product development and distribution. Therefore, any move to become more brand-orientated would require substantial changes in the activities of these areas. In particular, the company would itself need to have a greater understanding of consumer preferences instead of relying on its customers to do the market research for them.

The Marketing Group therefore shifted its attention to consumer preferences. This led Seaside to redefine its grouping of products according to consumer needs. The new product groupings, plus a range of possible new product options, were then evaluated against the company's long-term business objectives. The results clearly identified priorities amongst existing product groups and between the various new product options.

The final stage of the Action Learning programme consisted of a full weekend meeting at which both marketing and manufacturing strategies were brought together and evaluated in the light of the overall, long-term needs of the business. The Manufacturing Group put forward a list of 25 proposals for changes in the company's manufacturing operations. This included short-term measures, such as re-organising the shift system, and a greater emphasis on standardising and improving line-by-line working methods. The list also contained proposals for longer-term changes, such as the establishment of a special section to deal with selling damaged and poorly-wrapped biscuits to market traders, and major investment in new plant.

The Manufacturing Group also reported that when the Action Learning programme commenced, production levels were below expected standards. However, due to the programme, these had improved considerably, which put earlier investment proposals, especially the Managing Director's preference for a new factory, in a different light.

The Marketing Group presented their report and asked the Manufacturing Group to consider the manufacturing implications of their proposals. The report set down production targets, over a one-, three- and ten-year period, which would have to be achieved if the marketing proposals were to be successfully implemented. In particular, these related to the development of Seaside Biscuits' own brands.

The outcome

Inevitably, at the conclusion of the Action Learning programme, much was left to be done and some issues remained unresolved. Possible marketing plans were outlined which contained a series of options representing best and worst expectations. The Manufacturing Group's work had improved short-term performance, thereby easing capacity problems and 'saving' a £3 million investment programme. It had, at the same time, produced detailed manufacturing proposals for the following year and three-year period. Above all, the company's new strategy was market-led, a new departure for Seaside.

Both marketing and manufacturing proposals contained deadlines. In the case of manufacturing, a whole series of dates were proposed for the introduction of new supervisory systems and the recruitment of new managers. Likewise, the marketing plan contained deadlines when, after consultation, decisions would be made and policies reviewed.

The implementation, consultation and communication of these proposals were considered. It was decided that the whole plan and its various implications would be discussed by the company's Works Council, and each separate element would then be communicated to the work groups concerned. Although this agreement was reached, it was not discussed in detail and probably deserved more consideration than it was given.

The consultants' terms of reference, therefore, had been substantially carried out:

- At the end of the six-month Action Learning programme, a strategic plan existed and initial proposals for its implementation had been agreed. The company recognised that in many respects the plan was incomplete, but appreciated that strategic planning was a dynamic process which had to be continually worked at. In recognition of this, they suggested that the consultants should become involved in a six-monthly review of progress.
- Potential market growth areas had been identified and plans were devised for producing appropriate products.
- A manufacturing strategy, providing for short-term, as well as long-term efficiency improvements had been agreed and was being implemented.
- Proposals for management development were only at a preliminary stage, but there were firm proposals for changing the role of supervisors and giving them appropriate training. There were also proposals about the role of particular managers and ways in which various functions could be reorganised and related.
- Decisions had been made about how these various changes should be communicated to trade unions and the workforce.

The Action Learning programme had, therefore, produced the basis of a self-generated, market-led strategic plan. As the programme had developed, initiatives were increasingly undertaken by the directors and managers involved. Short-term, tangible results had been achieved and longer-term proposals agreed. However, perhaps the most significant developments were that the senior managers now worked as a team, and had gained confidence in their own ability to shape the company's future, rather than relying on outsiders to do it for them.

Conclusions

As the case studies show, strategic management can bring considerable benefits to organisations; nevertheless, it is fraught with pitfalls and dangers. However, the alternatives – to do nothing, or to adopt a reactive, fire-fighting mode – are a recipe for decline and, at the very least, necessitate the eventual replacement of senior management. This is illustrated by the cases of PCI and FFT, whose fortunes waned and whose chief executives were replaced, though to differing effect.

The cases of ING and Seaside Biscuits, on the other hand, show that companies can embark on strategic management without the need to replace senior managers, except in terms of planned succession. ING appears to have developed the ability to construct and pursue strategic objectives consistently and successfully over the long term. During the last 20 to 30 years, its senior management has changed in a planned manner; however, its strategic objectives have been consistent. Seaside Biscuits' exposure to strategic management has been considerably shorter than ING's, but it does demonstrate that senior managers can, without the spur of poor performance, choose of their own free will to change from a reactive to a strategic mode of operation.

From the case studies, a number of important conclusions can be drawn regarding strategic management:

- It is not a once-and-for-all solution to organisational problems. Rather it is a continuous, and never-ending process of creating, implementing, reviewing and recreating strategies in pursuit of an organisation's long-term objectives.
- Implementing strategies designed to transform organisations radically requires a careful, consistent and well-thought-out programme of change management.
- There is no guarantee that a strategic approach will be successful, but the alternatives tend to be blinkered and do not lead an organisation forward.

- The key to strategic management lies not in detailed and complex mathematical analysis, but in the willingness of senior managers to work together to develop, promote and consistently pursue a common strategic view of their organisation's future.

Discussion points

These case studies and strategic management will be discussed further in Part Four; however, the following discussion points will assist the reader to understand the issues involved more clearly.

1 Compare and contrast the approaches to developing strategic plans of PCI and Seaside Biscuits, and identify the factors which caused them to experience different outcomes.
2 Compare and contrast the approaches of ING and FFT to strategy implementation, and distinguish the lessons that they could learn from each other.
3 What are the implications for strategic management of the roles played by the management teams in the four case studies?
4 Is teamwork necessarily a precondition for the successful development and implementation of strategy?
5 Are there noticeable differences in the cultures of the four companies, which contributed to their experience of strategic management?
6 To what extent can functional-level strategies be seen as being separate from and independent of corporate- and business-level strategies?
7 Compare and explain the effect on the strategic management process of the openness and willingness to listen of the chief executives in PCI, FFT and Seaside Biscuits.
8 Is there convincing evidence to support the argument that organisations need to develop a strategic vision or intent as a necessary component of strategic management?
9 What is the case for arguing that ING and FFT represent prime examples of Mintzberg's (1987) concept of 'crafting strategy', as averse to seeing them as the arch-exponents of pragmatic and reactive management?

Part Three

The management of change –
Theory and practice

6

Change management:
approaches and techniques

Introduction

Whilst the previous chapter was concerned with how organisations identified their long-term objectives, the focus now shifts to how the changes necessary to achieve such objectives are managed. The chapter begins by investigating the theoretical foundations of change management. In particular, it is shown that the three main theories that underpin models of change management can be distinguished by their respective concentration on individual, group and organisation-wide issues. This leads on to an examination of models of change management themselves, which reveals that the principal ones all stem from the work of one person, Kurt Lewin. The various techniques and tools for implementing change, and how different writers have classified these, are then discussed.

The chapter concludes by presenting a classification of change management which proposes that it is the focus of the change project, whether it be to bring about alterations at the individual, group, inter-group or organisation level, which determines the theory and techniques to be applied, and the degree of involvement necessary from those who will experience the change. It is then argued that the classification helps to resolve two further issues: the principle to be applied when sequencing the various techniques and tools which are necessary to achieve change; and the relationship between large-scale, organisation-wide change programmes and smaller, more localised change projects.

Nevertheless, despite the large body of literature devoted to it, change is such an ever-present feature of organisational life that some

might ask: why comment on it at all? Such people could be forgiven
for believing that organisations are so used to change that they take it
in their stride. The reality though, according to many observers, is
different. Organisations can and do experience severe problems in
bringing about change (Howarth, 1988).

The reason for this is two-fold. Firstly, change comes in many
shapes and sizes, though most forms can be categorised as either radical or incremental. Radical change relates to large-scale, organisation-
wide transformation programmes involving the rapid and wholesale
overturning of old ways and old ideas and their replacement by new
and unique ones. Such forms of change are also referred to as revolutionary or discontinuous, thus emphasising not only the scale of the
change involved but also that it represents, for the entire organisation, a decisive break with the past. However, though radical change
is characterised by its speed, scale and break with the past, this cannot be achieved quickly or solely by recourse to wholesale changes to
structures and systems. Particularly when new forms of behaviour are
called for, it also requires a co-ordinated programme of smaller and
more localised projects, spreading over a longer period and designed
to bring about, reinforce and act as the building blocks for the overall
programme.

This, therefore, leads on to the second category: incremental
change. These types of change projects are relatively small-scale,
localised, and designed to solve a particular problem or enhance the
performance of a sub-section or part of an organisation. Such forms of
change are also referred to as evolutionary or piecemeal, thus emphasising the less dramatic and often uncoordinated nature of these
forms of change. By themselves, incremental change projects can only
bring an ad hoc and localised improvement in performance. Though a
long-term, co-ordinated programme of such improvements can clearly
achieve more than this, it can never bring about radical transformation without large-scale and organisation-wide change as well.

This brings us on to the second point. It is clear that to change,
even in a small way, can be complex and difficult. The literature
abounds with examples of changes that have gone wrong, some disas-
trously so (Burnes and Weekes, 1989; Cummings and Huse, 1989;
Kanter, 1989; Kelly, 1982).

Therefore, managing change is problematical, though it is difficult
to come to grips with the scale of the issue – do only a few organisations experience problems, or is this a common occurrence? However,
there are two types of change which have been well documented in recent years and where estimates of the scale of the problem have been

made – the introduction of new (computerised) technology and the adoption of Total Quality Management.

Over the past decade, the introduction of new technology has been one of the most common, and important, forms of organisational change. It has also, in Britain at least, been fraught with problems. A recent study, by the management consultants A T Kearney, found that of the leading industrial nations, Britain was at the bottom of the league table in achieving successful change. They concluded that out of the £1.9 billion spent on technology-related change by manufacturing companies in Britain each year, approximately one-third is wasted (Kearney, 1989). Though this is not a purely British problem (Howarth, 1988), other studies support the view that it is particularly acute here, and suggest that the failure rate for new technology change projects is anywhere between 40 per cent and 70 per cent (Bessant and Haywood, 1985; McKracken, 1986; New, 1989; Smith and Tranfield, 1987; Voss, 1985).

The move to adopt Total Quality Management (TQM) by British companies has gathered pace in the last few years. TQM, at its simplest, is an organisation-wide effort to improve quality through changes in structure, practices, systems and above all attitudes (Dale and Cooper, 1992). Though seen as pre-eminently a Japanese innovation, TQM techniques were originally developed in the USA in the 1950s and 1960s (Crosby, 1979; Deming, 1982; Juran, 1988; Taguchi, 1986). TQM is now proving to be one of the most potent forces for organisational change in the UK. However, despite the growing number of adherents worldwide, the reality is that many companies find great difficulty in adopting TQM. Indeed, one of the founders of the TQM movement, Phillip Crosby, argued that over 90 per cent of TQM initiatives by organisations fail (Crosby, 1979).

Although the above examples deal with change related to new technology and TQM only, they carry implications for all forms of change. This is because, firstly, such forms of change include all types of organisational transformations, ranging from job redesign, through the introduction of new reward systems, to full-scale changes in organisational structure and culture. Secondly, there is general agreement that such changes do not fail because of faults in the technology or techniques employed per se, but because of companies' lack of ability in terms of planning and managing change, motivating and involving employees, and designing and implementing suitable job and work structures – all key aspects of any type of organisational change (Blackler and Brown 1986; Burnes, 1989; Clegg and Symon, 1991; Crosby, 1979; Dale and Cooper, 1992; Deming, 1982; Juran, 1988 and Kearney, 1989).

Therefore, the issue of change management is not marginal or unimportant. Indeed, if organisations are to change in the radical manner that some writers envisage (Handy, 1989; Kanter, 1989; Peters and Waterman, 1982), then the management of change (both radical and incremental) will be one of the key factors that distinguish the successful from the less successful organisations.

Over the years, much of the literature on change management has been derived from the practice of Organisational Development (OD). This has been defined as 'a systemwide application of behavioral science knowledge to the planned development and reinforcement of organizational strategies, structures and processes for improving an organization's effectiveness' (Cummings and Huse, 1989:1). However, it has attracted a number of criticisms, not least that it is too manipulative and is concerned mainly with incremental rather than large-scale radical change (Dunphy and Stace, 1988).

To rectify this, new theories and approaches have been developed or added to the change management portfolio. In particular, these have sought to deal with the organisation in its entirety, especially in terms of large-scale, transitional change, rather than dealing only with discrete parts (French and Bell, 1984).

Change management: theoretical foundations

Change management is not a distinct discipline with rigid and clearly defined boundaries. Rather, the theory and practice of change management draws on a number of social science disciplines and traditions. Though this is one of its strengths, nevertheless it does make the task of tracing its origins and defining its core concepts more difficult than might otherwise be the case.

The task is complicated further by the simple fact that the social sciences themselves are interwoven. As an example, theories of management education, an important component of change management, cannot be fully discussed without reference to theories of child and adult psychology. Neither can these be discussed without touching on theories of knowledge (epistemology), a veritable philosophical minefield.

The challenge, then, is to range wide enough to capture the theoretical essence of change management, without straying so far into its related disciplines that clarity and understanding suffer. In order to achieve this delicate operation, we shall limit our examination to the three schools of thought that form the central planks of change management theory:

- The Individual Perspective school
- The Group Dynamics school
- The Open Systems school

The Individual Perspective school

The Individual Perspective school, in investigating organisational change, focuses on the individual. However, members of this school are split into two camps: the Behaviourists and the Gestalt-Field psychologists. The former view behaviour as resulting from an individual's interaction with their environment. Gestalt-Field psychologists, on the other hand, believe that this is only a partial explanation. Instead, they argue that an individual's behaviour is the product of environment and reason.

In Behaviourist theory, all behaviour is learned; the individual is the passive recipient of external and objective data. Among the earliest to work in the field of behaviour conditioning was Pavlov (1927). In an experiment which has now passed into folklore, he discovered that a dog could be 'taught' to salivate at the ringing of a bell, by conditioning the dog to associate the sound of the bell with food. Arising from this, one of the basic principles of the Behaviourists is that human actions are conditioned by their expected consequences. Behaviour that is rewarded tends to be repeated, and behaviour that is punished tends not to be. Therefore, in order to change behaviour, it is necessary to change the conditions of which it is a function (Skinner, 1974).

In practice, behaviour modification involves the manipulation of reinforcing stimuli so as to reward desired activity. The aim is to reward immediately all instances of the wanted behaviour, but to ignore all instances of the unwanted behaviour (because even recognition can act as a reinforcer). This is based on the principle of extinction; a behaviour will stop eventually if it is not rewarded (Lovell, 1980). Not surprisingly, given the period when it emerged, the Behaviourist approach mirrors in many respects that of the Classical school, portraying humans as cogs in a machine, responding to the external stimuli provided by the machine.

For Gestalt-Field theorists, learning is a process of gaining or changing insights, outlooks, expectations or thought patterns. In explaining an individual's behaviour, this group takes into account not only a person's actions and the responses these elicit, but also the interpretation the individual places on these. As French and Bell (1984: 140) explain:

Gestalt therapy is based on the belief that persons function as whole, total organisms. And each person possesses positive and negative characteristics that must be 'owned up to' and permitted expression. People get into trouble when they get fragmented, when they do not accept their total selves ... Basically, one must come to terms with oneself ... must stop blocking off awareness, authenticity, and the like by dysfunctional behaviors.

Therefore, behaviour is not just a product of external stimuli; rather it arises from how the individual uses reason to interpret these stimuli.

Consequently, the Behaviourists seek to achieve organisational change solely by modifying the external stimuli acting upon the individual. The Gestalt-Field proponents seek to help individual members of an organisation change their understanding of themselves and the situation in question, which in turn will lead to changes in behaviour (Smith *et al.* 1982).

Both the approaches of the Individual Perspective school have proved influential in the management of change; indeed, some writers even advocate using them in tandem. This is certainly the case with those advocating new paradigm-type organisations. Here the emphasis is on the use of both strong individual incentives (external stimuli) and discussion, involvement and debate (internal reflection) in order to bring about organisational change (Peters and Waterman, 1982).

This approach, once again not surprisingly, shares many characteristics with the Human Relations school, who (through the work of Maslow, 1943) stress the need for both external and internal stimuli in order to influence human behaviour. However, though acknowledging the role of the individual, the Human Relations school also draw attention to the importance of social groups in organisations, as do the Group Dynamics school.

The Group Dynamics school

In terms of change theory, this school has the longest history (Schein, 1969). Its emphasis is on bringing about organisational change through teams or work groups, rather than individuals (Bernstein, 1968). The rationale behind this, according to Lewin (1958), is that because people in organisations work in groups, individual behaviour must be seen, modified or changed in the light of prevailing group practices and norms.

Lewin (1958) postulated that group behaviour is an intricate set of symbolic interactions and forces which not only affect group structures, but also modify individual behaviour. Therefore, he argued that individual behaviour is a function of the group environment or 'field', as he termed it. This field produces forces and tensions, emanating from group pressures on each of its members. An individual's behaviour at any given time, according to Lewin, is an interplay between the intensity and valence (whether the force is positive or negative) of the forces impinging on the person. Because of this, he asserted that a group is never in a 'steady state of equilibrium', but is in a continuous process of mutual adaptation which he termed 'quasi-stationary equilibrium'.

To bring about change, therefore, it is useless to concentrate on changing the behaviour of individuals, according to the Group Dynamics school. The individual in isolation is constrained by group pressures to conform. The focus of change must be at the group level and should concentrate on influencing and changing the group's norms, roles and values (French and Bell, 1984; Cummings and Huse, 1989; Smith *et al.* 1982).

- *Norms* – are rules or standards that define what people should do, think or feel in a given situation. For the Group Dynamics school, what is important in analysing group norms is the difference between implicit and explicit norms. Explicit norms are formal, written rules which are known by, and applicable to, all. Implicit norms are informal and unwritten, and individuals may not even be consciously aware of them. Nevertheless, implicit norms have been identified as playing a vital role in dictating the actions of group members.
- *Roles* – are patterns of behaviour to which individuals are expected to conform. In organisational terms, roles are formally defined by job descriptions, though in practice they are also strongly influenced by norms and values as well. Even in their work life, individuals rarely have only one role. For example, a production manager may also be the company's safety representative, a clerical officer may also be secretary of the company's social club, and a supervisor may also be a shop steward. Clearly, where a person is required to conform to a number of different roles, the scope for role conflict or role ambiguity is ever-present. Unless roles are both clearly defined and compatible, the result can be sub-optimal for the individual – in terms of stress – and for the organisation – in terms of poor performance.
- *Values* – are ideas and beliefs which individuals hold about what is

right and wrong. Values refer not so much to what people do or
think or feel in a given situation; instead they relate to the broader
principles which lie behind these responses. Values are a more
problematic concept than either norms or roles. Norms and roles
can, with diligence, be more or less accurately determined. Values,
on the other hand, are more difficult to determine because individuals are not always consciously aware of, or cannot easily
articulate, the values which influence their behaviour. Therefore,
questioning them and observing their actions is unlikely to produce
a true picture of their personal values. Nevertheless, the concept itself is seen as very important in determining, and changing,
patterns of behaviour.

Despite its limitations, the Group Dynamics school has proved to be
very influential in developing both the theory and practice of change
management. This can be seen by the very fact that it is now usual for
organisations to view themselves as comprising groups and teams,
rather than merely collections of individuals (Mullins, 1989).

As French and Bell (1984:127–9) have pointed out, the importance
given to teams is reflected in the fact that:

> ... the most important single group of interventions in OD are
> team-building activities the goals of which are the improved and
> increased effectiveness of various teams within the organization
> ... The ... team-building meeting has the goal of improving the
> team's effectiveness through better management of task demands,
> relationship demands, and group processes ... [The team] ana-
> lyzes its way of doing things, and attempts to develop strategies to
> improve its operation.

In so doing, norms, roles and values are examined, challenged and,
where necessary, changed. Nevertheless, despite the emphasis that
many place on groups within organisations, others argue that the correct approach is one that deals with an organisation as a whole.

The Open Systems school

Having examined approaches to change which emphasise the importance of groups and individuals, we now come to one whose primary
point of reference is the organisation in its entirety. The Open Systems school (as mentioned in Chapter 2) sees organisations as composed of a number of interconnected sub-systems. It follows that any

change to one part of the system will have an impact on other parts of the system, and, in turn, on its overall performance (Scott, 1987). The Open Systems approach to change is based on a method of describing and evaluating these sub-systems, in order to determine how they need to be changed so as to improve the overall functioning of the organisation.

However, this school does not just see organisations as systems in isolation; they are 'open' systems. Organisations are seen as open in two respects. Firstly, they are open to – interact with – their external environment. Secondly, they are open internally: the various sub-systems interact with each other. Therefore, internal changes in one area affect other areas, and in turn have an impact on the external environment, and vice versa (Buckley, 1968).

The objective of the Open Systems approach is to structure the functions of a business in such a manner that, through clearly defined lines of co-ordination and interdependence, the overall business objectives are collectively pursued. The emphasis is on achieving overall synergy, rather than on optimising the performance of any one individual part per se (Mullins, 1989).

Miller (1967) argues that there are four principal organisational sub-systems:

1 *The organisational goals and values sub-system* – this comprises the organisation's stated objectives and the values it wishes to promote in order to attain them. To operate effectively, the organisation has to ensure that its goals and values are compatible not only with each other, but also with its external and internal environments.
2 *The technical sub-system* – this is the specific combination of knowledge, techniques and technologies which an organisation requires in order to function. Once again, the concern here is with the compatibility and appropriateness of these in relation to an organisation's particular circumstances.
3 *The psychosocial sub-system* – this is also variously referred to as organisational climate and organisational culture. In essence, it is the fabric of role relationships, values and norms that binds people together and makes them citizens of a particular miniature society (the organisation). It is influenced by an organisation's environment, history and employees, as well as its tasks, technology and structures. If the psychosocial sub-system is weak, fragmented or inappropriate, then instead of binding the organisation together, it may have the opposite effect.

4 *The managerial sub-system* – this spans the entire organisation. It is responsible for relating an organisation to its environment, setting goals, determining values, developing comprehensive strategic and operational plans, designing structure and establishing control processes. It is this sub-system that has the responsibility for consciously directing an organisation and ensuring that it attains its objectives. If the managerial sub-system fails, so does the rest of an organisation.

The Open Systems school is concerned with understanding organisations in their entirety; therefore, it attempts to take a holistic rather than a particularistic perspective. This is reflected in its approach to change. According to Burke (1980), this is informed by three factors:

1 Sub-systems are interdependent. If alterations are made to one part of an organisation without taking account of its dependence or impact on the rest of the organisation, the outcome may be sub-optimal.
2 Training, as a mechanism for change, is unlikely to succeed on its own. This is because it concentrates on the individual and not the organisational level. As Burke argues, 'although training may lead to individual change and in some cases to small group change, there is scant evidence that attempting to change the individual will in turn change the organisation' (1980:75).
3 In order to be successful, organisations have to tap and direct the energy and talent of their workforce. This requires the removal of obstacles which prevent this, and the provision of positive reinforcement which promotes it. Given that this is likely to require changes to such things as norms, reward systems and work structures, it must be approached from an organisational, rather than individual or group, perspective.

Though the Open Systems perspective has attracted much praise, attention has also been drawn to its alleged shortcomings. Butler (1985:345), for example, while hailing it as a major step forward in understanding organisational change, points out that: 'Social systems are extremely dynamic and complex entities that often defy descriptions and analysis. Therefore, one can easily get lost in attempting to sort out all the cause-and-effect relationships'. Beach (1980:138), in a similar vein, argues that Open Systems theory:

> ... *does not comprise a consistent, articulated, coherent theory. Much of it constitutes a high level of abstraction. To be really*

useful to the professional practice of management, its spokesmen and leaders must move to a more concrete and operationally useful range.

Despite these criticisms, the level of support for this approach, from eminent theorists such as Burns and Stalker (1961), Joan Woodward (1965), and Lawrence and Lorsch (1967), is formidable. This is why, as explained in Chapter 2, it has proved so influential.

Summary

In looking at the three schools which form the central planks of change management theory, two major points stand out. Firstly, not only do they stand, generally, in sharp contrast to the mechanistic approach of the Classical school towards organisations and people, but also, in their approach to individuals, groups and organisations as a whole, they form a link to the emerging organisational paradigms that were discussed in the previous chapter. Indeed, it might be possible to go further and say that these three schools provide many of the core concepts of the new paradigms. If this is so, the claim (by Kanter, 1989, and others) that these new forms of organisation are a radical break with the past may have to be reconsidered.

Secondly, though each school puts itself forward as the most effective, if not the only, approach to change, they are not necessarily in conflict or competition. Indeed, it could well be argued that they are complementary approaches. The key task, which will be examined in more detail later, is to identify the circumstances in which each is appropriate: does the problem/objective of change lie at the level of the organisation, group or individual? Can any of these levels be tackled in isolation from the others?

In practice, the Open Systems perspective may be correct: change at one level or in one area should take into account the effect it will have elsewhere in the organisation. However, whether the perspective adopted is organisation-wide, or limited to groups and individuals, in the final analysis, what is it that is being changed? The answer, surely, is the behaviour of individuals and groups, because organisations are, as the proponents of these perspectives admit, social systems. To change anything requires the co-operation and consent of the groups and individuals who make up an organisation, for it is only through their behaviour that the structures, technologies, systems and procedures of an organisation move from being abstract concepts to concrete realities. This is made even plainer in the next section, where we examine the models of organisational change that various theorists have put forward.

Models of organisational change

The practice of change management, as shown above, is dependent on a number of factors, not least the particular school of thought involved. Not surprisingly, therefore, a number of different approaches to change management have arisen over the years. Most of these were devised to meet the needs of particular organisations, or arose from a specific school of thought.

Despite the proliferation of such approaches, most observers seem to agree that these can be related to three basic models of the change process, which in turn arise from the pioneering work of one person – Kurt Lewin. Lewin was a prolific theorist, researcher and practitioner in interpersonal, group, inter-group and community relationships. In 1945, he founded and became the first director of the hugely influential Research Centre for Group Dynamics. The models of the change process which emerged from his work are:

- The Action Research model
- The 3-Step model
- The Phases of Planned Change model

Action Research

Action Research (or Action Learning as it is sometimes called) was designed as a collective approach to solving social and organisational problems. Though developed in America by Kurt Lewin in the 1940s, it was adopted, soon after its emergence, by the Tavistock Institute in Britain and used to improve managerial competence and efficiency in the, then, newly-nationalised coal industry. Since then it has developed strong adherents on both sides of the Atlantic (French and Bell, 1984).

According to French and Bell (1984:98–9):

> *Action Research is research on action with the goal of making that action more effective. Action refers to programs and interventions designed to solve a problem or improve a condition ... action research is the process of systematically collecting research data*

about an ongoing system relative to some objective, goal, or need of that system; feeding these data back into the system; taking action by altering selected variables within the system based both on the data and on hypotheses; and evaluating the results of actions by collecting more data.

Action Research is based on the proposition that an effective approach to solving organisational problems must involve a rational, systematic analysis of the issues in question. It must be an approach which secures information, hypotheses and action from all parties involved, as well as evaluating the action taken towards the solution of the problem. It follows that the change process itself must become a learning situation: one in which participants learn not only from the actual research, the use of theory to investigate the problem and identify a solution, but also from the process of collaborative action itself (Bennett, 1983).

An Action Research project usually comprises three distinct groups: the organisation (in the form of one or more senior managers), the subject (the people who make up the area where the change is to take place), and the change agent (a consultant who may or may not be a member of the organisation). These three distinct entities form the learning community in and through which the research is carried out, and by which the organisation's or group's problem is solved.

The three entities must all, both individually and collectively, agree to come together, as a group, under mutually acceptable and constructed terms of reference. This, usually small, face-to-face group constitutes the medium through which the problem situation may be changed, as well as providing a forum in which the interests and ethics of the various parties to this process may be developed. It is a cyclical process, whereby the group analyses and solves the problem through a succession of iterations. The change agent (consultant), through skills of co-ordination, links the different insights and activities within the group, so as to form a coherent chain of ideas and hypotheses (Heller, 1970).

The method of data gathering, analysis and diagnosis is dependent on the nature of the problem; but in all cases, these are carried out participatively. The change agent provides the methods of investigation in accordance with their understanding of the problem. The organisation contributes its understanding of the specific situation and its idiosyncrasies. This data is then presented to the subject for consideration. The response is fed back to the other two parties, and a series of iterations begins. The knowledge and understanding gained from this exchange of views and perceptions of the issues often result in a redefinition of the situation and of the problem. This in turn demands new action planning, if the outcome is to be followed up, fed back and evaluated. From this fact-finding process, hypotheses are framed, the line of action decided upon, implemented and evaluated. All this happens within the group and with the consent of every member.

Action Research is, therefore, a two-pronged process. Firstly, it emphasises that change requires action, and is directed at achieving this. Secondly, it recognises also that successful action is based on analysing the situation correctly, identifying all the possible alternative solutions (hypotheses) and choosing the one most appropriate to the situation at hand (Bennett, 1983). This two-pronged approach, by stressing action as well as research, overcomes the 'paralysis through analysis' syndrome that can occur with some techniques (Peters and Waterman, 1982). The theoretical foundations of this approach lie in Gestalt-Field theory, which stresses that change can only successfully be achieved by helping individuals to reflect on and gain new insights into their situation. However, it also has a strong affinity with Group Dynamics, given that it uses teams to solve problems and stresses the involvement of all those concerned. This is not surprising given Lewin's role in developing both Action Research and Group Dynamics.

Nevertheless, though Action Research has enjoyed a large following over the years, one of the barriers to its use is the need to gain the commitment of both the organisation and the subject of the change. This becomes especially difficult when dealing with large organisations. A common strategy is to use a top-down approach, establishing senior management agreement as a first step. But this does not always work, as compliance at the top does not always guarantee co-operation at other levels in the organisation (Clark, 1972).

Co-operation, though, is not enough. There has also to be a 'felt-need'. Felt-need is an individual's inner realisation that change is necessary. The need must be felt by all those involved if progress is to be made. If felt-need is low in the organisation, introducing change becomes problematic – especially where the principles of Action Research are being applied. Also, even when the need for change is accepted, this may not override anxieties about the implications of change. This can be particularly so when there exists a close relationship between personal identity, position at work and social standing, which is threatened by the proposed change (Bennis, 1966).

Even taking these drawbacks into consideration, Action Research is still a highly-regarded approach to managing change (Cummings and

Huse, 1989). However, this did not prevent its originator, Kurt Lewin, from seeking to improve upon it.

The 3-Step model of change

In developing this model, Lewin (1958) noted that a change towards a higher level of group performance is frequently short-lived; after a 'shot in the arm', group behaviour may soon revert back to its previous pattern. This indicates that it is not sufficient to define the objective of change solely as the achievement of a higher level of group performance. Permanence of the new level should also be included in the objective. A successful change project, Lewin (1958) argued, should involve three steps:

1 Unfreezing – the present level.
2 Moving – to the new level.
3 Refreezing – the new level.

This recognises that before new behaviour can be successfully adopted, the old has to be discarded. Only then can the new behaviour become accepted. Central to this approach is the belief that the will of the change adopter (the subject of the change) is important, both in discarding the old, 'unfreezing', and 'moving' to the new. This once again stresses the importance of felt-need.

Felt-need is not the only similarity that the 3-Step model shares with Action Research. Indeed, it is not too much to argue that the first two steps of the model, unfreezing and moving, roughly approximate to Action Research. This can be seen from the techniques used.

The step of unfreezing usually involves reducing those forces maintaining the organisation's behaviour at its present level. According to Rubin (1967), unfreezing requires some form of confrontation meeting or re-education process for those involved. This might be achieved through team-building or some other form of management development, in which the problem to be solved (changed) is analysed, or data presented to show that a serious problem exists (Bowers *et al.* 1975). The essence of these activities is to enable those concerned to become convinced of the need for change. Unfreezing clearly equates with the research element of Action Research, just as the next step, moving, equates with the action element.

Moving, in practice, involves acting on the results of the first step. That is, having analysed the present situation, identified alternatives and selected the most appropriate, action is then necessary to move to the more desirable state of affairs. This requires developing new behaviours, values, and attitudes through changes in organisational structures and processes. The key task is to ensure that this is done in such a way that those involved do not, after a short period, revert back to the old ways of doing things.

Refreezing is the final step in the 3-Step model and represents, depending on the viewpoint, either a break with Action Research or its logical extension. Refreezing seeks to stabilise the organisation at a new state of equilibrium in order to ensure that the new ways of working are relatively safe from regression. It is frequently achieved through the use of supporting mechanisms that positively reinforce the new ways of working; these include organisational culture, norms, policies and practices (Cummings and Huse, 1989).

The 3-Step model provides a general framework for understanding the process of organisational change. However, the three steps are relatively broad and require further development in order to enhance the practicable value of this approach.

Phases of planned change

In attempting to elaborate upon Lewin's 3-Step model, writers have expanded the number of steps or phases. Lippitt *et al.* (1958) developed a seven-phase model of planned change, whilst Cummings and Huse (1989), not to be outdone, produced an eight-phase model. However, as Cummings and Huse (1989:51) point out, 'the concept of planned change implies that an organization exists in different states at different times and that planned movement can occur from one state to another'. Therefore, in order to understand planned change, it is not sufficient merely to understand the processes which bring about change; there must also be an appreciation of the states that an organisation must pass through in order to move from an unsatisfactory present state to a more desired future state.

Bullock and Batten (1985) developed an integrated, four-phase model of planned change based on a review and synthesis of over 30 models of planned change. The model describes planned change in terms of two major dimensions: change phases, which are distinct states an organisation moves through as it undertakes planned change; and change processes, which are the methods used to move an organisation from one state to another.

The four change phases, and their attendant change processes, identified by Bullock and Batten, are as follows:

1 *Exploration phase* – in this state an organisation has to explore and decide whether it wants to make specific changes in its operations and, if so, commit resources to planning the changes. The change processes involved in this phase are: becoming aware of the need for change; searching for outside assistance (a consultant/facilitator) to assist with planning and implementing the changes; and establishing a contract with the consultant which defines each party's responsibilities.

2 *Planning phase* – once the consultant and the organisation have established a contract, then the next state, which involves understanding the organisation's problem or concern, begins. The change processes involved in this are: collecting information in order to establish a correct diagnosis of the problem; establishing change goals and designing the appropriate actions to achieve these goals; and getting key decision makers to approve and support the proposed changes.

3 *Action phase* – in this state, an organisation implements the changes derived from the planning. The change processes involved are designed to move an organisation from its current state to a desired future state, and include: establishing appropriate arrangements to manage the change process and gaining support for the actions to be taken; evaluating the implementation activities and feeding back the results so that any necessary adjustments or refinements can be made.

4 *Integration phase* – this state commences once the changes have been successfully implemented. It is concerned with consolidating and stabilising the changes so that they become part of an organisation's normal, everyday operation and do not require special arrangements or encouragement to maintain them. The change processes involved are: reinforcing new behaviours through feedback and reward systems and gradually decreasing reliance on the consultant; diffusing the successful aspects of the change process throughout the organisation; and training managers and employees to monitor the changes constantly and seek to improve upon them.

According to Cummings and Huse (1989), this model has broad applicability to most change situations. It clearly incorporates key aspects of many other change models and, especially, it overcomes any confusion between the processes (methods) of change and the phases of change – the sequential states which organisations must go through to achieve successful change.

Summary

As with Action Research and the 3-Step model, Bullock and Batten's model stresses that change is a cyclical process involving diagnosis, action and evaluation, and further action and evaluation. Their approach also recognises that once change has taken place it must be self-sustaining (i.e. safe from retrogression). In addition, they also stress the collaborative nature of the change effort: the organisation and the consultant jointly diagnose the organisation's problem and jointly plan and design the specific changes.

It is at this point that there appears to be a change of emphasis in Bullock and Batten's model in comparison with Lewin's Action Research model. Action Research aims to solve organisational problems through social action (dialogue). It seeks the active participation of the change adopter (the subject) in understanding the problem, selecting a solution and implementing it. The change agent is a facilitator, not a director or a doer. More important even than the solution to the problem, the consultant's real task is to develop those involved, and to create a learning environment that allows them to gain new insights into themselves and their circumstances.

Bullock and Batten's model, and to a lesser extent the 3-Step model, gives the consultant a more directive and less developmental role. Their model seems to place a greater emphasis on the consultant as an equal partner rather than as a facilitator; the consultant is as free to direct and do as the others involved. Those involved are more dependent on the change agent, not just for their skills of analysis but also for providing solutions and helping to implement them. Therefore, the focus is on what the change agent can do for and to those involved, rather than on seeking to get the subjects to change themselves.

Action Research, as mentioned earlier, is an off-shoot of the work of the Gestalt-Field theorists, who believe that successful change requires a process of learning. This allows those involved to gain or change insights, outlooks, expectations and thought patterns. This approach seeks to provide the change adopter with an opportunity to 'reason out' their situation and develop their own solutions (Bigge, 1982). Bullock and Batten's approach, and to a lesser extent the 3-Step model as well, on the other hand, appear to owe more to the Behaviourist approach. The emphasis is on the consultant as a provider of expertise that the organisation lacks. The consultant's task is not only to facilitate but also to provide solutions. The danger in this situation is that the learner (the change adopter) becomes a passive recipient of external and objective data, one who has to be directed to the 'correct' solution. Reason does not enter into this particular equation; those involved are shown the solution and motivated, through the application of positive reinforcement, to adopt it on a permanent basis (Skinner, 1974).

In linking the previous section, on the theoretical foundations, to this one, it was argued that no matter which theory or level of focus (the individual, the group or the organisation) was adopted, the end result was the same: the need to change the way individuals and groups behave. This is as true for situations which involve changes in technology and structures as it is for those that solely involve changes in tasks. If the changes in structures and tasks are not accompanied by changes in behaviour, then the objectives of the change process are unlikely to be fully met (Burnes, 1991).

However, as the next section will argue, the degree of behaviour change required will be dependent on the form of change (or intervention, as it is often referred to) that is proposed. Some interventions will only require surface changes in behaviour, such as the person moving from one department to another or a slight change in the tasks they perform. Other interventions, particularly where they concern interpersonal relationships, may require much more fundamental changes in behaviour, even necessitating the individual's reassessment of their personality and value system.

In examining various models of change, it was argued that, whilst there are some obvious similarities between the approaches on offer, the fundamental difference revolves around the degree of positive involvement of those who are expected to change. Action Research sees them as driving the process and being fully involved, albeit aided by a change agent. The Step or Phase approaches appear to see the change adopters in a less pro-active light; the aim is for the consultant to play a much greater role in providing solutions for them to accept rather than helping them to identify the solution for themselves. The difference is not a technical or minor one; rather it strikes at the very core of managers' values and beliefs, and reflects the dominant culture that exists in each and every organisation. On the one side are those managers and organisations whose values, beliefs and cultures belong to a Tayloristic, Behaviouristic ethos. On the other side, are those who are imbued with a more Organic ethos that sits more happily with those theories which stress full involvement, whether the level of focus is the organisation, the group or the individual.

Though the subject of organisational and managerial culture will be dealt with more fully in the concluding chapter, it should be noted that most of the techniques used to achieve change, which are discussed in the next section, can be applied regardless of the level of involvement of those concerned. However, this does not necessarily imply that they will achieve their objective.

Managing change

The actual process of organisational change, no matter what theory or approach is being applied, requires someone or some group to intervene in the running of the organisation to effect this change. The intervention could be led by the people who are the subject of the change process. More often, it is led by someone from outside the department/area concerned, or even from outside the organisation. However, regardless of who leads the process, French and Bell (1984) and many others argue that such interventions must be planned and structured activities initiated in response to a recognised need for change, and having as their objective a direct or indirect improvement in organisational performance.

As described above, Bullock and Batten (1985) argue that successful interventions involve moving an organisation through several distinct states in order to achieve a higher level of performance. Each of these states requires the application of certain processes (methods and techniques). However, whilst the number and sequence of the states is relatively clear, the actual processes involved are less so. This is because the various techniques and methods which are available have been developed in response to specific problems or opportunities which organisations face from time to time. Therefore, the techniques and methods which can be used to achieve a successful outcome are situation-specific; i.e. a technique such as team building, which may be the appropriate response in one situation, may be entirely wrong in another.

This is both a strength and a weakness: a strength, because for almost any situation an organisation might face, an appropriate response exists; a weakness because there are a vast array of these responses, and choosing or being aware of the appropriate option is not easy. Too often the temptation is to choose the response which is easiest or nearest, rather than searching for the most appropriate (Simon, 1957).

In order to overcome this difficulty a number of writers have tried to classify the main techniques and methods in relation to the specific conditions in which they are best used. However, before discussing these classifications, it has been argued that there are certain conditions which must be met if interventions are to be effective, regardless of the methods or techniques involved.

Conditions necessary for successful change

Argyris (1970) argues that interventions must:

1 Generate valid information.
2 Provide free, informed choice for those involved.
3 Create a commitment on the part of those involved to the choices made.

These conditions are considered by Argyris to be integral parts of any intervention activity, no matter what the substantive objectives are. Burke *et al.* (1981) added a fourth condition to this list, insisting that interventions must also:

4 Lead to cultural change.

Whilst the first three conditions flow clearly from the theoretical foundations discussed earlier, the justification for this fourth one is less clear. The origins of the argument for cultural change being an integral part of organisational change arise from work over the last 20 years investigating the role of culture in organisations. It is argued that socio-structure (organisational structures, practices and procedures) is supported and legitimised by organisational culture (Allaire and Firsirotu, 1984; Burnes, 1991; Handy, 1986). It follows from this that any change in the former must be accompanied by a concomitant change in the latter, otherwise it risks being rejected. As mentioned above, the issue of organisational culture is discussed further in the concluding chapter of this book, but for now it is necessary to note that though organisations do have sub-cultures which may be specific to certain departments or functions, these are encompassed within and subordinate to the wider organisational culture. It follows that if changes take place in the culture at one level, then this will have effects on culture at other levels. Therefore, if culture change is to be an integral part of every form of organisational change, the process of change becomes much more complex and wide-ranging, with success being less certain (Burnes, 1991).

   To achieve the above four conditions, French and Bell (1984) proposed that the change agent should structure the intervention process so as to ensure that:

1 Those to be affected by the problem or the opportunity are involved.
2 The intervention is orientated to the problems and opportunities identified by those involved.
3 The objective and the way to reach it are clear.
4 There is a high probability of success.
5 It contains both experience-based learning and conceptual/cognitive/theory-based learning.
6 The climate of the activity is arranged so that individuals are relaxed rather than anxious or defensive.
7 The participants both learn how to solve a particular problem and learn 'how to learn' at the same time.
8 The activities are arranged so that individuals can learn about both the task (what the group is working on) and the process (how the group is doing it).
9 Individuals are engaged as whole persons not segmented persons. This means that the demands of an individual's job, and that person's thoughts, beliefs, feelings and ambitions should all be called into play, not just one or two of these.

Classification of techniques and methods of intervention

Having listed the suggested conditions for successful interventions, the classification systems which have been put forward for the techniques and methods of intervention can now be examined. French and Bell (1984) categorised these in terms of the activities they are meant to perform:

- *Diagnostic activities* – fact-finding activities designed to ascertain the state of the organisation and the status of the problem.
- *Team-building activities* – designed to enhance the effective operation of teams.
- *Inter-group activities* – designed to improve effectiveness of interdependent groups. These activities are often called organisational mirroring when more than two groups are involved.
- *Survey feedback activities* – related and similar to the diagnostic activities, but different in the sense that these activities centre on using the data produced by a survey, and designing action plans based on it.
- *Education and training activities* – designed to improve the skills, abilities, and knowledge of individuals.

- *Techno-structural or structural activities* – designed to improve the effectiveness of individuals or groups by redesigning/reorganising the technology and/or structures of the organisation.
- *Process consultation activities* – activities by a change agent which help those involved to perceive, understand, and act upon social processes which occur in their organisation. The main emphasis is on such processes as communication, leadership and authority, group norms, and inter-group co-operation and competition.
- *Grid organisation development activities* – invented by Blake and Mouton (1969), these constitute a six-phase change model involving the total organisation. The model is very comprehensive, covering everything from the skills of individual managers to corporate planning and culture change.
- *Third party peacemaking activities* – conducted by a skilled, neutral party, these are designed to help two members of an organisation manage their interpersonal conflict.
- *Coaching and counselling activities* – these entail the change agent or other organisation members working with individuals to help them: (a) define learning goals; (b) learn how others see their behaviour; and (c) learn new modes of behaviour to see if these help them to achieve their goals better.
- *Life- and career-planning activities* – these enable individuals to focus on their life and career objectives and how they might go about achieving them.
- *Planning and goal-setting activities* – these include theory and experience in planning and goal setting, utilising problem-solving models, planning paradigms, and discrepancy analysis – comparing the way the organisation should operate with the way it actually operates.
- *Strategic management activities* – to help key policy makers reflect systematically on their organisation's basic mission and goals in order to develop long-range pro-active plans.

Blake and Mouton (1969), on the other hand, developed a different classification scheme. They list the major types of change in terms of their underlying themes:

- *Discrepancy intervention* – that calls attention to contradictions in actions or activities of particular individuals or groups within an organisation.
- *Theory intervention* – where the aim is to explain present behaviour and actions, and the assumptions which underlie these, through behavioural science theories.

- *Procedural intervention* – critically examines organisational methods and procedures to determine their efficiency.
- *Relationship intervention* – aims at improving or correcting interpersonal relationships.
- *Experimental intervention* – in which two or more action plans are tested for their consequences in order to determine which one to choose.
- *Dilemma intervention* – where dilemmas are used to force an examination of the choices available and the assumptions underlying them.
- *Perspective intervention* – puts an organisation's present situation in perspective by setting it in the context of past performance and future objectives. The aim is to assess whether the organisation is still on target to meet its objectives.
- *Organisation structure intervention* – evaluates and examines the structure of an organisation to determine causes of ineffectiveness.
- *Cultural intervention* – examines the tradition, norms, values, and practices of an organisation (the components of culture) in order to judge their appropriateness.

Blake and Mouton (1976) later developed these nine themes into a 100-cell cube called the 'Consulcube', which they claimed depicted virtually all change situations and their corresponding intervention activities. A number of other attempts have been made to classify methods and techniques in this manner (e.g. Bowers *et al.*, 1975; White and Mitchell, 1976). Although these tend to be similar, there is one which raises important questions with regard to change adopter involvement.

Prior to Blake and Mouton (1976), Schmuck and Miles (1971) produced their own 'cube' which classified methods and techniques under three headings: (1) the diagnosed problem (e.g. goals, communication, role definition); (2) the focus of attention (e.g. person, group or total organisation); and (3) the mode of intervention (e.g. training, coaching and counselling, techno-structural activities). Though not as comprehensive as Blake and Mouton's, the stated aim of this cube was to categorise and match organisational problems with the methods and techniques best suited to their solution.

As well as providing a different classification system, their work also cast a new light on the issue of the required or necessary level of involvement of those who have to adopt the necessary changes in order for the solution to be achieved. Schmuck and Miles (1971), unlike others, did not see full involvement as necessary in all situations. Instead they saw involvement as a continuum related to the type of change taking place. This continuum runs from 'acceptance', based on prescriptive modes of intervention, to 'theory and principle', which is where the change agent provides the change adopters with advice on which they can make their own free choice. This is a significant development, not because it challenges one of Argyris' conditions for successful change, but because it relates the level of involvement to the impact the type of change has on the people concerned.

Huse (1980) developed this distinction further. Building on earlier work by Harrison (1970), Huse categorises change interventions along a continuum based on the 'depth' of intervention, ranging from the 'shallow level' to the 'deepest level'. The greater the depth of the intervention, Huse argues, the more it becomes concerned with the psychological make-up and personality of the individual, and the greater the need for the full involvement of the individual if they are to accept the changes.

1 *The shallow level* – is concerned with techno-structural issues external to the individual, such as:

- Changes in the organisation's structure.
- Survey feedback.
- Quality of working life programmes.
- Blake and Mouton's OD grid.

2 *The deep level* – is primarily concerned with activities that allow the individual to analyse their own behaviour, including:

- Job design.
- Role analysis.
- Management by objectives.

3 *The deeper level* – is concerned with activities geared to helping the individual to discover hidden aspects of their personality and relationships, such as:

- Process consultation.
- Team building.
- Role negotiation.
- Inter-group conflict resolution.

4 *The deepest level* – is concerned with activities which relate to fundamental aspects of the individual's personality, which include:

- Life and career planning.
- Sensitivity training.
- Personal consultation/counselling.

Therefore, it becomes possible to link levels of involvement to the types of change involved. The key is that the greater the effect on the individual, especially in terms of psychological constructs and values, the deeper the level of involvement required if successful behaviour change is to be achieved.

Summary and conclusion

This chapter has examined the theory and practice of change management. It has argued that its theoretical foundations cover the entire spectrum of organisational life, ranging from group and individual behaviour to overall structure and practices. These theories are given life and put into practice through a number of models of change, each of which tends to stress the process from a different vantage point. Action Research, for example, stresses free and full involvement of those concerned; whilst the Step and Phase approaches concentrate less on involvement and more on methods of positive reinforcement, which are directed not just towards achieving behaviour change, but also towards maintaining it.

In the final section, we examined types of change in relation to the objectives being pursued. This was prefaced by Argyris' (1970) and Burke *et al.*'s (1981) view of the conditions necessary for successful change, especially the need for 'free informed choice for those involved'. However, in looking at the classification of types of changes, a new approach to involvement emerged – one based on the depth of the impact on the individual of particular changes, rather than on the belief that all changes required the same level of involvement.

This might appear to leave us in a position where we have a number of contradictory and incompatible themes and approaches towards change – some aimed at the level of the individual, some at the group and some at the organisation. Some stress full involvement and others less. Some are clearly concerned with incremental, localised change, especially those relating to individual or group improvement activities, whilst others are more concerned with radical, organisation-wide change, especially those relating to cultural or structural developments. Some are based on behavioural science theory, whilst others owe their life to mainstream organisational theory. Some appear to suggest that change can be seen as an isolated event, whilst others stress that change must be seen as part of a strategic plan.

The way to resolve these apparent contradictions is to view the various theories and approaches as partial and particularistic. Open Systems theory is a good example of this. It focuses primarily on the appropriateness of overall organisational structures and the external and internal environments. Its objective is to improve overall organisational performance by realigning structures so that they are appropriate to the organisation's situation. From a Contingency Theory perspective, this may require moving the organisation from a Mechanistic structure to an Organic one. The resulting change in structure may be quite radical, but the impact on most people's role in the organisation, in terms of their behaviour, norms and beliefs, may be much less profound. In this situation, to use Huse's (1980) terminology, individuals are only being affected at the shallow level, so the level of involvement necessary to get them to accept the changes is much lower than would be required if their intrinsic beliefs were being questioned. This is only to be expected, given that Open Systems theory does not pretend to relate to individual or group behaviour. Therefore, Open Systems theory is partial in that it does not cover all organisational life, and particularistic in that it focuses almost exclusively on one aspect.

What is clearly needed is a classification of change management theories, approaches and techniques which not only brings them all together but also shows the level of involvement required of those concerned. An attempt at such a classification is illustrated in Table 6.1, which draws on the work of Blake and Mouton (1969), and French and Bell (1984) on types of change interventions, and of Huse (1980) on involvement.

Under the headings Focus, Approach, Techniques and Involvement, it shows that different approaches, techniques and levels of involvement are required depending on whether the focus of the change activity is at the individual, group, inter-group or organisational level. It illustrates that, for example, if the objective of change is to improve individual effectiveness, then the approach to be applied might be Gestalt-Field theory and the techniques to be used would include role analysis, coaching and counselling. Clearly, for change to be successful in this case, the individual would have to be fully involved. On the other hand, if the objective of change is to improve overall

Table 6.1   A classification of change management approaches

Focus	Approach	Techniques	Involvement
Individual	Behaviourist or Gestalt-Field	Life- and career-planning activities Role analysis technique Coaching and counselling T-group (sensitivity training) Education and training to increase skills, knowledge in the areas of technical task needs, relationship skills, decision-making, problem-solving, planning, goal-setting skills Grid OD phase 1 Job redesign	High
Teams and groups	Group Dynamics	Team building Process consultation Third party peacemaking Grid OD phases 1, 2 Quality Circles Survey feedback Role analysis Education in decision making, problem solving, planning, goal setting in group settings	Medium – High

Table 6.1 *cont.*

Focus	Approach	Techniques	Involvement
Inter-group relations	Group Dynamics	Inter-group activities – Process-directed – Task-directed Organisational mirroring Techno-structural interventions Process consultation Third-party peacemaking at group level Grid OD phase 3 Survey feedback	Medium – Low
Total organisation	Open Systems	Techno-structural activities Confrontation meetings Strategic planning activities Grid OD phases 4, 5, 6 Culture change Survey feedback	Low

organisational effectiveness, the theory to be applied would be Open Systems, and the techniques used would include strategic planning and techno-structural change. Whilst these might have a significant impact on the organisation, most people might find their own roles relatively untouched. If this was the case, then the required level of involvement might be quite low, i.e. passive acceptance.

It has already been argued that many companies may need to embark on a programme of radical change if they are to remain competitive. Such a programme will involve many separate, but interlinked, change activities (often small-scale and localised) affecting all levels and functions within an organisation and extending over a considerable period of time. The classification presented in Table 6.1 indicates how a change programme of this nature might be constructed *and* put into operation. Once an organisation had decided upon its objectives, using the classification it could then identify how these could be put into operation at each level of the company by selecting the approaches and techniques most suitable to the type of change required. Approaching change programmes in this manner brings two additional benefits. The first is that it becomes possible to establish the sequence and to estimate the timescale of the various change activities involved. The second benefit is that the degree of involvement necessary to gain the support of those who are affected by the various changes is spelled out clearly in Table 6.1.

An example of such a radical change programme would be where an organisation recognised the need to change its culture in order to improve its performance. At the organisation level, this could take the form of changes to practices, rules and reward systems in order to give positive reinforcement to the new culture. Although this might involve negotiations with trade unions, the level of actual participation from most people would be quite low. However, once the implementation phase has begun, other techniques, such as team building, might be used to effect actual changes in individual and group behaviour. At this stage a medium–high level of involvement would be required. If it then became necessary to challenge and change the deep-seated values and beliefs of individuals, using techniques such as sensitivity training, then a high level of involvement on the part of the individuals concerned would obviously be called for.

It is also clear that whilst some of these changes can and should be initiated more rapidly than others, none will be entirely successful without the others. Therefore, though restructuring and changes in reward systems are a necessary part of culture change and can be initiated relatively quickly, it is only when the behaviour of individuals and groups changes that the culture begins to change. Seen in this way, it becomes possible to begin determining the sequence and times-cale of the assorted change activities; with structural and low-involve-ment activities, usually, preceding and creating the conditions for deeper-seated and more difficult changes to group and individual be-haviour.

Another point to note is that it is the objective that determines the level of involvement and not the particular technique being applied. Therefore, if structural change is used at the organisation level to re-configure the relationships between departments and functions, the level of involvement required would be low. However, if it is applied at the inter-group level, with a view to restructuring groups, then this begins to impinge more on individuals and their jobs and group norms and behaviour – in which case a higher level of involvement would be required.

The above argument, concerning the sequencing and timing of change programmes, also shows that radical change can be viewed as a co-ordinated sequence of incremental changes covering an extended time period. Therefore, radical change is inextricably linked with in-cremental change; however, the reverse is not the case. Incremental change, unless it is part of a larger plan, is unlikely to add up to rad-ical change because of its piecemeal and uncoordinated nature. In this respect, as it should be, the definition of radical change is analogous to Mintzberg's (1987) view of strategy – a consistent pattern of actions taken over a period of time to achieve a desired objective. It is the con-sistency and the pattern which separates radical from incremental change rather than differences in the actual tools and techniques themselves.

7

Case studies in change management: *strategy-driven change*

Introduction

The previous chapter examined the development of, approaches to, and techniques for managing change. It showed that there is no one all-encompassing theory of change management. However, it was argued that, taken together, the three key approaches which deal with change at the individual, group and organisational levels do constitute a unified approach capable of embracing all forms of change.

This chapter and the next will present a total of six case studies of change management, in order to compare the practice of change management with the theory, as outlined in Chapter 6. These case studies cover a variety of organisations and a range of change situations. The major distinction drawn is between those companies, described in this chapter, where the change projects are set in the context of a longer-term strategic change programme, and those, described in Chapter 8, where each change project is a one-off event, treated in isolation from other changes, and where no co-ordinated or strategic change programme exists.

This chapter begins with case study five, G K Printers, which describes how the company introduced a computerised business system as part of its efforts to transform itself from a traditional and declining printers to a company which can compete with the best in the business. In particular, it shows the benefits of allowing those most closely affected to drive the change process.

The following study, Pope Construction Vehicles, reinforces the message that involvement is crucial. In this case, the company's failure even to communicate with those affected threatened and greatly delayed the change process.

The final case study in this chapter, Dolphin Electronics, shows once again the benefits of involving those who are affected. However, it also demonstrates that not everyone is equally affected and, therefore, there is a need to target key groups for special attention in order to gain their commitment.

The chapter concludes by arguing that whilst there are clear benefits to be gained from deriving individual change projects from a longer-term programme of strategic change, this alone does not guarantee success. There is also a need to plan and execute change thoroughly, and especially to involve those most closely affected. However, it can also be seen that there is a less distinct and evident separation of the phases of change than the previous chapter suggested, particularly the final phase, which deals with integration and consolidation.

Case study five: G K Printers Limited

Background

G K Printers Limited is a small, family-run printing business. It was established just after the Second World War by the present Managing Director's father. The company was originally a jobbing printers; which is to say they would print anything. 'No job too large or too small', might well have been their motto, although in fact, the mainstay of their business was producing stationery, business cards and publicity brochures for local companies.

This work was moderately profitable and provided a reasonable living for the owners and their workforce, some 20 people. However, by the beginning of the 1980s, this situation began to change. Firstly, the recession had a strong negative effect on their traditional customer base, and orders began to fall off dramatically. Secondly, the advent of newer, computerised printing techniques, which G K had not adopted, meant that rivals could offer a quicker, cheaper and often better-quality service. Thirdly, the advent of small printing bureaux (such as Prontaprint), often situated in prime city centre locations, and portraying an up-to-date image, further eroded G K's business. Lastly, it was clear that many of their customers were no longer going to a printer directly. Instead, in the image-conscious 1980s, they were putting their work out to graphic designers who, having finalised the design, would then sub-contract out the printing. In such a situation, there was no guarantee that the work from their traditional customers would eventually end up with them. It depended upon the preference of the particular graphic designers concerned.

All these factors combined to threaten the financial viability of G K and, for the first time ever, the company lost money. The loss was only small, £20,000, but it came as a major shock to a company which had grown used to making a reasonable, if not spectacular, profit. The result of this was that the Managing Director and the company's Printing Manager, along with other members of the owning family, formed a 'crisis committee' to review the future of the business.

It rapidly became clear that to do nothing was not an option; the result would be to go out of business. The two main options considered were whether to sell the business, or, in some way, to change it to secure a viable future.

Without exception, the crisis committee preferred the second option, if only because it was clear that it would be very difficult to find a buyer for the company. However, no one was sure what it was they needed to do to change the fortunes of the business.

In desperation, almost, they approached a lecturer at the local polytechnic who was a friend of the Printing Manager. His suggestion was that one of their business studies students should undertake a project to examine the company's options. This took two months, during which the Managing Director and Printing Manager worked closely with the student.

The student's final report had a dramatic impact on the company. Its main findings were as follows:

- The printing market was expanding rather than contracting. This was mainly due to companies recognising the need to promote themselves more and in a better way than in the past.
- The market expansion was mainly at the higher-value-added end of the market; in the area of high-class, glossy promotional material.
- The newer print bureaux were not as strong competitors as the company had thought. Their product quality was both variable and, at best, no better than G K's. Also, their costs appeared to be higher.
- G K's existing customer base would prefer to continue to do business with them, but perceived them as old-fashioned, lacking in key capabilities – mainly graphic design – slow, and not particularly flexible.
- G K's printing equipment was not capable of producing the higher-value-added products that customers were increasingly demanding.

These findings were met with some astonishment and a great deal of relief by the crisis committee. Without exception they had steeled themselves for a report which would be doom-laden. Instead, they could see that a future did exist, and possibly a very profitable one. But some major changes would be required. However, before making any decisions, the Managing Director and Printing Manager insisted that the findings should be discussed with the workforce.

Employee relations were very good in the company and, whilst not being paternalistic, the tendency was to see the company almost as an extended family. The print workers, who made up the majority of the workforce, were all union members, and two of them were prominent activists in their local union branch. The workforce knew that a review was taking place; it would have been almost impossible to keep it from them, given the nature of the company, but in any case the management had been very open about it. Like the crisis committee, the workforce were relieved that the findings were more optimistic than many had believed possible. However, they wanted to know what the management intended to do to change the company in order to take advantage of the opportunities that appeared available.

The Managing Director was slightly taken aback by the workforce's apparent eagerness to change; he had expected some resistance, especially from the print workers. Instead, the reverse was the case – the two union activists were the strongest advocates of new equipment. As one later said: 'We knew what was happening elsewhere; skilled workers were being replaced by glorified typists. But we also knew that we needed new equipment. The deal we struck with management was that we would accept anything they bought, but we would be trained for it and we would operate it'.

Indeed, they went beyond this – they actually told the management what to buy and from whom.

On the basis of the report from the student, the management constructed a strategy for rejuvenating the company. The strategy had three main elements:

1 The appointment of a Marketing and Design Manager to develop the company's customer base and provide a graphic design capability.
2 Upgrading the company's image. The above appointment was part of this process, but it also involved remodelling the company's frontage and reception areas, redesigning its stationery and creating a company logo.
3 Progressively replacing old printing machines with newer, more capable equipment.

Though the company never formally created a 'vision' of its future, the Managing Director later said:

> ... *after the student's report I began to see a picture in my own mind of what I would like the company to be. I wanted it to be a one-stop shop for all our customers' printing needs. In the past, if we could not do it ourselves, or if we were too busy, we turned people away. Not any more. If we could not do it, we sub-contracted, just like the graphic designers. But we would ensure that we could do the money business in-house [the high-value-added business] and eventually only sub-contract out the cheap stuff.*

Therefore, the company began its transformation by the appointment of a Marketing and Design Manager and upgrading its image. Initially, it did not buy any new equipment, but took the decision to sub-contract work they could not do until such time as the volume of work necessitated new investment. This allowed them to turn round the business without having to borrow large sums of money from the bank.

Nevertheless, within 12 months, such was the success of the strategy that the company began buying new equipment. After that, as the economy grew in the 1980s, the company's fortunes also grew. By 1989 G K employed 40 staff (double its previous number) and had quadrupled its turnover to £4 million. In the process, it has managed to improve its profitability substantially.

However, it grew concerned that the increased volume of business, made more complicated by both the need to design as well as print, and having to co-ordinate their sub-contracting activities, was having an adverse effect on customer service. The main problems related to controlling paperwork (especially orders and invoices), the company's costing system, and production scheduling. Therefore they undertook a review of these activities to see how they could be improved. This resulted in the purchase of a computerised business system. The review process and the subsequent changes which took place form the focus of this case study.

Reasons for change

As can be seen from the above, market, product and operational changes meant that the company needed to provide a quicker and better service to its customers. While much had been done to achieve this, three years ago it was also realised that better business systems were required, especially in the area of costing, invoicing and production control. Given that G K is only a small company, it was relatively easy for the Managing Director to bring together the six people who were responsible for these activities and, in effect, state the problems and give them the authority to come up with their solution.

The people concerned agreed to meet for two hours each Friday afternoon to review the issues involved and come up with options. They were clear that they did not want to rule anything out, but rather identify all the available alternatives and choose the one that suited them and the company best.

After three weeks, they had come to a common view of the root cause of their problems: they were all being asked to do more and more without any additional resources. Not only did this mean that backlogs occurred, but the greater need to communicate across functions, which the company now required, was also not taking place.

Given this analysis, their first inclination was to ask for more staff. However, they also looked at other options, the main one of which was better systems – ones which reduced duplication. This threw up the additional question: manual or computer systems?

Eventually they agreed a number of key objectives which any option must be tested against. These were that any new system should provide:

- A quicker and better response to customers' requests for quotations.
- Speedier invoice and better debtor control.
- Better record keeping and a reduction in duplication.
- An increase in productivity of clerical staff.
- Better control of production, resulting in reduced lead times and quicker and more reliable service to customers.
- System integration.

Having decided upon these criteria, the people involved then asked the Printing Manager if he would approach his contact at the local polytechnic for assistance. This he did, and once again the assistance came in the form of a student project. The student evaluated the company's existing operations and looked at alternatives. Her report stated that it was possible to improve the existing systems but that this would not allow them to achieve their objectives. Instead, she advocated introducing computer-based systems instead.

As they had witnessed the successful introduction of computerised printing equipment during recent years, staff were neither overawed nor complacent about computerising their systems. They discussed with the local polytechnic how best to approach evaluating the benefits of and selecting computer systems.

The group then prepared a written report for the Managing Director which detailed their investigations, their initial objectives, and the advice they had received. Their recommendation was that the company invite a number of computer companies to visit them to discuss their needs. A long discussion took place between the Managing Director and the group, which resulted eventually in their report being accepted. However, the Managing Director did add one proviso. This was that the group should be responsible for deciding whether to computerise, and, if so, what system to select and whom to purchase it from. The Managing Director said he would sit in on any negotiations that took place with computer companies, but that he would not take the decision away from them; rather he would bolster their authority by his presence.

Therefore, a number of computer companies were invited to discuss the company's requirements with them. In total, some 20 companies visited them. The upshot of these visits was that the company became convinced that their needs could best be met by purchasing a computerised business system which could perform and integrate their existing manual systems. However, the cost of this was likely to be between £20,000–£30,000, which, for a company of G K's size, was significant. The Printing Manager and others pointed out that such an amount spent on printing equipment would greatly extend their capabilities. Nevertheless, after much discussion, the decision was taken to go ahead with purchasing a computerised business system (CBS).

Though it took a number of meetings to reach this conclusion, which was subject to much discussion throughout the company, the final decision was almost unanimous. The reason for this was that the company was performing well on all fronts except in the areas covered by the proposed changes. Late and inadequate quotations, poor debtor control and erratic delivery performance were all causing the company problems. These were not as yet major problems, but could be expected to get worse as the company expanded.

Introduction and development of CBS

Once the decision had been made, the original group were given the responsibility, as the Managing Director had earlier stated, for specifying and deciding which equipment to purchase. Their task was made difficult because, whilst it was clear that standard software packages were suitable for such tasks as sales ledgers, wages and invoicing, special software would need to be written to accommodate the company's production control needs. The CBS 'steering group', as they jokingly referred to themselves, spent a number of months identifying and writing a specification for exactly what they required from a production control system. They then asked the computer companies to quote for a CBS on the basis of this specification. However, of the original companies who had shown interest, only two were prepared to provide the bespoke software the company required. The company wished to ensure that both the hardware and software were supplied by the same vendor, not only to avoid any incompatibility problems but also to have only one organisation responsible for any problem that might arise. Further discussions took place with the two companies in which the software specification was further refined and eventually a supplier was chosen. The entire process, from the Managing Director raising the issue, to placing the final order, took over a year.

The computer for running the systems, and the standard packages, were delivered almost immediately, but it was another six months before the production control package was installed. This was because it had to be specially written. The company ensured that it closely monitored the writing of the software and that the final package met the specification. It then took some three months to bring the production control package on-line. During this period, manual records were still kept in parallel to the computerised system. After this, it took a further three months before the total CBS package was up and running satisfactorily. Therefore, in total, it took two years from the inception to the completion of the project. Nevertheless, no one regretted the time spent. As the Managing Director said: 'If you'd told me at the beginning it would take so long I'd have laughed at you. But now we've ended up with a system that gives us all we want – and more. It's a system that "belongs" to the people who work it – it's not my system, it's theirs. They made it work and they're dying to improve it'.

Though the company only bought one workstation initially, it had specified that the CBS should be capable of networking. This was done with the intention that once the CBS had proved itself, further workstations would be acquired. Since then three more workstations have been purchased and the company has also doubled the memory capacity of the system. In total, some £35,000 has been spent on the CBS.

As with other aspects of the CBS, the company was careful to ensure that adequate training was provided to those who would use the system. Once again, this was made easier because it was the users who had selected the system and they knew what it could do and what training they required. This ranged from three days to a week, depending upon the user's requirement. The training was provided by the equipment supplier. Training took place in stages, allowing users to become familiar with one aspect of the system before being trained on another aspect of it. Training was provided for clerical staff who would use and maintain the system, and also for senior managers who needed to access it for information.

As might be imagined, staff appear to have taken to the CBS very well. Though initially there was an additional workload for them in terms of inputting information into the system, they now find that it is better and quicker than the previous manual system. Their workload is no less than before, but they take satisfaction from being more effective by using 'their' system. Obviously, the system has had a knock-on effect elsewhere in the company, both in the collection and use of information. This appears to have been accomplished with little or no difficulty.

The outcome

The CBS has not transformed the fortunes of G K; no single system will do that for any company. However, it has made a significant contribution, in the areas it covers, to improving the service G K provides to its customers and meeting its own requirements.

The company believes that computerising its business systems has brought the following benefits:

- Better and more accurate records.
- Quicker access to information.
- Better control of resources.
- Speedier and more accurate response to quotation requests.
- Higher productivity from clerical staff.
- Reduced lead times.
- Quicker and more reliable deliveries.
- A greater integration of business functions.
- An improvement in staff morale and skills.

Though this appears to be a case of successful technical change, it would be wrong to perceive it exclusively in this light. Certainly, that is not how those involved see it. Rather they believe that CBS is an aid to allowing them to deploy their skills and commitment more effectively. They are the ones who know what customers and the company require; all CBS does is to mechanise some of the more routine elements of their work – in any case they chose and control the system, not the other way round. Whether their perception is true or false may not matter. The real issue is that they believe it to be so. This has clearly had a substantial effect on their effectiveness, self-esteem and morale.

Conclusions

To the outsider, at least, this appears to be an almost textbook case of how to manage change. However, the staff involved, whilst clearly pleased with their role, are also not uncritical of their performance. With hindsight, they say that they should have completed the process in a year rather than two years. They also believe that they should have included additional features in the CBS.

Whilst these criticisms may be true, they are only so from the vantage point of having gone through the process of change and having gained confidence and experience from it. They also reflect a key reason for the success of the process: a willingness to be open and critical about themselves and their requirements, and a belief that they all needed to be convinced of what was required before proceeding.

Nor should the role played by the Managing Director be undervalued. In a company where – a few years earlier – change, of any sort, was very rare indeed, it takes considerable courage for a senior manager to delegate authority to users. Indeed, at one point he openly told the group that 'if you succeed, it's your success – not mine. If you fail, I carry the can – not you'. This created the climate of trust and responsibility which made those involved determined to succeed.

Nevertheless, it would be remiss not to draw attention to several other factors which contributed to successful change in this instance. These were as follows:

- The company had a strategy for its future development and therefore was able to take an overview of all areas of its business in relation to future objectives.
- Because the company was strategy-driven, it was able to establish not only where there were problems in the company, but also whether the problems were high, low or medium priority.

- In this instance, it meant that the company could establish that there was a need to improve business systems and that this was a priority.
- The company did not rush into making a decision about what exactly was the problem, what solution to adopt or what equipment to purchase.
- The company clearly identified where standard packages were sufficient and where bespoke software was required.
- It clearly documented its requirements.
- It carefully selected a supplier in whom it had confidence and with whom it could work closely.
- It constructed a timetabled implementation plan with clear objectives for the introduction of CBS.
- It ensured that the appropriate training was provided.

Two further points should be stressed about this case study. Firstly, the company is in the process of moving from being an organisation where change was the exception, to one where it is becoming a continuous activity. In this situation, it is impossible for change to be controlled exclusively by management or 'experts'. The sheer volume of work would overwhelm them. Without devolving the responsibility to those affected, change either would not take place or would be unsuccessful. Nor would it be possible for senior managers to concentrate on the longer-term strategic aspects of their business.

Secondly, devolving responsibility in this way ensures that those who have to live with the change take ownership of the process, and are committed to it. It allows those involved to develop their skills and confidence. It also ensures that once the changes do take place, they become fully operational as rapidly as possible.

Case study six: Pope Construction Vehicles Limited

Background

Pope Construction Vehicles, as its name suggests, makes products for the construction industry. However, these particular products are extremely uncommon; no one else in the UK now makes them and, worldwide, its competitors can be counted in single figures. Its products are gigantic earth-moving vehicles for major construction and, to a lesser extent, mineral extraction projects.

The price of Pope's vehicles can be in excess of £2 million each, and it is not unusual for them to sell five or ten vehicles per project.

Because the construction industry is cyclical and Pope, like all companies, does not always win the contracts it bids for, its business is subject to great peaks and troughs. One year it may gain, literally, hundreds of millions of pounds of business, and the next very little at all.

Nevertheless, in its particular market, its name is better known, and its reputation higher than those of its competitors. However, because, in many export markets, contracts are awarded by government rather than private companies, name, reputation, price and even product may be subordinate to political considerations in winning orders. In the 1960s and 1970s, because many of its markets were more pro-British than they are now and there were fewer competitors, political and other considerations in export markets tended to favour Pope. However, by the late 1970s, particularly in Africa and the Middle East, Pope's British origins became a severe drawback.

This also coincided with an increase in competition, both by companies who previously had not entered the export market in a serious way, and by attempts in some countries to establish their own domestic industries. Allied to this was the worldwide recession of this period, which was especially severe in Britain.

The result of all these factors was that Pope's fortunes diminished. Its order book reached an all-time low, and the prospects of winning new, substantial orders began to seem remote.

In response to this situation, in 1980, a new Chief Executive was appointed. He reviewed the company's performance and diagnosed four main problems:

- The company operated in a volatile market, which varied between very high demand and almost none at all. This was compounded by a narrow product range and limited sales and marketing expertise.
- The workforce was too large and its composition wrong. There were too many white-collar staff and relatively few shop-floor operatives; a substantial number of the latter were engaged on a hire and fire basis in order to cope with the volatile workload.
- The company's factory was large, old and very ramshackle. Layout was inefficient and heating and lighting costs were too high.
- A separate company, a member of the same group, provided computer facilities at a cost of £500,000 per year. However, these facilities were not only costly but also inflexible and no longer met the company's modern-day needs.

Having diagnosed the problems, the Chief Executive and his senior managers developed a strategy to secure the company's future. The object of the strategy was to create an organisation which had the capability to meet high levels of demand, whilst having the cost base which allowed it to be profitable in times when work was scarce. This not only meant restructuring the company to remove unnecessary costs, but also developing a smaller, but more skilled and committed workforce; one capable of high levels of performance. In addition to this, it was necessary to extend its product range and to be able to win orders in countries where political and domestic production considerations, at present, worked against them.

In order to meet these objectives, the main components of the strategy were:

1 The construction of a new, purpose-built factory. This cost £11 million, but paid for itself within two years through a reduction in overhead costs.
2 Cutting the workforce by 400 white-collar staff. Hire and fire employment policies were modified, and a core workforce was retained regardless of fluctuations in product demand. This was achieved by sub-contracting work when demand was high and undertaking its own sub-contract work when demand for the principal products was low.
3 The creation of a new Sales and Marketing Department, with the twin objectives of developing joint ventures with overseas companies in the same line of business, and identifying new product opportunities.
4 Discontinuing the computing facilities provided by the outside company and instead introducing in-house, low-cost/low-risk systems. These did not need the services of external specialists or a separate internal computer department. New computing systems were located in each department where tangible benefits justified the investment. The departmental staff took responsibility for running the systems.

Therefore, since 1980, the company has gone through a major reorganisation in terms of location, organisation, products and technology. A further major change took place in the late 1980s when it took over its main competitor in the UK. The takeover resulted in the doubling of the workforce (to 1,650) and the trebling of turnover (to £150 million). The company now operates on two sites, some 100 miles apart, and at present is in the process of integrating the management structure and product range.

The merger was very much a product of the company's strategic aims to develop key alliances, extend its product range, and increase its competitive position in the market-place. The subject of the case study, the introduction of Computer Aided Design (CAD), was also a product of the strategy.

Reasons for change

In the mid-1980s, the company began to look at the possibility of acquiring a CAD system. This was partly due to staff cuts in the Technical Department which raised doubts about its capacity to meet existing workloads, partly due to a larger product range increasing the workload of the department, and partly due to the need to produce more complex designs in less time. After much discussion at senior management level, a project team was established to assess the case for CAD. This comprised a senior engineer, the Technical Director and an outside consultant. Over a period of 18 months, the systems offered by 25 suppliers were evaluated. This information was gathered by a number of methods, the main one being a detailed questionnaire sent out to potential suppliers.

By this process, Pope was able to assess the capabilities of CAD, and so decide whether or not its purchase would benefit the company, and – if so – in what ways. The project team's recommendation was that a CAD system should be purchased. Its recommendation was based on the expectation that the following benefits would be achieved:

- The streamlining and speeding-up of the design process.
- The ability to handle more new product designs at any one time.
- The reorganisation of the design and drawing office to achieve higher levels of productivity.
- Improved quality of output.
- Quicker updating and modification of drawings.
- The establishment of a library of standard components which would rationalise vehicle construction.
- Long-term benefits from the introduction of three-dimensional solid modelling, though initially the company expected the main benefits to come from two-dimensional CAD.
- The eventual extension of the CAD system to include Computer Aided Manufacture (CAM) which was expected to bring large benefits in this area.

The project team's recommendations were accepted, and they were told to proceed with the selection and purchase of a CAD system. From their original investigations, the team drew up a short list of six potential suppliers.

These companies' systems were then subjected to a stiff benchmark test. From this, two systems appeared to be better than the rest. Both of these were turnkey systems, i.e. the supplier was responsible for the provision of both hardware and software.

Finally, one system was preferred to the other. There were four reasons for this:

- The software was written in the UK and by a local company, and therefore it would be relatively easy to handle any problems which might crop up.
- It was judged to be a sound, reliable product.
- The technical support offered was rated as very good.
- It was rapidly becoming the standard system for the industry (when the new company was acquired, it was found that they also were using the same system).

Introduction and operation of CAD

Even after the decision to purchase the CAD system was taken, the system was not installed for another 18 months due to various delays. The system comprised a mini-computer, four workstations and a database management package at a cost of £600,000. Originally a cheaper system, based on micro-computers, had been considered but it was realised that this would have neither the power nor the database management facilities to meet the company's requirements.

The Technical Department, in which CAD was to be based, was organised into a number of separate sections. It was felt that it would not be feasible to base CAD solely in one of these or to split it up amongst them all; it was therefore decided to establish a separate CAD section to be used as a common facility by the rest of the Technical Department. This CAD section has three specialist staff to develop and run the system.

Despite the care taken in selecting and introducing the system, there were problems. As soon as it was operational, it was blacked by the trade unions. This was because, although they knew it was being introduced, there had been no negotiation or discussion about pay rates or conditions of work. Management expected that employees would operate the system without any more pay and that shift work could be introduced without resistance. On both counts, they were wrong. This resistance was eventually overcome when the shift-work proposal was dropped, and additional allowances were paid for undertaking training and using CAD: employees received an extra payment for training on CAD, and another payment when they reached a specified standard. Nevertheless, this did not provide an auspicious start to the CAD system, and appeared to leave an undercurrent of suspicion with regard to CAD.

Another problem was lack of senior management support for the CAD system. The Technical Director, who had been involved in purchasing the system, left the company shortly after it was introduced, and he was not replaced for 18 months. This meant that there was no one at director level to take responsibility for the introduction of CAD, or for resolving managerial conflicts within the Technical Department. This manifested itself clearly when the CAD section set up its first training course. It experienced great difficulty in getting the rest of the Technical Department to release employees for training. Even when staff were made available, they would often withdraw from the course at the last minute and, as a result, the training programme which had been painstakingly developed, but without involving users, collapsed.

Managers of the various sections within the Technical Department argued that their workload did not allow time for CAD training, and as there was no Technical Director to intervene, there was no way of remedying this situation. For some time the CAD section existed in a vacuum. It lacked support from the rest of the Technical Department, and in consequence implementation of the CAD system ground to a halt. This led the Personnel Manager to comment later that: 'Most companies have islands of automation, we had mountains of it'. This was a reference to the fact that, six months after its arrival, much of the CAD equipment and associated training material was still packed up in boxes and stacked up in the CAD section.

Eventually, senior managers overruled sectional resistance, instigated training and insisted that the system be used. After this, more and more staff undertook training and, despite the difficulties in getting people to attend courses, the training provided by the equipment supplier was said to be excellent. At the time of writing, the supplier is still being used in addition to the company's own in-house training. The training programme for new operators has two parts. The first consists of a one-week training course at the equipment suppliers'. Then follows an in-company package which takes approximately 100 hours to complete. The training can be spread over two or three months depending on the motivation of the individual and the workload of their section. On satisfactory completion, employees are classed as CAD operators and paid accordingly.

The CAD system has now proved successful and has been expanded. Eighteen months after its installation, a second mini-computer and two more workstations were added, and six months later a further two workstations were purchased. Recently, a further mini-computer and another workstation have also been obtained. In total, therefore, the company has spent some £1.4 million in developing its CAD system.

The outcome

Recently the company carried out a post-audit of the CAD system to see whether its purchase had been cost-effective, and they concluded that the main benefits had come from three-dimensional solid modelling of vehicle bodies. While they had expected this to bring benefits in the medium to long term, they were surprised at how quickly the benefits were achieved. This was mainly due to the work of a member of staff with three-dimensional solid modelling experience, and the influence of a manager in a user section who had put a great deal of effort into developing this aspect of CAD.

CAD had substantially speeded up the design phase of new product introduction. As an example, on one vehicle, design time was reduced from 45 weeks to 30 weeks. Moreover, in the past, assembly had always been problematic because, owing to design faults, parts often did not fit and needed to be altered for correct assembly. This was expensive and time-consuming. The advent of three-dimensional solid modelling, however, ensured that the parts were designed to fit.

The gains from two-dimensional drafting were probably not as great as was anticipated. Some companies have claimed that the productivity of staff has doubled or even trebled by the introduction of two-dimensional drafting. However, in this instance, the increase was only 10–25 per cent. The reason for this was said to be the type of product manufactured by the company. Nevertheless, the speed of modification and retrieval of drawings had been greatly increased by CAD.

It appeared that the database management system had not been as efficient as was originally envisaged. For this reason, a new database management system was being introduced which would be shared with the recently-acquired company.

Some of the expected benefits from CAD had not been achieved at all. It had been hoped to use the CAD system to produce a full bill of materials for each vehicle automatically, thus easing the task of the Purchasing and Production Control Departments. This, however, had not come about, partly because the design process was lengthy, and therefore a finished design from which a bill of materials could be derived might not be ready for months. This was also partly due to design modifications taking place during production. It was still intended eventually to automate the bill of materials.

Another aspect was the failure to produce a standard parts catalogue which would reduce and standardise the parts used to build vehicles. A parts catalogue would have obvious benefits in the management of stores, and for production control. The ordering of materials would become easier, more efficient and cheaper. Categorising all the parts in use was a difficult task, but disagreements between departments over where responsibility for this should rest had so far prevented standardisation.

CAD development had also not, as was originally intended, been extended into production engineering. It was originally expected that the system would be used by jig and tool draughtsmen and programmers producing tapes for CNC machines. CAD staff were aware of the need to expand and link the system into other areas but, due to other priorities, the finance had not been available. This had been compounded by resistance from other departments, and the purchase of computer systems which were not compatible with CAD. Also, within some sections of the drawing office, there were still doubts about the benefits of using CAD. The result of this was that some sections and project managers – who had discretion in this matter – were not using CAD on new projects. In one instance, a major new vehicle design had incurred serious design problems because it was not put on the CAD system. Resistance by some staff might also account for the fact that only some 20–30 per cent of current production drawings were being produced through the CAD system.

Despite disappointments, there were major gains from CAD. At the time of writing, there were nine workstations and some 45 users, and further workstations had been ordered. There were also 20 other terminals in the Technical Department which could access, but not manipulate, information from the CAD system. As a result, the Technical Department could now produce designs and drawings more quickly and cope with much greater and more varied workloads. In the past, the drawing office had only been able to cope with three design projects at any one time, but it could now cope with many more. As has been mentioned, only 20–30 per cent of drawings were being produced using CAD, but, as the system was expanded and developed, it was expected that this would increase considerably.

Conclusions

Though the company made significant gains from the introduction of CAD, clearly greater benefits could have been obtained. Therefore, there are both positive and negative lessons that can be learnt from how Pope Vehicles managed this particular change project. The positive points are that:

- The process was driven by the strategic needs of the business.
- Pope established a project team, representing senior management, the department concerned, and – from outside the company – someone with CAD experience.
- The team's initial remit was to establish whether, and how, CAD could benefit the company. Only when the benefits were established and agreed was the decision taken to purchase a CAD system.
- The investigation of suppliers and their systems was very thorough, and the final choice of system appears to have been an excellent one. This is especially the case in the light of Pope's takeover of their rival company who, it transpired, used exactly the same system.
- The company recruited staff to run the system who had the necessary skills and experience to make it work.
- The training programme for CAD users was thorough and detailed.
- The company has not stood still, but has continued to develop the system.
- The company carried out a post-audit to evaluate the benefits gained and the progress made with the introduction of CAD.

Having stated the positive steps Pope took to achieve successful change, we can now examine the causes of the negative consequences, which are as follows:

- Failing to consult and involve users and managers sufficiently; and, especially, taking for granted that they were willing to use the system and to change to a shift-working arrangement.
- Establishing CAD as a separate entity, with its own staff and manager, rather than fully integrating it into the various sections of the Technical Department.

- Failing to convince all the section managers within the Technical Department that they should use CAD.
- Failing to ensure that there was senior management responsibility for the CAD introduction process.

No doubt other positive and negative aspects of Pope's experience could be identified. However, the main point which should stand out is that the areas where the company failed relate exclusively to employee relations and management competence. The failure to involve, consult and gain the commitment of staff was crucial, as was the failure of both senior managers and section managers to share a common view of CAD and agree common objectives.

The irony, as the Personnel Manager remarked, was that 'If we had followed the same procedures for change that applied to shop-floor staff, most of the problems would not have arisen. We didn't. We took the Technical Department staff for granted. Our attitude was outdated. In effect, we thought, they're white collar, they're on our side. We won't make that mistake again.'

Case study seven: Dolphin Electronics Limited

Background

Dolphin Electronics is a subsidiary of the American-owned Whale International Incorporated (WII), and specialises in the manufacture of process control equipment for the petrochemical industry. Within Britain, the parent company operated on three sites until 1980, when one of these was closed and the work transferred to Dolphin. In 1981, the company introduced new control-room instrumentation products. As demand for these grew, there was an increase in employment levels around the new product, but employment decreased in relation to older products. By 1983, the new and the old products were being manufactured separately, and those responsible were operating as semi-autonomous units, with most functions duplicated. At this point, a decision was taken to sell off the part of the company manufacturing the older products, and to concentrate on the newer ones. Since then, the control-room instrumentation business, now known as process control, has continued to grow and Dolphin now employs some 400 people.

As a result of the growth in business and employment levels, the company outgrew its original site, and in 1985 approval was given to construct a new manufacturing facility. The company began moving into the new factory in late 1985, and completed the move by April 1986. The site is now the European headquarters of the business, and controls two other factories, one in France and one in Germany.

Given that it is operating in new premises, making products designed since 1980, and relying, in many instances, on staff recruited since that date, the rate and scale of change at Dolphin have clearly been very fast, and this is expected to continue. This has meant that the company had, and will have, to cope with a rapid rate of change. It is the view of the company's senior management team that past and future progress is only possible because the company has a clear and well-thought-out strategic plan for its future. The company believes that strategic planning – setting future overall company objectives – is essential in order to maintain and increase competitiveness. Their strategic plan is constructed by examining both external developments – changes in markets, technology and products, and internal requirements – structures, technology and, above all, people.

Their strategic business plan looks five to ten years ahead; within this is a more immediate one- to two-year budget-type plan which deals with the company's short-term future. These two are interlocked: the strategic business plan gives a broad view of the medium- to long-term future and allows short-term, one- to two-year developments, to be seen in this perspective.

In constructing the plan, the key indicator they examine is the market – especially in the chemical, gas and oil industries they serve – to see how the level of demand and customer requirements are changing and also the type of demand in terms of products. It is especially important to identify declining and emerging markets and products in order to plan moves from one to the other. Given that these are essentially medium- to long-term developments, they can only be effectively managed in the context of a medium- to long-term business plan.

An essential element of the strategic business plan is to establish how and where products are to be manufactured. Having established where the company is going in terms of markets and products, it is then essential that these can be manufactured to the correct design, quality, price and delivery. Therefore, the manufacturing element of the strategic plan covers everything from quality requirements to methods of manufacture, e.g. which tasks are to be automated and which will continue to be performed manually. The company needs to be aware of changes in technology, both in products and in production methods. In its industry, technology and components are continually changing, which means that it has to be aware of not only what it wants to manufacture, but also what its suppliers want to sell.

Dolphin also needs to be aware of the key competitive factors in its industry: whilst price is always important, the key to success in its markets revolves around quality (Dolphin's aim is zero defects) and delivery. Therefore, the mechanism to ensure that these can be achieved must be built into the manufacturing operations.

Given the pressures that always exist for change, it is important to identify and prioritise where changes need to be made. It is also important that this process is driven by the overall objectives of the company. Nevertheless, implementing change, in Dolphin, is considered to be the responsibility of all employees. This is because Dolphin believes that success comes through people, and this is reflected in the human resources element of their strategic plan. The company's approach to people is to treat them as assets to be developed rather than as a liability to be minimised. This is illustrated by the company's annual training plan, which states that:

- It is the objective of the company to improve the performance and develop the potential of individual employees at all levels in order to promote the effective conduct of the business.
- Training is a collaboration of mutual benefit. It should generate enthusiasm for new ideas and provide opportunity for learning. All managers and supervisors have a direct responsibility for seeing that their subordinates are effectively trained.
- Also, use must be made of the potential ability and ambitions of staff by giving those concerned appropriate development training to meet future requirements of the company.

This approach goes beyond training and development of individual employees; it also extends to ensuring that jobs and organisational structures are designed in such a way as to motivate employees and facilitate effective working practices. An example of this is the process of assembling the company's product. In the early 1980s, this was a highly fragmented process split into nine separate operations, performed by separate groups of workers. These tasks have been amalgamated, and are now performed by two groups of workers rather than the previous nine. This gives the workers involved more control over their work, a greater range of skills and higher pay. Similar developments have taken place elsewhere. The result is not only a more motivated workforce, but also simplified material flows, better production control and better quality. Where changes such as these take place in the company, those affected are always involved, in order both to draw on their knowledge and to ensure that they 'own' the change process.

The approach of the company to change is illustrated by its recent introduction of a new production control system, called Manufacturing Resources Planning (MRP2), which is the subject of this case study.

Reasons for change

The predecessor to MRP2 was introduced into the company when it moved into its new factory in 1986. The main reason for the decision to replace it was the company's poor delivery record to customers and sister plants. At this time, the delivery record to sister plants in Germany and France was only 38–45 per cent of products delivered on time. To final customers, the performance was slightly better, some 60–70 per cent of products being delivered on time. Given that one of the main competitive factors in their market is delivery, this obviously was not acceptable. Indeed, as one of the company's key strategic objectives is to achieve 100 per cent delivery reliability, this was obviously a priority issue for Dolphin.

The reason for the poor deliveries was that the original production control system operated in isolation from the other systems in the company, especially sales forecasting. Because of this, no one knew whether production plans were achievable and therefore had little faith in them. Instead of using the information the system provided, staff preferred to use their own judgment of what was required. In any case, the Marketing Department themselves had little faith in their own forecasting ability and, indeed, on occasion, orders were accepted irrespective of the company's ability to deliver in the times promised.

The result was that production was driven by a shortage list rather than an achievable plan in which staff had confidence. This could not continue; the senior management team themselves reviewed the company's poor delivery record and concluded that, in order to rectify the situation, three steps needed to be taken:

- The forecasting and production systems needed to be integrated.
- Forecasting needed to be made more rigorous and accountable – some marketing staff were surprised that forecasts should be expected to be treated seriously.
- Staff needed to stop overriding the information provided and instead work to it.

This latter point, in particular, meant that staff had to accept new ways of working – a new philosophy. The suggestion to examine the benefits of MRP2 came from the company's Materials Manager. He had examined what the company required and what was available, and suggested that MRP2 was the correct way forward. He went on an MRP2 awareness course himself, and convinced other managers to do likewise. Nevertheless, senior managers insisted on reviewing all the options before making a decision. This took six months, including visiting other WII plants in the USA and the Middle East, but eventually, it was agreed that MRP2 best met their overall requirements.

Given the changes that MRP2 would involve, not least in terms of staff commitment, the company established a five-person project team to examine the benefits and drawbacks of MRP2, and to produce a blueprint for its introduction. MRP2 is a company-wide system that affects all functions (i.e. it is not just a materials control system, but links sales and marketing, production management, management information services and even personnel). Therefore, the need for a multi-disciplinary group, which spanned a wide range of functions, was clear. The project team consisted of a manager from the engineering services department, the plant's Materials Manager, a manager from the company's sales and marketing group, a senior analyst programmer from the company's management information services group, and the plant's Management Accountant. The project team reported directly to Dolphin's senior management team.

The team were initially given 12 weeks to produce their report, but this was extended to 20 weeks to allow full consultation to take place with all the departments affected. The team's first task was to familiarise themselves with MRP2, which involved going on a training course and acquiring video training material. They then began to examine and discuss with the relevant departments the implications of its introduction.

Each member of the team took a section of the company with which they were familiar, and worked with that area to examine the benefits and problems of applying MRP2, and what changes would need to be made. Presentations were made to, and discussions took place with, department and section leaders in an attempt to consult them fully; in turn, they were expected to discuss the ideas with their staff.

Despite their vigorous efforts to consult with people, in retrospect the project team felt that they should have given staff within departments longer to discuss the proposals before being asked to comment on them. Nevertheless, the team were satisfied with their final report which confirmed the recommendation to purchase MRP2 – and this was accepted by the company's management team, who gave the go-ahead to introduce it.

Introduction and operation of MRP2

The company appointed two members of staff to act as project managers for the introduction of MRP2: one responsible for the manufacturing side and the other for the support side. The target was to become a full MRP2 user within 18 months (though due to changes in product-mix and quantities this had not been achieved by the end of this period).

Dolphin used an outside consultant, with an international reputation in the field of MRP2, to help them set the objectives and timetable for introducing it. The timetable and programme was broken down into easily-understood goals for each area involved. The company had already introduced some measures which assisted the development of MRP2: these mainly involved stock reduction and better inventory controls. Obviously, there was much else to do. On the manufacturing side, there was the need to introduce capacity planning and resource control, though software problems meant these were delayed somewhat. In turn, this reduced the impetus behind the introduction of MRP2.

The company's own Management Information Services group was given the responsibility of introducing and developing the necessary software and, despite teething troubles, the final product appears to have been satisfactory. The MRP2 system is based upon a bought-in software package which the company customised to its own needs. Previously, the company had used outside resources for developing software packages, but the difficulty of this is that when the outsiders leave, so does much of the expertise that has been gained. With MRP2, the company was determined to use internal resources in order to retain the expertise developed during the introduction of the system.

The Management Information Systems group also developed a training package which was used to test the software and to train staff. Training, even for those not directly concerned, was seen as a major element in the development of MRP2. There were two clear objectives underpinning this:

- To enable staff to be able to use the system.
- To instil in staff the MRP2 philosophy so that they had confidence in the system rather than reverting to the previous working practices.

This latter point was especially important, given that staff in all areas of the company had previously exhibited a lack of confidence in the company's sales forecasts, production schedules and production control methods. If the system was to work, then not only must sales forecasts, production schedules, stock control, etc. be reliable, but also staff must have sufficient confidence in them not to override them.

To achieve these twin aims, a training programme was established for the whole company. A seminar room was set aside solely for the MRP2 courses and, over a period of nine months, every member of staff, from director to assembly worker, went through some form of MRP2 training. The actual training material was divided into modular elements which allowed appropriate training courses to be provided for each category of staff. However, all staff went through a standard two-day initial appreciation course, designed to familiarise them with the operation and benefits of MRP2.

Three key groups of staff were targeted for special attention: senior managers, supervisors and all marketing and sales staff. Senior managers were considered important because they set the climate and priorities for the company. If they were seen to understand and consistently support MRP2, then others in the organisation, it was argued, would follow. However, if they did not give it their full support or were seen not to understand it, as the outside consultant argued, others would see no reason to make the effort to adjust to the new system. Therefore, though senior managers did not need an intensive course, over a period of nine months, all senior managers had three weeks' intensive training on MRP2. As one of the two project managers later commented, 'the result was remarkable. Managers not only talked to staff about the system but are knowledgeable and are seen to be openly committed to it. They understand its capabilities and how difficult it is to use.' Perhaps for the first time, supervisors are finding that senior managers listen to them and understand their problems. This appears to have raised morale, especially amongst supervisors.

The supervisors, in total, had six weeks' training. Once again, this was more than they actually needed to carry out their jobs, but it was clear that if they did not believe in the system and understand its benefits then MRP2 could not work. This training also involved taking them off-site to other user companies. The intention in doing this was not to create a rosy picture of MRP2. Instead, the idea was to give them a realistic appreciation of its benefits (for both the company and themselves) and the difficulties in getting it up and running.

The third group, the marketing and sales staff, are the ones responsible for forecasting future production requirements. If these forecasts are not accurate, then neither are the production schedules developed by MRP2. Once again, this group received more training than they actually needed – in their case some three weeks. However, as part of their training, the importance of their role was stressed time and again. Indeed, one entire day was devoted to a joint meeting of the marketing and sales staff and production supervisors. This allowed both groups to appreciate the other's difficulties, and left the marketing and sales staff with a much clearer idea of the damage that poor forecasting could do.

At the end of the nine-month training programme, the company had a workforce not only committed to MRP2, but also with a better overview of their individual role in the company.

The training programme was only one element, though perhaps the most important one, of a detailed 18-month programme for introducing MRP2. The programme laid down clear objectives and timescales for each element of the introductory process. This was overseen by the two project managers who reported directly to the company's senior management team. The two project managers saw their role as both to monitor and to facilitate the change process. Therefore, they worked closely with the managers and staff who were involved, as well as organising the training. In this way, both through training, and by involvement in the planning of the introduction and use of the new system, staff at Dolphin became committed to making MRP2 a success.

Despite this, the MRP2 introduction did not run to schedule. This had little to do with any lack of commitment on the part of staff, and much to do with an increase in demand for Dolphin's products. The result was that increasing output, for a time, overshadowed all else. This detracted from the effort needed to introduce MRP2, but was only a temporary hiccup.

The outcome

The introduction of MRP2 led to a significant improvement in delivery and throughput times. Delivery accuracy increased to almost 100 per cent. In addition, throughput times were reduced from four or five working weeks to one and a half or two working weeks; it was hoped to reduce this to one working week in the near future. MRP2 also gave the company a complete overview of delivery requirements and materials availability, which meant that products are assembled only when required and not until all the material is available. Previously, supervisors on each section decided on priorities, regardless of whether materials were ready for the next operation, or the next section required that item. The changes also reduced inventory significantly: before MRP2, inventory totalled some £5.1 million. This was reduced to £3.9 million, despite the fact that Dolphin significantly increased its workload during the process of introducing MRP2.

Not surprisingly, one of the biggest areas affected was the stores. It is important for them to achieve inventory accuracy, both in terms of assembling products and ordering new material. Without stores accuracy, the production control system crumbles. Therefore, major efforts were made to train stores staff and to help them appreciate the importance of their role. The stores staff admitted that the changes had been difficult but, realising the importance of their role, they subsequently achieved a 95 per cent inventory accuracy – which in the industry is considered to be extremely good. Their efforts facilitated a reduction in overall stock level and work in progress. A knock-on effect of this was to reduce, by 84 per cent, the amount of space occupied by the stores, thus releasing valuable space for production needs.

Nevertheless, it is important not to be blinded by the improved statistics. Senior managers believe the key change was in the attitude of the workforce. Before MRP2, there was an almost universal cynicism about believing delivery schedules. Everyone made their own personal assessment, which often conflicted with others'. If this attitude had continued with MRP2, then no improvements would have been made. Instead, because of being consulted and involved, staff became committed to making it work and to operating by its schedules rather than against them. It became seen as a tool to aid their effectiveness rather than something which hindered it, which was how the previous service had been perceived.

Conclusions

Despite some setbacks – inevitable given the complexity of the project – the company made successful progress in introducing MRP2. This appears to have been for seven main reasons:

- The company did not rush into the introduction of MRP2; rather it carefully examined it in terms of strategic and operational requirements.
- It recognised that the successful assessment of MRP2 required a broad-based project team, which reflected the areas that would be affected and comprised the required skills and competences.
- The project team sought to involve all those who would be affected by the new system.

- A detailed written report was produced, which allowed the company's management to appreciate fully what was involved in introducing the new system and what the benefits would be.
- Having given the go-ahead, a carefully constructed and realistic implementation programme was developed.
- Training needs were accurately considered and provided for.
- It was recognised that the key to success was to convince staff, especially supervisors, of the need for the new system and the importance of their role. Indeed, one of the benefits of the system's introduction was that it gave company staff – from salesmen to assemblers – a clearer idea of the importance of their role, and in so doing raised motivation and morale. As one store keeper put it: 'This has raised the level of awareness of the store keepers and what they can do for the company and also made the rest of the company aware of what store keepers can do for them. It also feeds back into morale, and morale is now very high'.

Underlying the above are two fundamental features of the way the company operates. Firstly, the company is committed to strategic planning. This ensures that it knows where it is going, and what changes need to be made and when. It allows any problems that occur to be judged in the light of the long-term, and overall, needs of the company. This prevents it from going off at tangents and ensures that the company is always focused on its strategic objectives.

Secondly, the company's attitude towards people – the fact that it sees them as assets to be developed – facilitates successful change. The company's attitude ensures that staff not only take pride in their work, but also take joint responsibility for identifying their own training and education needs. This feeds back into morale, reflected in extremely low staff turnover, and a willingness to be flexible and make changes.

Conclusion and discussion

The case studies show that whilst managing change is never easy or straightforward, it is always possible, as in the instance of Pope Vehicles, to make it more difficult and complicated than it need be. To avoid creating unnecessary problems for themselves, organisations need to adopt a positive, open and systematic approach to managing change. Such an approach, as argued in the previous chapter, recognises that the key phases in achieving successful change are:

- Identifying the need for and type of change.
- Planning how the change is to be executed.
- Implementing the change programme.
- Consolidating and integrating the new arrangements.

Even if it is accepted, as the case studies seem to show, that the lines between these phases are blurred, especially with regard to the final phase, the need to treat them all with equal seriousness and attention cannot be underestimated. If one or more of the above phases is missed or treated lightly, then the outcome will almost certainly be sub-optimal and possibly, as the next chapter will show, disastrous. In addition, the case studies show that successful change can only be achieved where there is:

- Senior management commitment and encouragement.
- An atmosphere of openness and trust which enables frank discussion of all the available options, including maintaining the status quo.
- The appropriate blend of skills and expertise amongst those charged with managing the change process.
- The close involvement of those who will be most affected by any proposed change.

The importance of these conditions can be seen from the three case studies in this chapter. The first study, G K Printers, shows that when all these conditions are met, the change process gathers a momentum of its own, and those involved become fully committed to making it a success. In a similar fashion, the last case study, Dolphin Electronics, shows that in organisations where change is the norm, staff exhibit a positive attitude towards change and a readiness to accept it; although, even in such companies, there is still a need to include rather than exclude those concerned, and a need to avoid becoming complacent or making assumptions about what is or is not acceptable to people.

This latter point is well illustrated by the second case study in this chapter, Pope Construction Vehicles. This company assumed that office staff, unlike shop-floor staff, did not need to be consulted about change. Their assumption was demonstrably wrong; the introduction of an expensive and necessary computer system was delayed, and the benefits it could bring were threatened.

The outcome of each of these case studies is described above. However, the general lessons which can be drawn from all three are:

- Successful change cannot be achieved by diktat or coercion; rather it depends upon co-operation and involvement.
- Those who are likely to be most affected by any proposed change possess a reservoir of knowledge about their work and a potential contribution to the success of the change project which organisations ignore at their peril.
- The level of involvement from those concerned will vary depending on the numbers concerned, the type of change envisaged and their past experience of change. However, it is unlikely that involvement can ever be dispensed with entirely.

Obviously, different organisations have different needs and start from different places. Some organisations have strong cultures which stress flexibility, trust and innovation. In such cases, as with Dolphin Electronics, there may not be such a need for high levels of involvement. Other organisations, such as G K Printers, are in a less fortunate position; they are still developing such cultures. Yet for them, having to secure a high degree of employee involvement in change projects is not a distraction or additional burden; it is rather one of the prime ways that they can develop their culture. Seen in this light, Pope's failure to involve its staff not only threatened the anticipated benefits from this project but also damaged its chances of establishing a new and more co-operative relationship with its staff.

These case studies will be discussed further in Part Four, but in addition there are also a number of discussion points at the end of the next chapter to aid the reader's further understanding of change management.

8

Case studies in change management:
stand-alone change projects

Introduction

This chapter presents three case studies of stand-alone change projects, which, though significant in themselves, are one-off, isolated
events in that they do not form part of any strategic or concerted programme of change or transformation for the organisations concerned.
Indeed, in these three companies, the lack of any clear strategic direction appears to have resulted in their initiating, or having initiated for
them, change projects whose benefits were unclear and for reasons
which owed more to faith, bias and expediency than to any provable
need. Not surprisingly perhaps, given this situation, the companies
were all to a greater or lesser extent disappointed by the results of
their efforts, though none of them appears to accept that they bear
any great responsibility for what went wrong.

This is certainly the case with the first study, Fort Vehicles. It was
their parent company who triggered the change process at Fort, by
transferring equipment from another of its companies, for reasons of
expediency. The transfer of equipment was carried out at short notice
and without any consultation with Fort. They were, therefore, unpre-
pared for this occurrence, and to a large extent proved incapable of
dealing with it. It took them a considerable period of time to come to
terms with what was required of them in order to operate the equipment efficiently and effectively. Even then there was still a marked
reluctance to provide staff with the training that would equip them
with the skills they required.

In the instance of Mining Equipment Worldwide (MEW), the second case study in this chapter, it was the company itself that took the
decision to embark on change. For reasons which remain unclear,

MEW took the decision to purchase a Computer Aided Design/Computer Aided Manufacturing system. Though much effort was put into choosing the technology and planning its introduction, much of this appears to have been misdirected. This was especially the case with the company's structural arrangements for managing and using the system. For these reasons, together with a lack of clear objectives and the failure to involve and win over users, this particular change project was not so much a failure as an unmitigated disaster.

The last case study in this chapter, Global Financial Services, reveals the problems that can arise when an organisation initiates change for reasons which are untested and, to an extent, kept secret from users. In this instance, the company felt that the introduction of a computer system would allow them to upgrade their image with customers and gain or regain a tighter control over staff. Decisions taken during the development process negated the first of these aims, even if it had ever been achievable, and the second objective also proved elusive.

The chapter concludes by arguing that these case studies show the problems which arise when:

- the objectives of a change project are unclear and/or unrelated to the wider, strategic needs of the organisation;
- there is a failure to consult or be honest with those affected;
- there is a lack of systematic evaluation and planning of what is required;
- there is no impartial outsider who can facilitate the change process.

Case study eight: Fort Vehicles Limited

Background

Fort Vehicles employs some 280 staff and has an annual turnover of £10 million. It manufactures a wide range of tarmac-laying vehicles used in the repair of roads and motorways. These are highly specialised pieces of equipment which few other companies manufacture. For this reason, Fort has carved out a relatively protected niche in the market for construction equipment.

Their main customers are road repair contractors, local authorities and plant hire specialists. It is a peculiarity of their market niche that their main 'competitor' is the second-hand vehicle market. This is because many road repair contractors do not own their own equipment; they buy it for a particular contract and then dispose of it. This means that when a contractor wins an order, they have to assemble the necessary workers and equipment quickly; therefore, they may not be able to wait for a new vehicle to be supplied.

The corollary of this is that the contractor gets rid of the equipment as soon as possible after the end of the contract, thus helping to create and sustain a thriving second-hand vehicle market. However, given that these vehicles often need to be custom-made to suit a particular contractor's requirements, second-hand vehicles are not always appropriate. Consequently, price is not always the main factor when selling to contractors, though it tends to be when dealing with local authorities and plant hire specialists.

In addition, because Fort is involved in the repair rather than the new-build end of the market, it is to a degree insulated against the wilder fluctuations in demand that affect the construction industry in general. Nevertheless, its market has shrunk in the last few years, mainly due to local authorities cutting back on road repairs.

Over the past four years, it has remained viable, partly due to the large amount of sub-contract work it undertakes for its parent company in America, and partly due to improved internal efficiency.

Fort has had a somewhat chequered history; it was under the control of a number of different companies and in the mid-1980s went into receivership. It was then taken over by an American company who had sold it ten years previously, and who manufacture similar products for the American market. Prior to receivership, the company was owned by a Swedish conglomerate. The Swedish owners appear to have managed the company badly; investment was low, and owing to over-ambitious sales forecasts, stocks were allowed to build up to an unrealistic and expensive level. The company had employed 450 people; this was reduced to 180 by its new owners, but at the time of writing this had been increased to 280.

The new owners have instigated new conditions of employment which have led to greater labour flexibility, and have reorganised the company and invested heavily in new plant and systems. By the beginning of the 1990s, investment was running at over £1 million per year. Given that the company had only a £10 million turnover, this amount of capital investment is indicative of the pace of change in the company, and the lack of investment in the past.

Most of the new investment was concentrated in the area of computerised business systems and manufacturing equipment. However, this left the company in something of a dilemma. To manage and operate the equipment successfully, it needed to upgrade the skills of its workforce, but it was reluctant to do this for two reasons. Firstly, they were afraid that their staff would then be 'poached' by other local companies; this appears to be a common practice in the area of the South-East where they are located. Secondly, their American owners, while being supportive on most issues, do not believe in spending money on training. Apparently, it is not their practice in the USA to train workers, and they do not see why they should adopt this practice in Britain. Instead, they prefer to recruit fully-trained workers.

The company's dilemma, therefore, was that it needed to train to get the benefits from its capital investments, but for a variety of reasons it could or would not do so. The result was that employees were often left to their own devices in terms of managing/operating the new equipment that had been introduced. In addition, the company had attempted to recruit experienced staff but this had merely had the result of pushing up wages for these types of employees in the area, and forcing other companies to poach staff from Fort.

The morale of the workforce, which was high after the new take-over, had now declined. This was partly due to the company being willing to spend money on equipment but not on training people, and also to the pressure on staff to get new equipment up and running, even though they might not have the knowledge to do so. Mainly, though, it appeared to be due to the company's perceived lack of direction. The workforce had no confidence that the company had a long-term future.

This brings us to the issue of strategy. It might be assumed that Fort's new owners, having rescued them from receivership and embarked on a relatively large investment programme, would wish the company to have a clear and well-thought-out strategy for its future. Unfortunately, this was not the case. Fort's owners required them to produce a three-year, rolling business plan. However, this was admitted to be little more than a paper exercise involving projecting current sales into the future, and ensuring that all the figures add up.

Management exhibited a marked fatalism towards the company's future. This was summed up by the Managing Director's comments: 'We have to take what the market gives us, and that's unpredictable'. There was no attempt to look for new markets, or develop new products for the British market, although the sub-contract work they carried out for their American parent company was for products different in many respects to their own. Nor was there any attempt to forge closer links with their existing customers, or consistently to attack delivery times and costs in order to increase sales.

Even the investment programme, though ambitious, was piecemeal. It was not part of any overall plan; rather it was dependent on each function in the company, in isolation, bidding for funds. Such changes as were taking place were not supported by any complementary, or necessary, changes elsewhere. This was exemplified by the company's investment in Computer Numerically Controlled (CNC) machine tools.

Reasons for change

Though the company's main expenditure in the last five years had been on the upgrading of its business systems, it was also aware that its manufacturing facilities were outdated and needed to be upgraded. Therefore, it began to purchase new manufacturing equipment which included CNC machine tools. However, given that the company had only limited experience of CNC, and that each machine had to be justified on its own merits, the intention was to introduce them one or two at a time over a period of years, rather than attempting a wholesale move to CNC.

In line with this intention, the company introduced three CNC machine tools over a three-year period at the rate of one per year. However, in 1990, at the end of this period, none of these were operating particularly successfully. The operators were still trying to train themselves, and the person responsible for programming the machines had other duties which took up most of his time. Also, the company tended to operate in a 'fire-fighting' mode, which meant that its management's attention span was relatively short. Despite the money spent, no one appeared to accept responsibility for getting the CNCs up and running to their full capacity.

It was at this point that another British subsidiary of their American parent company was closed down and the decision was taken, at short notice, to transfer a number of CNC machines to Fort. This appears to have been a case of expediency rather than strategic thinking; the parent company needed to find a new home for the equipment and Fort was judged to be a convenient place to locate it. Fort were instructed that they would have to pay for these machines on a commercial basis, and that they were to have the equipment running as quickly as possible, meaning weeks rather than months. This equipment comprised nine CNC machines, none of which were similar to the ones already installed in the company.

The company had a matter of weeks to react to this new situation before the CNCs were delivered. Nevertheless, their parent company expected to see the equipment fully operational shortly after its arrival. Even in ideal circumstances, it would normally take months, perhaps even over a year, for such equipment to be fully operational (Burnes, 1989). Therefore, in this case, the expectation was not just ambitious; it would appear to have been almost impossible to fulfil.

This, combined with the late delivery of CNC machinery which had previously been ordered, and the transfer of work, left the company inadequate time to plan their introduction or to train new staff to operate and programme the machines.

Introduction and operation of CNCs

The introduction of the new CNCs caused major problems for the company. It had to absorb, introduce and operate highly complex equipment whilst maintaining existing output and introducing new and modified products – 60 per cent of the company's products had been introduced in the previous two years (mainly as sub-contract work for its American parent company).

In reality, this meant that the company had not been able to make available either shop-floor or office staff for training on the new equipment. Nor, even if they were available, had it been able to recruit experienced CNC operators, because this would merely have resulted in other shop-floor staff being made redundant when the CNC equipment became fully operational, and existing conventional machines and their operators were no longer required. Redundancies might well result in any case because the CNC equipment was much more productive than conventional equipment. Therefore, even without recruiting new staff, the new CNC equipment could be expected to displace some of the shop-floor workers. However, to recruit staff to, in effect, take the jobs of people who would then be made redundant would not only have caused industrial relations problems, but would also have been far more expensive, taking into account recruitment and redundancy costs, than retraining existing workers.

The problems with the CNCs were further exacerbated by the fact that they were introduced at a time when the company's management was already overloaded with work, and did not always have the time to devote to resolving the problems thrown up by the rapid delivery of the machines.

It can be seen that the introduction of the new machines was dealt with in a very hurried and ad hoc manner. No external training was sought for either operators or the person responsible for programming and, in addition, very little information was transferred with the machines, and there was little back-up from the machinery suppliers. The result was that many of the machines were under-utilised for lack of operators, programs and tooling. Indeed, most of them stood idle for over six months. Clearly, the company should have purchased equipment from suppliers who could provide the necessary back-up, but they had little choice in the matter and had to obtain most of the CNCs from their parent company's British subsidiary.

Where machines were operating, the operators were poorly trained and had difficulty in understanding what was expected of them. Not surprisingly, this had caused frustration and dissatisfaction among staff and operators, especially as the CNCs, because of these problems, appeared to be producing less efficiently than some conventional equipment.

It took the company some time to come to grips with the need to approach CNC use in an organised fashion. In particular, the company only had one CNC programmer, and the vastly increased demand for programs overwhelmed him. There was a weekly requirement for some 30 to 40 new programs, and at one point a backlog of 500 programs existed, though this was reduced later to below 100. In order to overcome the programming bottleneck, the company decided to introduce a computer system for the production of programs. Though this had been installed, it was too early at the time of writing to evaluate how successful it would be. Nevertheless, it should have gone some way to speeding up the production of programs, provided that the programmer received adequate training to operate the system. In addition, the company also sub-contracted out some programming, and this was expected to reduce the backlog significantly.

Maintenance on the new equipment was also causing problems. The company's own maintenance staff had little or no experience of this type of equipment, particularly on the electronics side. Initially, the company employed outside contractors at a cost of some £12,000 per year. However, it later recruited maintenance staff with electronics experience and was retraining existing staff. Nevertheless, the company had still not resolved the issue of the training of operators for the equipment, or indeed decided what these operators would do.

It is apparent that there was considerable disarray over the introduction and use of this equipment, which resulted in a failure to pinpoint the cause of the problems and to take adequate remedial action. Though, as described above, some action was eventually taken, progress to resolve the problem was dependent upon management rather than shop-floor staff.

The outcome

The introduction of such a relatively large number of CNCs represents a considerable investment by the company, not all of it voluntarily. The total cost of the transferred equipment and the CNCs already purchased was nearly £2 million. Any company which invests this amount, particularly when its turnover is only £10 million, should expect to see a considerable improvement in its performance. However, in this case, it is clear that, to say the least, their introduction was unsatisfactory. Even without the transferred machines, the company was having difficulty in gaining the benefits from its first three CNCs. The transferred machines greatly exacerbated this situation.

Though the initial reason for these problems was the lack of time given to the company to prepare for their introduction, this was compounded by the company's failure to deal rapidly and effectively with the problems that arose. The main causes were the lack of training for operators and supervisors, the reliance on external maintenance staff, and the company's inability, internally, to meet the demand for new programs. With regard to the latter, the company introduced a computer system which should, once the backlog had been fully eliminated, be able to deal with the company's normal programming needs – provided, that is, that the equipment worked as expected.

The difficulties and costs of contracting out CNC maintenance were being resolved by retraining the company's existing staff and recruiting new staff with appropriate skills. Operator training, though, still appeared to be the most urgent, immediate problem facing the company. There was no doubt that unless machine operatives were sufficiently skilled, the CNC's level of performance would remain unsatisfactory. It has been emphasised by many observers that operatives, in competitive companies, will need skills beyond the jobs they perform (NEDO, 1987). A successful CNC company must have employees who understand what they are doing, and how their job relates to the system as a whole. They must be able to take initiative and operate efficiently to the benefit of the entire system.

These standards cannot be achieved without excellent levels of training and supervision. Therefore, as a matter of urgency, Fort needed to initiate a training programme for the people who operated and supervised the CNC machines. Indeed, this ought to have been a priority for the company from the outset.

Conclusions

The case of Fort is perhaps a typical example of many traditional engineering companies faced with unaccustomed forms of change (Burnes and Weekes, 1989). The key issue in Fort's case was not the technology per se, rather the approach of the company's management. There was no indication that managers in the company thought beyond the day-to-day problems that they faced.

There was certainly no strategic overview which allowed changes in one area to be related to the overall needs of the company. Nor was there a view of how the company should develop over time. Rather, Fort's management operated in a reactive, indeed sometimes passive, mode rather than a pro-active one. Therefore, with CNC or any other development, there was no sense in which the company's management considered that such a development would bring overall benefits which would allow the company to compete more efficiently in the market-place. This lack of strategic intent or purpose, as mentioned earlier, was causing morale problems amongst the company's existing staff, and might even be contributing to their inability to recruit new employees.

Even without a strategic plan, it is still possible for companies to deal effectively with the major issues that Fort handled so badly. The main issues in this case are the interlinked ones of training and change management. With regard to training, the company found itself in a vicious circle all of its own making. It would not, for a variety of reasons, train and it could not attract enough staff who were already trained. The result was that they had very expensive equipment standing idle. The cost of training to use the equipment was minimal – the cost of the equipment standing idle for lack of trained staff was enormous.

In the case of change management, the company appears to have handled the CNC situation very badly, to say the least. Putting aside the question of training, there was no attempt to put together a team to manage the change. Nor was a timetable or list of tasks produced. Instead, everything was dealt with on a piecemeal basis, with no sense of consistency, planning or urgency.

It should be pointed out that the key tasks concerned not the technology as such, but rather how the introduction process should best be planned and how the company should organise itself to use the new equipment. In both areas, there was little or no work done; therefore, the change process was more unplanned than planned, and more mismanaged than managed. The result was that the people who were least able to affect the situation, and the least responsible for it, the operators and supervisors, were left to deal with the mess, and – to a certain extent – carry the can.

Case study nine: Mining Equipment Worldwide Limited

Background

Mining Equipment Worldwide (MEW) Limited was established in the early 1970s and grew rapidly with the expansion of its main customer, British Coal. In 1990, the company employed 500 staff and had a turnover of £20 million per year. Both numbers employed and turnover had fallen from their high point in the mid-1980s, due to the contraction of British Coal.

The market for coal mining equipment in Britain was, and still remains to a large extent, protected from foreign competition by British Coal's 'buy British' policy. Also, there was, until the late 1980s, very little competition amongst domestic companies in Britain. This was for two reasons. Firstly, British Coal were reluctant to be reliant on one supplier for any type of equipment. Therefore, they encouraged at least two, and often three or four, companies to supply them by ensuring that they all got 'a slice of the action' – as one MEW manager put it. Secondly, partly for the above reasons, but mainly owing to British Coal's ability to pass its costs on to its customers, contracts with the company were very profitable. Therefore, no one had to work tremendously hard either to obtain work or for this work to be profitable.

This was certainly the case with MEW. Although it exhibited all the trappings of a successful company – a new building, new equipment, expensive cars for its directors – it did not exude a sense of efficiency or hard work. Instead, until the mid-1980s, there was an air of complacency amongst managers and lack of motivation amongst employees.

Although the company was in favour of capital expenditure – indeed, managers took great pride in being seen to be up to date – this was not part of any concerted plan to improve MEW's performance. New equipment tended to be treated as a status symbol – as something to impress customers, visitors and rivals.

On the subject of strategic management, the company were disparaging; they did not believe that a company of their size could affect its circumstances or future. As one director put it, 'We take what British Coal gives us, and we haven't done so badly'. Unfortunately, since then, British Coal has contracted in size considerably and MEW, and its competitors, are finding that less is being given than in the past.

This case study begins in the mid-1980s in the period when the company's market was still buoyant and prosperous. It concerns the purchase and use of a Computer Aided Design/Computer Aided Manufacturing (CAD/CAM) system. These systems are designed to automate the production of drawings and related technical data; however, they are costly, complex and have an associated long learning curve (Clegg and Symon, 1991).

MEW bought such a CAD/CAM system at a cost of £350,000 for the equipment and an associated running cost of £200,000 per annum. The Managing Director was later to refer to their experience of CAD/CAM as 'a disaster'.

One final background point: the company's relations with its employees are very traditional. 'Managers manage and the rest do as they are told', would seem to sum up their attitude. Though they seem perfectly willing to negotiate with trade unions over relevant matters, the concept of communicating directly with employees, or involving them in decision making, is alien to them. Having said that, morale in the company is not particularly low, and the workforce do not blame the management for the decline in the company's fortunes in the late 1980s.

Reasons for change

It is not clear what the company's aims were in purchasing the CAD/CAM system; no written justification for the decision was ever produced, and the memories of those involved are somewhat hazy. However, three main factors appear to have influenced the decision. Firstly, the company was rapidly expanding in the mid-1980s and wished to be seen as 'up to date'. Secondly, in the early 1980s, there was much talk in the press about the benefits of new technology. This led to a general belief in manufacturing industry that such technologies as CAD/CAM were essential in order for companies to remain competitive. This was reinforced by talk in the mining industry that British Coal were about to computerise their design function and that any of their suppliers who did not follow suit would lose out. Thirdly, the company had considerable amounts of money available to invest in new equipment.

Therefore, by a process which is not clear, but appears to have been based almost on an act of faith, the company's Board of Directors took the decision to purchase a CAD/CAM system. The decision was taken before any investigations were made into either the suitability of such systems for their company or what benefits a CAD/CAM system might bring.

Having taken a decision in principle, the Board established a two-person project team to make a recommendation on which particular system to purchase. The two people were a senior manager and a computer specialist. Surprisingly, neither of the two departments who were to use the system, the Design Drawing Office and the Production Services Department, was involved or consulted.

The project team made their recommendation a year later, and shortly afterwards an order was placed for the new system, which was installed in the following year. In order to set up and maintain CAD/CAM, a new department was established. Although the two main users of CAD/CAM were the Design Drawing Office and the Production Services Department, the new CAD/CAM Department operated separately from both. Its remit was to set up the necessary databases, to maintain and manage the system and to train Design Drawing Office and Production Services staff to operate the system. As with so many of the company's decisions, the rationale for this one is not clear, and indeed the decision, along with the lack of user involvement, seems to have contributed significantly to the system's eventual failure.

One of the benefits claimed for such systems as CAD/CAM is that they integrate the operation of functions within companies. This is based on the premise that two or more departments using the same system will be forced to work closely together if the system is to operate successfully. Nevertheless, in this case rather than bringing the Design Drawing Office and the Production Services Department closer together, it put another department between them, which in effect blocked opportunities for co-operation and in fact made the relationship more distant and difficult.

When the company announced that they had purchased a CAD/CAM system, it came as a surprise to the departments concerned. It also elicited some suspicion: why were they only told after the decision was taken? What were the implications for job numbers? Who was to operate the system? Why was it being run by a separate department?

Introduction and operation of CAD/CAM

This suspicion died down to an extent until the system physically arrived in the company. Even then, the Design Drawing Office and the

Production Services Department were not involved in its implementation and development. The new CAD/CAM Department took responsibility for setting up the system, and concentrated on training its own staff before moving on to train the people who would actually use the system.

In most companies, users are the first to receive training, often in advance of the system's introduction. This helps to overcome many of the apprehensions that computer systems can raise. It also ensures that the system is being used as soon as it is practicable. Nevertheless, the manager of MEW's CAD/CAM Department saw it as a priority to train his staff, which took three to four months. Only then did staff from the user departments receive any training.

Also, it was the CAD/CAM Department, rather than the user departments, who decided which features of the system would be developed first. Indeed, their main aim, which they did not achieve, was to have all the features of the system up and running at the same time. Once again, this is unusual. Normally, features are developed one at a time, and only when one is successfully developed will the next one be started. Also, it is highly unusual for user departments not to be involved in determining the order in which features are developed. The reasons why this approach is favoured are to reduce the complexity of the task, to ensure that what is developed meets the operational priorities of users, and to build user confidence in the system.

However, this approach was not adopted and, as time went by, the view emerged that the CAD/CAM system was something of a disaster. This was because:

- It was slow to set up. Two years after its introduction, when the CAD part of the system was taken out of operation, only one feature of the system was fully operational.
- It was complex and difficult to use; staff in the user departments considered the system very 'user-unfriendly' and disliked operating it.
- It was costly to run, with overheads of £200,000 per year. Much of this cost was for the full-time staff employed in the new CAD/CAM Department who were responsible for setting the system up but not for operating the system.

There were also other factors which contributed to this view. The system was unreliable; by the time the CAM part was finally taken out of operation, it only operated on two days out of five due to breakdowns.

Because the system was based in a separate department, those who wished to use it had to leave their own work location. Not only did staff find this irksome, but it created barriers between users and those responsible for the system. It also led to friction between managers of user departments and the CAD/CAM management about which should have the greater priority – immediate production requirements or the need to develop and bring on-line the various features of the system.

Also, there were only three workstations, which was insufficient for the number of staff trained and expected to use the system. Users had to book time in two-hour blocks in advance. Not surprisingly, this added to the frustration of those who were already trained and therefore expected to use their new skills and operate the system.

As mentioned, the CAD/CAM Department attempted to have all of the features of the system up and running at the same time. Some managers, however, felt it would have been better to tackle one feature at a time and therefore allow users to become proficient in that area and then to move on to new ones. They felt that attempting to do everything at once was counter-productive. Users complained that they never got the chance to consolidate their skills in any one aspect of the system before being hurriedly moved on to another. None of this was helped, the company claimed, by inadequate back-up from the equipment supplier.

Gradually, users and senior managers lost confidence in the system – the former because of the system's complexity and shortcomings, and the latter because of the time and cost of implementation.

The outcome

As can be seen, the outcome justified the view of many in the company that CAD/CAM was a disaster. The company spent £350,000 on the system and supported it at a cost of £200,000 per year, only to close the system down. This not only represents a considerable financial loss, but also a loss in time, expertise, opportunity and motivation.

- *Time* – the company spent three years and saw no return on this investment time.
- *Expertise* – as well as staff in the user departments, the company put a group of highly-skilled computer systems people together to develop CAD/CAM. What expertise they gained was lost when the system was closed down.

- *Opportunity* – the company had the opportunity to develop a lead over its competitors in this area, to have greater integration between departments and to enhance its competitiveness; none of these opportunities were realised.
- *Motivation* – any enthusiasm and commitment that existed for CAD/CAM was lost and became very difficult to regenerate. All this presented a substantial loss above and beyond any strictly financial loss.

Instead of a fully-functioning CAD/CAM system, capable of reducing design and production lead times, not to mention overall costs, the company spent more than three years to end up back where it had started. The CAD/CAM department was closed down and most staff lost their jobs. In its place, the company bought five personal computers and divided these between the Design Drawing Office and the Production Services Department. These were low-cost, stand-alone systems – easy to operate but limited in what they could do. The cost of each computer with its attendant software was £10,000, and cost was a big factor by this time. Not only did the company feel that it had invested and lost far too much in CAD/CAM already, but by this time its own financial fortunes were on the wane. Nevertheless, the fact that the company plumped for personal computers had the advantage of allowing the departments to be independent of any other body within the company and to decide for themselves how to use the equipment and for what purposes.

Training for the equipment was quick and cheap, and staff learned to use the systems relatively quickly. However, after the problems with CAD/CAM, there was a great deal of cynicism among staff. This was especially manifest on the occasions when suggestions for improvements in the new equipment were put forward and turned down, even when the cost was low.

The main problems with the new personal computer-based systems was that they were little more than electronic drawing boards, with information stored on floppy discs. Some of the more complex tasks still had to be done manually, and because the drawings were stored on floppy discs, it was difficult to keep track of all the information, given the considerable numbers of drawings that the company generated.

As far as the company's management are concerned, it is noticeable that they are now biased against expensive, and indeed cheap, computer systems. Having got their fingers burnt once, they do not intend to do so again. However, perhaps the most surprising aspect of the whole affair, concerns the apportionment of blame. As far as senior managers are concerned, though others tell a different story, the problem was purely technical. Their view is that the system supplier sold them equipment which was unreliable, over-complex and not suited to their needs. No one in the company was at fault, they say; the supplier let them down.

As mentioned, not everyone shares this view, and even senior managers admit that a sister company, who bought the same system at the same time, considers that this system is extremely reliable and beneficial.

Conclusions

Despite the views of senior managers, the central point to note is that the failure of the company's CAD/CAM system was not a technical one. The experience of the sister company belies this, as does much of the company's own experience. Failure appears to have occurred for six reasons:

1 There was no view of where the CAD/CAM system fitted into the overall plans of the company, which was because no strategic overview existed. Therefore, no clear objectives were laid down by which CAD/CAM's contribution could be either evaluated in advance, or measured, once introduced. This was a clear failure on the part of senior management which prevented the change project being established on a firm basis.
2 The remit and composition of the project team responsible for purchase of the system was inadequate. Its remit was to recommend the purchase of a system: it should have been to evaluate the benefits of CAD/CAM in the light of the company's overall needs. Also, the composition of the team should have included, and indeed been biased towards, users. This would have achieved three goals:

   • They would have chosen a system that fitted their needs.
   • They would have ensured that the way it was organised and used was efficient and effective.
   • User involvement would have resulted in them 'owning' the CAD/CAM system, and thus they would have been committed to making a success of its use.

3 The process was driven by computer specialists and not users. The latter knew systems but not what the needs of the users were. They

were, for this reason, more intent on making a 'technical' success of CAD/CAM, whereas users would tend to focus more on its operational success.

4 There was no pre-introductory planning or training for users, nor was there any consultation. Because of this, there was no clear timetable for its development, nor objectives for its use.

5 Instead of using CAD/CAM as a mechanism for breaking down barriers, the creation of a new department created more barriers. In addition, there was no unified management structure for CAD/CAM. One department managed the system and two other departments managed the users. In the best of situations, the chances of conflicts would have been high. In this situation, they were almost inevitable.

6 The lack of consultation, involvement and training of users acted to demotivate them. Therefore, though some of the above problems might have been overcome if users were committed to making CAD/CAM work, the motivation did not exist and the obstacles remained.

Therefore, the installation of the CAD/CAM system was a disaster, but not for the reason that senior managers gave.

Case study ten: Global Financial Services

Background

Global is a large financial services company dealing exclusively with clients in Britain. It was founded in the late nineteenth century, and until the 1940s dealt exclusively in the provision of personal pensions. After the Second World War, it began to offer a wider range of financial services to its clients. In the main this now involves investment, savings and insurance advice. The company does not offer any of its own products, but acts as an intermediary between its clients and those who do provide such products. Global makes its money from the commission it gains from selling other companies' products rather than from marketing its own. Therefore, as Global has no products of its own, the service (advice) it provides to its clients is vital in gaining and retaining their custom.

Though the company is still best known as a provider of pensions, its income is now split evenly between this activity and the provision of personal financial services. The company operates as two distinct divisions: a Pensions Division and a Financial Services Division. This split in the company's activities is the product of historical and practical considerations. When the company first began to offer a wider range of products in the 1940s, a small separate group was established to promote this activity. As time went by and financial services grew, the company formalised this arrangement by creating the present two divisions. The rationale for this was that the two divisions tend to deal with distinctly different products, even though to an extent their client base may overlap.

Pensions clients and their needs tend to be long term and stable. Once a client has taken out a pension, it is very difficult to withdraw from the arrangement, or at least it was until recent changes in pensions regulations. Therefore, 'once a client, always a client' is the motto of the Pensions Division. The Financial Services Division, on the other hand, deals with a much more volatile and short-term market. Clients' needs, whether for insurance or investment advice, can change rapidly – people move house, change jobs, buy new cars or, as in recent years, change their perception as to what constitutes a good investment. Similarly, products can and have changed rapidly. Therefore, the financial services business is more precarious and clients more prone to change companies than is the case with the pensions business. This is one of the main reasons why the company does not offer its own products but instead acts as an intermediary for others: the company is always in a position to offer the latest products on the market. Also, it does not have to become involved in the costly and precarious business of product development and launch.

The aim of the Financial Services Division is to secure the long-term loyalty of clients by offering them a range of products that meet all their financial service needs. Nevertheless, it is the company's view that though client loyalty depends to an extent on the type and performance of the products that are offered, it is also dependent on how the client perceives the organisation. To this end, like many of its competitors, the last ten years have seen it spruce up its image in order to project itself as an up-to-date concern. Nevertheless, many clients never visit the company's offices and only see its representatives (now called consultants). This means that the performance of the consultant (the ability to sell to the client) is often the main factor in gaining and maintaining a client's loyalty.

However, the consultants are neither highly regarded nor highly rewarded. Global's higher reaches are dominated by those from the Pensions Division and, to a large extent, a 'them and us' situation exists in the company. This split is also reflected in the way the company views its employees. On the pensions side, employees tend to be viewed as highly trained (which they are) and valuable people. On the financial services side, employees tend to be viewed as little more than sales staff, poorly trained and mainly motivated by commission payments. Consequently, employees in the Financial Services Division are deemed to require tight management control in order to ensure that they perform well.

Because of the need to process large quantities of information on pensions and financial services, the company acquired a mainframe computer in the 1960s and has upgraded this periodically. However, until several years ago, all the allied paperwork was manually processed and stored. It was at this point that the company began to consider introducing computers into its Financial Services Division.

Reasons for change

The 1980s was a period of unprecedented change in the financial services industry. This was fuelled by changes in government regulations, the rise and then fall of the economy, and the renewed interest in the stock market, followed by its collapse. Not only did this create a volatile environment, but it led to a host of new financial service products being launched, especially unit trusts, which in turn led to unaccustomed competition for business.

This affected Global as much as anyone else, perhaps more so. As regulations and the range of products changed and grew, its management and salesforce (consultants) had to keep up with the changes. As an intermediary, it found itself coming under the supervision of a number of new regulatory bodies; and as a supplier of products, it found itself constantly trying to keep up with the ever-increasing range of new, sometimes unique, products. It also found that many of its clients were more aware, due to advertising and media interest, of the products on offer, and their own financial needs, than in the past. Global responded to this in a number of different ways. It refurbished its offices, it renamed its sales staff as consultants, and spent large amounts of money on promoting itself through television and newspaper advertisements. In addition, it began to investigate the use of computers in the Financial Services Division.

The interest in computers, as was the case with other changes, was not prompted by any overall strategy, nor by a perceived need as such. Indeed, it was mainly a case of copying the opposition. Competitors were upgrading their image, spending more on promotion and computerisation; therefore, Global followed suit. Senior managers did not want to be left behind in what was perceived to be a booming market. The form of computerisation they looked at was termed an Immediate Service Information System (ISIS), designed to give clients rapid access to information and quotations. The benefits Global expected from its introduction were twofold:

- To impress potential customers: the company felt that customers would perceive them as a modern, efficient organisation if they saw sales staff using computers to answer their queries and process their policies.
- To increase (restore) control over the salesforce: the uncertain environment, especially in terms of products and regulations, created a situation where managers' knowledge (often gained from working as sales staff themselves) was out of date. The existing salesforce, therefore, often knew more than their managers about the product they were selling. Also, when consultants were at a loss, managers themselves were unlikely to know the answer. Not unnaturally, given the type of company concerned, managers saw their authority as being undermined by this perceived lack of competence.

For obvious reasons, it was the first of these benefits which was openly broadcast to staff, though the second was commonly seen as a key issue by senior managers. However, it should be understood that neither benefit was the product of any serious investigation and, according to senior managers responsible, the need for ISIS arose from 'us having our fingers on the pulse'.

Introduction and operation of ISIS

Once Global had taken the decision to introduce ISIS, a senior manager and two of the company's computer staff were given the responsibility for specifying and introducing the system.

This involved an examination of the existing practices and procedures of the Financial Services Division. Staff were consulted on what they wanted from the new system, though they saw this as something of a public relations exercise and, correctly as it turned out, felt that their views carried little weight. Before ISIS, records and documents (quotations and policies) were kept manually. All the information was kept in a client's file and added to and amended as necessary. Like all such systems it had its limitations; information was not always updated immediately, information was sometimes lost and only one person could consult the file at any one time. Nevertheless, staff saw it as having advantages, the main one being that they could gain access to all the information themselves.

Therefore, though on the surface the process was a prime candidate for computerisation, there was some resistance to change. This was bolstered by the fact that the company's consultants suspected, and in some cases were actually told by their managers, that ISIS would be used to gather information on them as well as their clients.

Nevertheless, the development of ISIS proceeded, though at a very slow pace. It took three years to develop the system and install the first terminals in one of their regional offices. Even with hindsight, it is not clear why the development of ISIS took so long. Certainly such developments should not be rushed, but given the relatively simple nature of the system, three years do seem a long time. A number of explanations were suggested by Global managers and staff for the time taken. The three main ones were:

- ISIS was not seen as a priority by management. The company was bogged down in the intense and confusing battle to select, promote and actually sell new products. In the flood of new products and potential clients, ISIS inevitably, given the nature of Global, took second, or even third or fourth place.
- There was no clear remit or clear objectives for the system and, therefore, those responsible for its development were unsure as to what was required. In Global, the prevailing sentiment appeared to be: 'Better to do nothing than to do something that's wrong'.
- The computer staff involved were more used to dealing with mainframe computers and large data processing departments rather than a relatively small, decentralised system such as ISIS. Consequently, they had to chart their way through unfamiliar territory.

These reasons, and others, could explain the slowness of the ISIS implementation programme. However, one thing is clear: the slowness did not arise from any attempt by the company to actively involve users in the change process or to take on board their views.

Even after the first system was installed, it took another 15 months for all their offices to get the system. The total cost was £300,000, to develop a system which could service all the Financial Service Division's 70,000 clients.

During the development process, a number of changes were made to the original concept. Originally, the idea was for each consultant to have their own portable computer, which they could take with them when they visited clients; this was eventually dropped on grounds of cost and complexity. Global's Financial Services Division has some 50 offices in the UK, each of which has between 20 and 30 consultants. This would have required some 1,200 or so computers in order for each consultant to have their own. Each consultant would have needed to be trained in computer and keyboard skills. In addition, each office would have to 'collect' the information from each consultant's computer in some way in order to pass it on to a central database.

To train staff adequately would, Global felt, be costly and time-consuming. To train them inadequately could have been disastrous. In the new era of financial service regulation, Global were aware that mistakes were more likely to be picked up and punished, often with a great deal of attendant publicity. To give consultants the power to generate their own quotations (rather than their being sent out by regional offices or the head office) seemed to be tempting fate. In addition, such a development could enhance the importance, and bargaining power, of consultants – the reverse of the original intention. It was also the case that if consultants took on an enhanced role, questions would be raised about the function of and requirement for other staff within Global.

Therefore, finally, the company backed away from giving each consultant their own computer. Instead, the consultants gather the information manually, as in the past, and pass it to a secretary who types it into the ISIS. If the consultant wishes to access the information, which they need to do regularly, they have to ask a secretary to print part or all of the file. However, as was originally planned, once in the system, the information can be manipulated in a variety of ways to gain information on clients and create mailing lists for new products.

The outcome

As is quite clear, the reality of ISIS was different to Global's intention. After each interview with a customer, the consultant filled in a form stating details of the customer, information needed, or policy details. It also recorded when the consultant saw the customer, for how long, and what the outcome was. This was then given to a secretary who input it into ISIS. The customer was then sent a print-out with the information they had requested or details of the policy they had taken out. Therefore, all the customers saw of the new system designed to impress them was a computer print-out which, in certain cases, might take longer to reach them than under the previous system. In effect, the consultant–customer interview was almost exactly the same as before ISIS.

In terms of increased management control, the result was hardly impressive either. It did not restore managers' knowledge of products and regulations; indeed, in some instances, managers were bypassed altogether. It did, however, provide a detailed record on a weekly basis of how many customers each consultant had seen, for how long and the result. In this way, managers could compare the productivity of each member of their salesforce and identify 'who is not pulling their weight'. But, given that the previous systems had allowed managers to see who was selling most and least policies, this was hardly a major step forward. It could possibly even be seen as a backward step, because managers had to wade through a mass of information on each consultant on a weekly basis, whereas previously they had received each month one list showing each person's sales performance. On top of this there had been, and still was, some resistance to ISIS from the salesforce which had increased friction between them and managers. Partly, this was due to its being a less flexible system than the previous one, but mainly because staff believed that it 'spied' on them.

Conclusions

Given the size, resources and professional image of Global, it might be assumed that the adoption of modern methods and technologies would be an almost commonplace event. However, this was certainly not the case with ISIS nor, unless there are major changes in the company, is it likely to be the case with future developments. The reasons for this are complex and deep-seated. First, the history of the company, its market and product has been one of slow evolution rather than fast revolution. At least, this was the case up to the 1980s, when rapid change and aggressive competition shattered the previously cosy and profitable world in which companies such as Global operated.

Global had never previously needed to take a strategic, long-term overview of its business; the former pace, and type of change, had never required it. Therefore, it is not surprising that Global fell back on reacting to change, which had stood it in good stead in the past, rather than attempting to construct a strategic overview. Neither is it surprising that it took to 'copying' the opposition. As one senior manager put it: 'It stops them stealing a march on us and, if it turns out wrong, we know they're in as much trouble as us'. Thus, one of the main reasons why ISIS failed to bring substantial benefits to the company – a lack of clear, strategic objectives for its purchase – was actually seen as a virtue by many of the company's senior staff.

Secondly, the structure and culture of the company ensured that the design and use of ISIS were always likely to be sub-optimal. The Pensions Division enjoyed much higher status than the Financial Services Division. The latter was seen as having an easy life, and its staff were perceived as a low-grade salesforce.

Given this context, it seemed perfectly natural for Global's management to see ISIS as, almost, a cosmetic development designed to create the right image. That at the same time it allowed greater surveillance of staff was seen by the company's management both as a tangible benefit and a more substantial reason for its adoption. Nevertheless, it was never seen as an urgent priority by Global's management. Nor, when it became clear that to issue each consultant with their own computer would be a very costly exercise, was it difficult for them to accept the revised arrangements.

Lastly, the twin objectives of ISIS – improved image and greater control over consultants – were incompatible. The former required each consultant to have their own personal computer. It required them to have enhanced skills and to take on greater responsibilities. However, this clashed in almost every respect with the control objective, and it was the former, rather than the latter, which inevitably suffered.

Clearly, therefore, ISIS was neither successful as a sales gimmick nor as a labour-control device. It might be argued that the company did need to introduce computerisation to create greater rather than less flexibility in order to cope with the uncertainties they faced. But without major changes at the top of the company, such an outcome was always unlikely.

Conclusion and discussion

As Burnes and Weekes (1989) and Burnes (1991) have shown, for many companies, undertaking change projects in isolation from, or in the absence of, a strategic plan is the norm rather than the exception. They argue that this usually undermines the chances of a successful outcome. In addition, they argue that it also makes it difficult to measure accurately the degree of success achieved. This is because there is little or no basis on which to measure its contribution to the organisation as a whole, or to assess whether or not the effort and resources would have been better directed at improvements elsewhere in the organisation.

Clearly, these points apply to the case studies in this chapter. If the companies had possessed the strategic vision of the organisations in the previous chapter, then it is doubtful if some of the projects would have been given the priority they received. If they were, it would have been in the certain knowledge that they were strategically necessary and their impact could be measured and monitored. It also seems possible that greater discussion and openness would have taken place before any of the projects were rushed into. However, in the light of the Pope Construction Vehicles study, this is not an automatic corollary.

Nevertheless, leaving aside the presence or not of strategic objectives, the way that change was planned and executed in these three companies also raises serious concerns. The first of these is the continuing issue of employee involvement. Neither in Fort nor in MEW was there any real attempt to involve, consult or even communicate with those affected by the changes. In Global there was some consultation with employees, but a lack of frankness on the part of its management and a corresponding suspicion on the part of employees prevented this leading to real participation.

The second concern relates to the need to develop realistic implementation plans which can be monitored in order to judge progress. In Fort's case, there was no plan at all; therefore, in their case, it was the absence rather than the inadequacy of a plan that was at issue. In MEW's case there was apparently a plan to start with, though only a few people appeared to have known what it was. However, it certainly must have been flawed and evidently there was no attempt to monitor it, otherwise the serious problems which arose would have been avoided or spotted earlier than they were. Global, like MEW, certainly had a plan for implementation but, given the outcome of the ISIS change project, questions must be asked as to how realistic the plan was and how well it was monitored.

The third and final concern, which does not only apply to the companies in these three case studies, relates to the use of outside consultants/facilitators. Though many companies employ external consultants, or staff from elsewhere, to provide technical or specialist assistance in managing change, few employ facilitators or consultants to aid them in managing the change process itself. Certainly, all three case study companies could have avoided many of the problems that arose if such assistance had been sought. However, the real point, given that the need for this kind of assistance has been advocated for many years (see Chapter 6), is why there is such a reluctance to seek this kind of assistance. Indeed, an answer to this question might also provide an answer to many more, especially those relating to the failure adequately and honestly to involve employees. This is an issue that will reappear in Chapter 10 when the role of managers is discussed more fully.

Discussion points

The case studies in this chapter and the previous one will be discussed in greater depth in Part Four; however, the following discussion points will assist the reader to appreciate the issues involved more thoroughly.

1 Compare and contrast the approach to change management of G K Printers (case study five) and MEW (case study nine), and identify the features which caused them to experience different outcomes.

2 Given that in both Fort Vehicles (case study eight) and Pope Construction Vehicles (case study six) the change process became stalled, examine the reasons for this in these companies and evaluate the steps they took to remedy this.

3 To what extent can individual change projects be seen as separate and independent of strategic objectives?

4 Are there noticeable differences between the cultures of the companies described in this chapter and the previous chapter which contributed to their approach to change?

5 To what extent can employee involvement (or lack of it) be seen as the major factor which distinguishes the more successful companies from the less successful ones?

6 To what extent were the problems experienced by MEW, Pope, Global and Fort caused by the complexity of the technology concerned?

7 What are the implications for change management of the roles played by senior managers and senior management teams in the case study companies?

8 Is change management necessarily a team activity?

9 What key steps did the more successful companies take to gain the commitment of their staff to the change programme?

10 How might an outside consultant/facilitator have made a difference to the way the case study companies approached change?

11 In the companies where serious problems arose, would earlier warning of these problems, through more effective monitoring of progress, necessarily have led to different and better outcomes?

Part Four

Managing change and changing managers – Conclusions

9
Managing change:
lessons and guidelines

Introduction

Part One of this book discussed the historical development of organisation theory and newly emerging approaches to it. This showed that in the past, and increasingly in the future, the effectiveness and efficiency of organisations depend to a great extent on managers identifying when change is necessary, what that change should be, and how it should it be implemented.

Parts Two and Three described and illustrated, through theory and practice, the importance of strategic management and change management in bringing about successful change. Without the former, it is difficult both to legitimise change and to assess whether or not its impact has a positive or negative effect on an organisation. Without the latter, a structured approach to change management, even the best-reasoned arguments for change are unlikely to be successful.

This chapter brings both theory and practice together in order to present a framework and guidelines for managing change. The chapter begins by comparing the theories of strategic management and change management outlined in Chapters 4 and 6 with the experience of the case study companies, described in Chapters 5, 7 and 8.

From this, lessons are identified and guidelines provided for successfully managing the process of change. These stress both the strategic and operational elements of change, arguing that both are vital if success is to be achieved.

The chapter concludes by arguing that it is the responsibility of management to create the conditions which promote the acceptance of and commitment to change within organisations, as well as managing the actual change process itself. It is their role and competence which determine whether or not the change process will be successful.

Lessons from theory and practice

In the 1990s, with the emergence of new organisational paradigms, the pace and magnitude of organisational change can be expected to increase rather than decrease. Organisations (of the future) are seen as rapidly changing coalitions whose (internal and external) boundaries are fluid. Organisations will be driven by their own vision, to which all staff must be committed. Strategy, in this context, is perceived as flowing both from the top down and from the bottom up. That is to say that strategy emerges from the actions and changes that staff at all levels identify and bring about. This creates organisations which, according to Peters (1989), are able not only to cope with continuous change but also to thrive on it.

The implications of these developments for managing change are almost the reverse of those prescribed by the Classical school:

- Senior managers must take responsibility for establishing the corporate vision and then committing the rest of the organisation to pursuing this.
- A key requirement is the creation of flexible and permissive cultures which allow organisations to achieve continuous change and improvement.
- It is a key role of managers to create the conditions in which individual initiative and teamwork thrive, rather than identify and prescribe in detail what individuals should do.
- Managers no longer identify and implement some ideal universal model. Rather they establish, jointly with those most closely affected, the structures and practices necessary to operate effectively under the conditions which prevail at any particular point in time.

Therefore, managing change under the new paradigms is less a question of managers telling people what to do and when to do it, and more a case of creating the space and conditions in which those most closely affected can also play a leading role in the process of change.

This is by no means an easy task for managers, but as the following will show, there is much to be learned from both theory and practice.

There are two basic types, or levels, of change project. The first is radical change, which operates at the organisation level and aims to transform and renew the entire organisation. This type of change is strategy-driven. The second type, or level, of change is small-scale, localised or incremental change, which aims to change or improve a small part of an organisation. The two can be, and indeed should be, connected.

Though radical change involves making major adjustments to structure, practices and procedures, for most members of an organisation the actual impact of these is through a series of small-scale, localised changes. This is similar to Peters and Waterman's (1982) idea of 'chunking': making large objectives manageable by breaking them down into small but interrelated chunks. Therefore, to be successful, radical change must encompass a whole series of small-scale, localised adjustments to the organisation.

It follows that small-scale change should be part of a larger, longer-term strategy if it is to contribute to the overall improvement in organisational performance.

Nevertheless, this is not necessarily always the case, as Chapter 8 demonstrated. Nor is it the case that just because a change project is strategy-driven, it will be successful.

The following will compare the theory of strategy development and change management with the actual practice, as demonstrated by the case studies in Chapters 5, 7 and 8. This will be done, firstly, by examining the theory and practice of strategic management. Then the approaches to change management discussed in Chapter 6 will be compared with the case studies of change management in Chapters 7 and 8.

Strategic management

As argued in Chapter 4, this has developed considerably in the last 20 to 30 years. Originally it was seen as being a very mechanistic approach, concerned primarily with achieving an optimum match between an organisation's products and its markets. Over the years, the approach has changed in three fundamental ways:

1 It is now as much concerned with the internal structures and operations of companies as it is with companies' external situations.
2 It has moved away from sole reliance on mathematical/mechanistic approaches to strategy development. Now a greater emphasis is placed on more qualitative methods, especially the development of organisational visions which identify an organisation's 'strategic intent'.

3 The actual strategy (or strategies) necessary to move towards the organisation's vision is not seen as being fully developed in detail in advance by a company's senior managers. Instead, strategy emerges from (is crafted by) all the organisation, out of the many day-to-day strategic decisions that companies take in pursuit of their vision. The actual strategy that evolves from this process can be seen as a consistent and long-term pattern of actions which are taken in pursuit of the organisation's vision/intent.

These new developments in strategic management can be seen in the case studies presented in Chapter 5.

Case study one: PCI

In this company, much effort was put into creating a vision, which then acted as a spur to the development of a number of specific strategies aimed at reorganising and renewing the company. As the case study demonstrated, though this approach has many benefits, in this instance it failed. The main reasons for its failure were:

- Lack of time to develop the vision and commit the full management team to it.
- Change of Chief Executive Officer at a crucial point.
- Management (and employee) resistance.

Case study two: ING

The experience of this organisation stands in sharp contrast to that of PCI. What can be seen is an organisation which developed, kept renewing, and pursued its strategy over an extended period. This case study demonstrates some of the key lessons for all companies:

- Strategy is not a one-off exercise. Rather it involves continually reviewing and amending (sometimes radically) the organisation's modus operandi and its objectives.
- This process requires consistent, competent and stable management.
- This process requires the building of commitment and competence throughout the organisation.
- This process requires a culture that sees people as an asset and not as a threat.

Case study three: FFT

This study demonstrates the dangers of failing to review and update a company's objectives continually. The company had become known as a 'sleeping giant'. Neither the management nor the employees demonstrated a commitment or desire to compete and progress. The culture of the organisation appears to have encouraged stagnation, supported the status quo and worked against change. It was only when the organisation was forced by its bankers to change its senior management that the turnaround began. The key elements in this turnaround were as follows:

• A new Chief Executive was appointed with a remit of renewing FFT.
• The Chief Executive developed a vision of the type of organisation he wanted FFT to become. This was not broadcast as such, but the Chief Executive used it as a template against which to measure proposed changes. The Chief Executive consistently and effectively pursued his vision over the next decade.
• The company was radically restructured both internally and externally – new operations were added, and FFT diversified into related markets.
• Whilst new blood was introduced into the organisation, FFT constructed a programme to develop existing staff as well.
• New values and beliefs, regarding people, work practices and competitiveness, were developed.

Case study four: Seaside Biscuits

Unlike either FFT or PCI, this was an organisation which was not considered to be in trouble. However, the management were concerned about the organisation's future development. They therefore embarked on an Action Learning programme to review their business and develop plans for the future. This programme appeared to succeed in developing a strategic vision and programme for the business. This was successful for three reasons:

• With the encouragement of the Action Learning facilitators, they reviewed every aspect of their business, and all assumptions were tested (and some dramatically changed).
• The process welded the management team together in full support of their shared vision and created a new attitude of co-operation rather than competition amongst them.

- The final strategy involved both short- and long-term elements designed to move them towards their strategic objectives.

Therefore, in reviewing the practice and theory of strategic management, a number of crucial elements emerge:

- There must be strong leadership from the top which is prepared to review and develop the organisation continually.
- Senior managers must develop a vision of where the organisation is going. This must be shared with, and used to motivate, the rest of the organisation.
- This is a long-term process which has to be pursued consistently over years rather than months. Similarly, when first embarked upon, the major pay-offs from this approach will tend to come in the medium term rather than the short term – though Seaside Biscuits shows that this is not exclusively the case.

The case studies in Chapter 7 also illustrate these points. However, they are primarily aimed at broadening our understanding of the management of individual change projects. Therefore, before discussing these, we will briefly review the theory of change management itself.

Change management

As argued in Chapter 6, there is no one accepted theory or approach to change management. Nevertheless, there are six guidelines which are generally accepted:

1 Arising from the above discussion of strategic management, any change project should be considered in terms of: (a) how it relates to the future objectives and priorities of the entire organisation; and (b) how it affects the operation and structure of the rest of the organisation.
2 Change should be considered in steps or phases. Whether the number of stages is three, five or more, all the approaches to change management stress the requirement to create the recognition of the need for change, to make the actual change, and to consolidate what has been achieved.
3 In order to gain their commitment and co-operation, those who are most closely affected by the proposed changes must be involved in planning and executing them, though the level of involvement will differ with the type of change concerned.

4 To be effective, change programmes must generate valid information, provide free, informed choice for those involved, and create a
personal commitment, by those involved, to the choices made.

5 To be successful, all change projects require individuals and groups
to change their behaviour to a lesser or greater extent.

6 A more contentious guideline is that any change project must involve cultural change. However, as argued in Chapter 6 and reinforced in the next chapter, this is only valid in situations where
radical change is taking place and the existing culture is inappropriate for the new arrangements.

As these guidelines represent the distillation of what the theorists
and practitioners in Chapter 6 regard as best practice, they can be
used to consider how well or badly the organisations in Chapters 7
and 8 initiated and managed change. In so doing, the validity of the
guidelines will also be tested and modified in the light of the companies' experiences of change.

However, before examining the experiences of these companies, it
should be noted that whilst the companies in Chapter 7 embarked on
their particular change project for strategic reasons, those in Chapter
8 were driven by less strategic and more impulsive reasons. Therefore, from the outset, the three companies described in Chapter 8 viol-
ated the first guideline, that change projects need to be judged in
relation to future strategic objectives. With that caveat, we can now
begin to examine how the case study companies' performance in managing change measures up in the face of the six guidelines described
above. We shall begin by examining the three companies described in
Chapter 7.

Case study five: G K Printers

Comparison between G K's actions and the six guidelines:

1 *Strategy* – the initiative to embark on the introduction of the CBS
was driven by strategic needs.

2 *Phased change* – quite clearly, there were distinct phases in the
process of change, though the interface between the phases, and indeed the actual number of phases in total, is less clear. A phase
where the company's management and those affected came to recognise the need for change can be identified. Similarly, after the
system had been installed, a period of consolidation can be discerned, though this was to an extent more disparate than the

theory suggests, given that it was also a period of system expansion. Indeed, it might be argued that the final phase, in this instance, could better be labelled 'continuous improvement' rather than 'consolidation'.

Nevertheless, despite the clarity with which the beginning and end of the change process can be seen, the portion in between is less clear. Was there one phase of change, comprising a number of component phases such as evaluation, choice of options, planning, installation and training, and implementation? This is more than an academic concern. If models of change are established we need to be able to discern the steps involved.

3 *Involvement* – in G K's case it is difficult to say how those most closely affected could have had a greater involvement, given that to all intents and purposes they formed the project team which decided upon, planned and implemented the change process. Nor was their involvement one of mere rubber stamping, or of being overawed by experts and/or senior managers. In a very real sense, the people who were most closely affected were the ones who took 'ownership' of the CBS.

4 *Choice and commitment* – it follows from what was said in point 3 above that the staff were given the information and power to make informed choices, and through this came to be committed to the choices they made.

5 *Behaviour change* – it can be seen that staff in the area affected certainly did change, both in what they did and how they did it. The first form of change arose out of the introduction of the new system itself; however, the second – changes in how they worked – appeared to reflect the wider behavioural and attitudinal changes taking place within the organisation, from which a new culture was emerging.

6 *Cultural change* – rather than seeing this particular change project as a spur to a change in culture, it would be better to view a change in culture of the organisation itself as the facilitating factor which made this particular change project so successful. Though there was no particular strategic objective within the company labelled 'Changed Culture', there is little doubt that a cultural change was taking place. This was leading to a more pro-active, flexible, innovative and co-operative approach within the company.

Therefore, the case of G K would seem to follow the guidelines which emerged from the literature. However, it is worth noting that, in this case at least, it was difficult to identify clearly the phases involved in the actual change project itself (Guideline **2**). Also, and more importantly, Guideline **5** (Behaviour change) and Guideline **6** (Cultural change) appear, in this instance, to relate more to company-wide changes in behaviour and culture and less to the individual change project under consideration. This would seem to bear out Handy's (1986) suggestions that: (a) individual change projects will succeed or fail depending on the extent that they fit in with the culture of the organisation; and (b) culture can only be changed by concerted and long-term strategic effort directed towards the entire organisation.

Case study six: Pope Construction Vehicles

Comparison between Pope's actions and the six guidelines:

1 *Strategy* – the decision to investigate CAD arose from the strategic need to improve the performance of the company's design facilities as part of its overall objectives.
2 *Phased change* – the change process at Pope can certainly be divided into a number of distinct phases. The first was the growing recognition amongst senior managers that the design function needed to improve its performance. This led to the next stage, which was to investigate the benefits or otherwise of CAD. However, neither of these two phases involved either the potential users or managers in the design office. Therefore, neither the recognition of the need for change nor the type of technology proposed was established amongst these groups. The third phase was one of implementation, which was long and drawn-out, and suffered a number of hiccups, the main one being the users' initial refusal to work the CAD system. Because the implementation phase was so drawn-out and because of the problems of getting people to work the system, it is difficult to identify a consolidation/continuous improvement phase because implementation, as it was originally envisaged by senior management, was never achieved.
3 *Involvement* – to all intents and purposes, there was no involvement at all by those who were to use and manage the CAD system and those who were responsible for selecting and implementing it. Clearly, this lack of involvement was a major cause of the many difficulties the company experienced in trying to implement the CAD system.
4 *Choice and commitment* – once again, because of the lack of involvement, there was no facility for users to become involved in any of the choices relating to the system nor, because of this, could they be expected to generate any enthusiasm for the new system. Strangely

enough, it appears that senior managers also lacked any commitment to the change process in this instance.

5 *Behaviour change* – the only behaviour changes that can be seen at
Pope were negative; users became apprehensive of the new system
and, initially, were reluctant to use it.

6 *Cultural change* – clearly no cultural changes took place. Indeed, it
may well be that the main problem experienced by Pope was that
their existing culture was inappropriate for the type of company
they were wishing to become. If they had a culture which stressed
involvement, commitment and communication, they would have
been unlikely to have made the major error that they did in failing
to involve users in this particular change project.

Therefore, unlike G K Printers, Pope's experience of change, though
driven by strategic objectives, can be considered at best disappointing.
The main reason for this was the lack of involvement of users, even to
the extent of not informing them that the company was contemplating
introducing CAD. A compounding factor was that the organisation's
culture seemed to be one where white-collar staff were taken for
granted, though this does not seem to have been the case with shop-
floor staff. It was assumed that as they were white collar-staff, they
would do as senior managers ordered them, without the need to consult or involve them.

Case study seven: Dolphin Electronics

Comparison between Dolphin's actions and the six guidelines:

1 *Strategy* – the priority given to the company's needs to improve its
delivery performance (and ultimately to introduce the MRP2 system) arose from its strategic objectives.

2 *Phased change* – it is possible to see a number of distinct phases in
the process of change at Dolphin. Phase 1 was the recognition of the
need for change; though initially identified as a problem by management, there later appeared to develop a general appreciation of
the need for improvement in this area. The second phase was one of
investigation and consultation. A project team was established to
identify what was required (though their main remit was to look at
MRP2) and to consult users as to their views. From this, a decision
was made to implement the new system. The next phase was one of
planning: the original project team was given the responsibility for
planning the introduction of MRP2. The fourth phase was one of
training, which spanned both pre- and post-introduction. At this

stage, key groups whose behaviour needed to change were identi-fied and special training was provided for them. The fifth stage was one of implementation. The final phase was one of consolidation and improvement, although it must be stated that during this last stage the company had not yet reached its anticipated objectives for the new system.

3 *Involvement* – a multi-disciplinary project team was established which sought to involve users and others affected by MRP2. How-ever, the project team did have a number of concerns with regard to the level of involvement which took place. These revolved around the limited duration of the period of consultation, and whether or not staff had enough knowledge of the proposed changes in order to make informed choices. Consequently, the exercise appeared to be one of communication rather than involvement.

4 *Choice and commitment* – clearly the information and time avail-able do not seem to have been adequate to allow staff to make in-formed choices. However, this does not seem to have affected the eventual commitment to ensuring that the introduction of MRP2 was a success. The reason for this appears to be that the existing culture within the company was one which encouraged innovation, flexibility and commitment.

5 *Behaviour change* – it was recognised quite early on that a number of key groups within the company – particularly senior managers, marketing staff and supervisors – would need to change their beha-viour with regard to scheduling if the new system was to work. Therefore, as mentioned above, special attention was paid to these groups in order to encourage them to change their behaviour. To a large extent, this appears to have been successful, and their beha-vioural changes also appeared to affect others in the organisation positively.

6 *Cultural change* – in this instance there was no discernible cultural change, but rather it appears that the existing culture within the organisation reinforced the types of change which were taking place.

So, this is another example, like G K, of successful change. Not all the objectives were achieved on time, but considerable and satisfactory progress was made. In addition, out of this process, the company rec-ognised that future change projects should perhaps accommodate a greater involvement of users at the evaluation stage, facilitated by more time and information. However, the lack of this appeared to have little adverse effect on the project. The main reason for this was that the culture of the organisation, and their experiences over the

previous few years, had conditioned staff to treat change as an everyday and almost welcome event, rather than something which was to
be resisted or regarded as exceptional.

As mentioned above, these three case studies show where change
can be discerned as emerging from the strategic objectives of the company. However, the following three case studies, which are fully described in Chapter 8, can more accurately be described as cases of
piecemeal and reactive change rather than proactive and strategic
change.

Case study eight: Fort Vehicles

Comparison between Fort's actions and the six guidelines:

1 *Strategy* – it is difficult to discern the strategic rationale behind
transferring the CNC machine tools to Fort at the time, or in the
way that they were transferred. It appears that the parent
company was closing down another company which it owned, and
looking for ways of disposing of its assets. Recognising that Fort
were investing in new manufacturing capability, the parent company decided to transfer the machine tools to Fort. There appeared
to have been no evaluation of whether or not Fort needed the tools
at that time, or whether they could actually cope with introducing
such a large number of tools simultaneously.

2 *Phased change* – when investigating Fort's experience in managing
this particular change project, if any phases at all can be identified,
then the first was one of paralysis – it did nothing at all for nearly
six months after the equipment arrived. Then, it began to try to use
the equipment, but on a piecemeal basis – trying to plug gaps as
they became apparent rather than taking an overview of what was
required. However, there was no real attempt to plan CNC machine
tools introduction or use, nor to train operators.

3 *Involvement* – not only were potential users and managers excluded
from assessing the need for or planning the use of the new equipment, neither were Fort's senior managers given any chance to be
involved in the decision to transfer the equipment to the company.

4 *Choice and commitment* – clearly there were no important choices
made about the change process because no one at Fort was involved
in deciding on the introduction of the new equipment. However,
once the equipment had arrived, neither did Fort's management attempt to involve anyone else in the company in planning what they
should do with it. Similarly, there appeared to be no great commitment either from management or users to making the new

equipment work effectively. This was illustrated by the continuing refusal of management to provide adequate, or indeed any, training for users.

5 *Behaviour change* – rather than changing behaviour, the way that this change project was managed appeared merely to reinforce the attitudes and opinions of many in the company that it had lost its way, and was likely to go downhill rather than prosper.

6 *Cultural change* – clearly there was no discernible change in culture, though it might be argued that there needed to be. Rather, as with the other cases we have discussed, the existing culture in the organisation influenced the way that the change process was managed and its ultimate effectiveness or, in this instance, ineffectiveness. The culture of the company appeared to be one which promoted a 'do nothing' attitude, by both management and the workforce.

As the above shows, the change process at Fort was not so much poorly planned as totally unplanned. The attitude of managers, who – it must be said – were both hard-pressed by other activities and constrained by their parent company, was a crucial factor in Fort's inability to bring about change successfully. Many factors contributed to this, not least the parent company's inability to recognise the need for training; yet what is most striking is the lack of urgency, which led the managers to allow the new equipment to stand idle for so long.

Case study nine: Mining Equipment Worldwide (MEW)

Comparison between MEW's actions and the six guidelines:

1 *Strategy* – not only did MEW not believe in strategic management, its entire approach was based on an almost fatalistic view of its own future.

2 *Phased change* – it is possible to distinguish phases in MEW's approach to the adoption of CAD/CAM. The first phase was the decision to purchase the system. The decision appears to have been one which, at best, could be called an act of faith. There appeared to be no general recognition either amongst senior managers or elsewhere in the company that CAD/CAM could bring specific benefits or that the existing system required such radical change. The second phase was the evaluation and purchase of a system. This was done in isolation from those who would be required to use the system and their managers. It was carried out by a two-person project team, who examined the systems which were available and made a recommendation on which one to purchase. They also made

recommendations on how the organisation needed to be restructured in order to accommodate CAD/CAM: they recommended that a new department be established. The third phase was one of installation and implementation. This was a phase during which it was not clear what the priorities were for the system, or who should have the greatest say in how it was used and what it was used for. This phase was never completed, and led to what we could call the fourth phase – the demise of the system. After struggling to try to make the system work, the company eventually admitted defeat and got rid of it.

3 *Involvement* – no staff or managers in the two areas affected were involved in the decision to purchase CAD/CAM, nor in its installation or how it should be used.

4 *Choice and commitment* – clearly users were not involved in any of the decisions regarding the purchase or use of CAD/CAM. Nor, because of this, and because of the establishment of a separate department to run CAD/CAM, could it be said that any of the users showed any great commitment to making the system work.

5 *Behaviour change* – if behaviour did change, then it was for the worse rather than the better. The establishment of a separate department led to friction between the user departments and the department responsible for running CAD/CAM. Eventually, senior managers themselves became hostile towards the system and disillusioned with it.

6 *Cultural change* – there was no discernible change in the culture of the organisation. Rather, the existing culture, which emphasised short-term fire-fighting and guesswork as well as seeming to promote a lack of trust within the organisation, appeared to have influenced the way that CAD/CAM was purchased and used.

It is quite clear, therefore, that in this case the change process was a disaster. The reasons for this are many; however, the attitude of senior managers towards decision making and employee relations appears to have been crucial. A more thoughtful and pro-active approach to the company's situation, coupled with the greater involvement of employees and communication with them, could have led to an entirely different outcome.

Case study ten: Global Financial Services

Comparison between Global's actions and the six guidelines:

1 *Strategy* – as mentioned, Global does not practise strategic management

and this particular change project does not appear to have been initiated as a result of any attempt to establish organisation-wide or
future objectives.

2 *Phased change* – a number of phases can be discerned with regard
to Global's introduction of ISIS. The first was the decision by senior
management that they needed to take action in order both to
reverse what they perceived as a lessening of management control
and also to upgrade the company's image in the light of what its
competitors were doing. The second phase was to investigate and
design a computer system to achieve both objectives. This involved
consulting staff within the company. The third phase was one of
implementation and training, and the fourth phase was one of consolidation.

3 *Involvement* – certainly Global did take the trouble to discuss users'
requirements with those staff who would operate and be affected by
the new system. However, there was considerable scepticism
amongst the staff as to Global's real aims. Many of them came to
realise that one of the aims was to increase management control.
Consequently they suspected, probably correctly, that Global were
not really listening to their comments. In any event, this could not
be construed as full involvement – rather more as a communications exercise designed to minimise resistance from users for the
eventual introduction of the new system.

4 *Choice and commitment* – it could not be said that information was
provided which allowed users to make informed choices. This was
especially the case given that the decision to introduce the system
had already been taken, and that what they were being asked
about were the nuts and bolts of how the system would operate. It
is noticeable that the decision to go back on the original intention,
to allow the consultants to use the system themselves, was taken
without consultation with users. Given the suspicions that users
had with regard to ISIS, it is not surprising that they showed a lack
of commitment to introducing this system and making it work.

5 *Behaviour change* – there appeared to have been no discernible
changes in behaviour within Global. Indeed, given that consultants
were required not to use the system itself but to pass information
on to those who would input it into the system, in a similar way to
their traditional method, it is hardly surprising that there were no
real changes in behaviour. Also, given their suspicions of the system, it is highly unlikely that they would be willing to change their
behaviour.

6 *Cultural change* – clearly the culture of Global was one which could

be described as being highly Tayloristic, in that management were very sceptical of the willingness of staff to work effectively without close management supervision and control. It was this culture which caused management to consider introducing ISIS as a management control method in the first place, and it was this culture which appeared to determine how management would approach this process, and indeed how staff would react to it.

Therefore, as described in Chapter 8, the introduction of ISIS does not appear to have been particularly successful; nor does it appear to have resulted in any great improvement in performance, managerial control, or staff motivation. Given what we know of the culture of the organisation, this is hardly surprising.

Managing change in the 1990s

In this chapter we have discussed the actual experience of the case study companies described in Chapters 5, 7 and 8 in the light of the theoretical approaches to strategy and change management described in Chapters 4 and 6. In relation to successful strategic management, three guidelines were identified:

1 Strategy should embrace the external and internal affairs of an organisation.
2 Strategy is more qualitative and less reliant on building mathematical models of an organisation's operations and markets.
3 Long-term strategy emerges out of the strategic actions that organisations take over time in pursuing their vision, rather than being preformed and detailed in advance.

In relation to change management, a further six guidelines were identified, as follows:

4 Change projects need to be considered in relation to the strategic requirements of an organisation.
5 Change should be planned and implemented in phases.
6 Those most closely affected should be involved in planning and implementing the change project.
7 To be successful, change projects must allow those involved to make free and informed choices in order to gain their commitment.
8 Individuals and groups will need to alter their behaviour if successful change is to be achieved.
9 Cultural change is a necessary part of any change project.

Having examined the ten case studies presented in Chapters 5, 7 and 8, it is now possible to present an approach to change management which encompasses lessons from both theory and practice. This approach comprises nine elements, but although these include the above guidelines, they have been substantially amended and reconfigured to incorporate lessons learnt from the case studies.

In presenting this approach to the change process, it is necessary to distinguish between those elements which create the conditions which allow successful change to take place (1–4 below), and those which actually comprise the stages (or phases) that individual change projects need to go through in order to be successful (5–9 below). However, this division does not present the full picture, because those elements which create the conditions for successful change are also affected, sometimes positively and sometimes negatively, by the process of change itself. It is the interplay between these two sets of elements which makes the change process so complex and difficult to manage. This can be seen more clearly by examining in detail the nine elements which constitute this new approach to managing change:

1 Creating a vision.
2 Developing strategies.
3 Creating the conditions for successful change.
4 Creating the right culture.
5 Assessing the need for and type of change.
6 Planning and implementing change.
7 Involvement.
8 Sustaining the momentum.
9 Continuous improvement.

The nine elements constituting a new approach

1   Creating a vision

As described in Part Two, the concept of organisations driving themselves forward by creating an ambitious vision (or intent or scenario) of where they wish to be in the long term has become increasingly influential over the last decade (Cummings and Huse, 1989). The argument, in brief, for this approach is that previous attempts to plan the future have either fallen foul of the difficulty of accurately translating past trends into future projections, or have not been ambitious enough because they have allowed future plans to be constrained by present resources (Hamel and Prahalad, 1989). The process of developing an organisation's vision attempts to overcome this by encouraging senior managers to think freely without considering present resource constraints, about where they would like to take the organisation in the long term.

This can produce very ambitious objectives, such as Honda's declaration in the 1960s (when it was barely more than a motorcycle producer little known outside Japan) that it wanted 'to become the second Ford'. The creation of visions is an iterative process whereby an initial vision is created, and the gap between this and the present circumstances is identified. Then the organisation considers its strategic options to bridge the gap and, in so doing, refines the vision itself. Part of this refining process is both to discuss the vision widely within the organisation and to gain employees' commitment to its objectives, thus using the vision as a motivating and guiding force for the organisation.

The organisational vision can best be described as a beacon shining from a faraway hillside at night that guides travellers to their destination. Travellers can usually only see a few feet ahead but are prevented from getting lost by the beacon. Occasionally, the traveller will have to make a detour, or sometimes even reverse course, but this is done in the certain knowledge that they still know their ultimate destination. The concept of the beacon is a useful analogy in that it highlights one of the main differences between vision building and other forms of long-range planning. Normally, it is only the leadership of an organisation that has a clear view of where the organisation is going in the long term. However, the vision, like the beacon, should shine clearly for everyone in the organisation to see, so that they all know where they are travelling to.

Cummings and Huse (1989) developed guidelines to help organisations construct visions. They argue that there are four aspects to constructing a vision:

- *Mission* – this states the organisation's major strategic purpose or reason for existing.
- *Valued outcomes* – visions about desired futures often include specific performance and human outcomes the organisation would like to achieve. These valued outcomes can serve as goals for the change process and standards for assessing progress.
- *Valued conditions* – this element involves specifying what the organisation should look like to achieve the valued outcomes. These valued conditions help to define a desired future state towards which change activity should move.

- *Mid-point goals* – mission and vision statements are often quite general and may need to be supplemented with mid-point goals. These represent desirable organisational conditions but lie between the current state and the desired future state. Mid-point goals are clearer and more detailed than desired future states, and thus, they provide more concrete and manageable steps and benchmarks for change.

By constructing a vision in this manner, the organisation not only has a picture of what it wishes to become but also some concrete targets to aim for. In the case of Honda, whose vision was to become 'the second Ford', they clearly knew they would have to produce a range of cars to match Ford's, and establish the necessary manufacturing, design and marketing facilities both in Japan and the rest of the world. With this vision they then began to put together a strategic plan for its achievement.

2   Developing strategies

Whilst organisations generally have only one strategic plan, this usually comprises a whole catalogue of intermediate strategies for each area of the company's activities. Such strategies would usually cover marketing, product development, manufacturing, personnel, finance, and – increasingly – information technology and quality. The characteristics of such strategies are that they generally look five years or more ahead, but only contain firm and detailed plans for the next 12 to 18 months. This is because most companies find it very difficult to be firm about their intentions for much more than that time.

These strategies are put together in one strategic plan which is, usually, formally reviewed annually, but is frequently reviewed informally and in the case of major and unexpected events. Because the strategies are not ends in themselves, but means to an end – the vision – they are, by necessity, both flexible and pragmatic. They will be constructed and pursued only to the extent that they facilitate the pursuit of the vision.

One way of viewing strategy in this respect is to see it as a series of links in a chain stretching from the present to the indeterminate future where the vision lies. Each link in the chain represents particular strategies or groups of strategies that organisations adopt to move themselves forward in the light of both their eventual target and the prevailing circumstances of the time. Therefore, the links (strategies) are continually having to be forged and reforged (to use Mintzberg's term, 'crafted') over time.

Once again, Honda's experience gives a useful insight into this process. In the early 1960s, it developed a series of strategies for producing cars and gaining a toe-hold in the American and European markets. These strategies were succeeded in the 1970s and 1980s by strategies to produce higher-quality and more Western-style cars, and also to improve its image in the eyes of a Western consumer. In addition, it needed to take into account the rising value of the Japanese currency and increasing production costs in Japan.

Part of achieving these strategies was to establish manufacturing bases in the USA and Britain. In Britain, this was initially achieved through a partnership with the Rover Group rather than building its own assembly plant. Undoubtedly, in the 1960s, it never envisaged exactly how it would move into Western car markets. These decisions did not need to be taken at that time, which is to say those particular links in the chain only needed to be forged when the preceding ones had been completed. It is also interesting to note that other Japanese car companies did not follow exactly the same strategies.

As an example, Toyota and Nissan both preferred to build their own manufacturing plants in Britain instead of going into partnership with British-based car companies. Mazda, on the other hand, have chosen to go into partnership with Ford in Europe, allowing Ford to build their cars for them.

The point of this is, hopefully, obvious. Strategies should not be considered as immutable or running forever. Rather, they should be seen as links in a chain that leads to the vision. As such, strategies will be forged or crafted in the light of long-term considerations and present necessities. Also, those strategies which suit a particular company at one point in time are unlikely to hold good for all time, nor for all companies.

Nevertheless, whilst not following the same strategies, Japanese car companies have been very successful in penetrating Western markets. In the 1960s, Japanese cars had the reputation of being cheap but unreliable. Now, though they are still highly competitive on price, they could not be described as cheap in the sense of quality, and their reliability leads the world.

This type of approach can also be seen at ING, described in Chapter 5, where successive strategies have been developed and implemented over two decades in order to move towards their vision. Similarly, though less successfully, PCI, also described in Chapter 5, began by creating a vision and then attempted to develop strategies to move them towards this vision.

One final point: it follows from this that organisations do not need to be able to see all the links in the strategic chain, merely those which will serve them over the next few years.

3   Creating the conditions for successful change

To move towards an organisation's vision, to implement its strategies, requires change – often quite radical change. This usually means that people in the organisation are required to do new things in new ways within new structures. For some, hopefully most, this will bring benefits, not least of which may be greater job satisfaction. For other people, though, the reverse may be the case. Whether at the top, middle or operational levels, there may be some who will lose out. The reorganisation of the senior management team at PCI was a case in point. Most managers felt that they had improved their lot but the three original team members felt slighted and effectively demoted.

Organisational change involves moving from the known to the unknown, with the possibility of loss as well as gain. Companies, therefore, need to create a readiness for change amongst their employees, and adopt an approach which is aware of the possibility and causes of resistance, and deals with these at an early stage.

In order to create a readiness for change, there are three steps an organisation should take:

- *Make people aware of the pressures for change* – the organisation on a regular basis should inform employees of its plans for the future, the competitive-market pressures it faces, and the performance of its key competitors. Obviously, promoting the vision and explaining the strategic plan are vital components in this. Through this approach, members of the organisation come to appreciate that change is not only inevitable but is being undertaken to safeguard rather than threaten their future.
- *Give regular feedback on the performance of individual functions and areas of activities within the organisation* – this allows a company to draw attention to any discrepancy between actual performance and desired present and future performance. It allows those concerned to begin to think about how this situation can be improved and prepares them for the need for change. In looking at the case study companies, it is noticeable that there was a greater readiness to change in those organisations where management was

open about its objectives and the company's current performance than in those organisations where information was guarded. This can be seen particularly in comparing Dolphin Electronics with Pope Construction Vehicles; in the former, the company's openness facilitated change, whilst in the latter its secrecy had the opposite effect.

- *Publicise successful change* – in order to create a positive attitude towards change, companies should publicise the change programmes which are seen as models of how to undertake change and the positive effects it can have for employees. This does not mean that mistakes should be hidden or poor outcomes ignored; these should be examined, explained and lessons learned. However, staff should be encouraged to expect and set credible and positive outcomes for change programmes. Once again, the experience of the case study companies illustrates this point.

  In ING, there was a long history of successful change, which produced a positive view of change. In PCI, on the other hand, its recent history had been one of the problems in introducing new products and making changes, and the dismissal of the Chief Executive clearly acted to demoralise staff and make them suspicious.

If the above steps help to promote a readiness for change, it must also be accepted that other steps need to be taken to deal with causes of resistance at an early stage. In this respect there are three steps which organisations can take:

- *Understand people's fears and concerns* – one of the major mistakes that Pope Construction Vehicles made was to fail to recognise the real and legitimate fears of staff when they introduced the CAD system. Their fears may have been groundless, but the fact that the company had failed to recognise their existence and take appropriate action caused Pope many problems. The same point could be made with regard to the resistance at PCI. Therefore, organisations need to recognise that change does create uncertainty and that individuals and groups may resist, or may not fully co-operate if they fear the consequences. It follows that managers need to pay special attention to those groups if adverse conditions are to be avoided.
- *Encourage communication* – one way of avoiding the uncertainty that change can promote is to establish a regular and effective communications process; one which both gives the context for and details and consequences of proposed changes. This should be a

regular rather than a one-off exercise. In some cases, such as G K Printers where all those affected were involved, this ceases to be an issue. However, G K's size makes it an exception. In most cases it is impractical to give everyone this level of involvement; therefore, as at Dolphin Electronics, it is important to communicate proposals from the outset.

• *Involve those affected* – this will be dealt with in greater detail below. However, as already demonstrated by contrasting the experiences of G K Printers and Pope Construction Vehicles, involvement promotes understanding and overcomes potential resistance; lack of involvement creates suspicion and leads to resistance.

Therefore, as can be seen, there are positive actions which organisations can and should take to promote a readiness for change and to avoid or overcome resistance. However, it should be realised that all this will be in vain if, as with Global Financial Services, an organisation embarks on a programme of change specifically in order to affect its employees adversely rather than to promote greater effectiveness.

4 Creating the right culture

Much of the above, and indeed what follows, require organisations to have cultures which encourage and support these types of activities. Handy (1986) pointed out that just as there are many types of organisational structures, practices and procedures, so too are there different types of culture. However, rather than being separate, Handy argues (as do others such as Allaire and Firsirotu, 1984) that each type of organisational structure has its own matching culture. These act to reinforce and legitimise each other. However, if the two are not matching, or if one changes and the other does not, then the likelihood is that conflict will arise. In any case, the types of behaviour and procedures involved in bringing about successful change require cultures which encourage flexibility, autonomy, group working, etc. If the organisation's culture does not support these types of activities, then change will be much more difficult and may not be successful. Therefore, if organisations do not have a culture which matches how they wish to operate in future, they must create one. This issue will be considered in greater detail in the next and concluding chapter.

5   Assessing the need for and type of change

In a major study of 15 companies, covering some 30 different change projects, Burnes and Weekes (1989) found that 20 of the projects either failed entirely or fell considerably short of their original expectations. There were a number of reasons for this, but two prime ones were that the companies either did not adequately assess the need for change or investigate other types of change than the ones they chose.

This can also be seen in some of the case studies presented earlier. It is evident that neither MEW nor Global Financial Services carried out any real assessment of the need for change. Nor, having decided to make changes, did they consider what alternatives were available. There is also a suspicion that even Pope Construction Vehicles and Dolphin Electronics fell into the trap of assuming that only one solution was appropriate to their situation. In cases such as these, doubt has to be raised about whether the organisation needed to make these particular types of changes.

Even in cases where changes were undoubtedly necessary, it was not always clear from the case studies whether these particular changes should have taken priority over other changes that could have taken place, or whether the particular types of change chosen were the best in that situation.

Burnes (1988) suggested an approach to assessing the need for and type of change which attempts to avoid these problems. This approach has four phases:

1 *The trigger* – organisations should only investigate change (other than minor projects which can be easily accommodated) for one of the following reasons:

   - The company's strategy highlights the need for change or improved performance.
   - Current performance or operation indicates that severe problems or concerns exist.
   - Suggestions or opportunities arise (either from the area concerned or elsewhere) which offer significant improvements.

   If one or more of the above arises, then this should trigger the organisation to assess the case for change, which leads to the next phase.

2 *The remit* – senior managers should draw up a remit for the assessment. This should state clearly the reasons for the assessment, its objectives and timescale, and who should be involved and

consulted. The remit should stress the need to focus as much on the social aspects as the technical considerations involved. In addition, it must make clear that those who will carry out the assessment must look at all options rather than merely considering one or two alternatives.

3 *The assessment team* – this should be a multi-disciplinary team consisting of a senior manager, representatives from the area affected (both managers and staff), specialist staff (finance, technical and personnel) and, where appropriate, an outside consultant or change facilitator.

4 *The assessment* – the first task of the assessment team is to review and, if necessary, clarify or amend its remit. Only then can it begin the assessment, which should comprise the following four steps:

- *Clarification of the problem or opportunity* – this is achieved by gathering information, especially from those involved. In some situations it might be found that the problem or opportunity is redefined, or does not exist, or can be dealt with easily by those most closely concerned. If so, this is reported back and probably no further action needs to be taken. However, if the clarification reveals that a significant problem or opportunity does exist, then the remaining steps need to be completed.
- *Investigate alternative solutions* – a wide-ranging examination should take place to establish the range of possible solutions. This should be tested against an agreed list of criteria covering costs and benefits, in order to eliminate those solutions which are clearly inapplicable and to highlight those which appear to offer the greatest benefit. This then leads on to the next step.
- *Feedback* – the definition of the problem or opportunity and the range of possible solutions should be discussed with interested or affected parties to obtain their views and to establish the criteria for selecting the preferred solution or solutions.
- *Recommendations and decision* – the team should present their recommendations to senior managers in a form which clearly defines the problem/opportunity, identifies the range of solutions, establishes the criteria for selection and makes recommendations. These recommendations should include not only the type of changes, but also the mechanics and timescale for making such changes and the resource implications, as well as performance targets for the new operation.

This then leaves senior managers in a position to assess, modify, defer or reject the assessment team's recommendations in the light of the strategic objectives of the organisation. If the decision is to proceed with the proposed changes, then it becomes necessary to begin planning the implementation process.

6 Planning and implementing change

Having established that change should take place and its form, it is then necessary to plan how this will be achieved and then to implement the plan. This process comprises a number of activities:

- *Establishing a change management team* – this must include some, if not all, of those responsible for the original assessment of the need for change, including the assistance of an outside consultant or change facilitator. However, it might also have a significant user input, especially at the implementation stage. Sometimes, for large change projects, a sub-group comprising primarily those affected by the changes, both managers and others, is established to handle the day-to-day implementation issues.
- *Activity planning* – this involves constructing a schedule for the change programme, citing specific activities and events that must occur if the transition is to be successful. Activity planning should clearly identify and integrate discrete change tasks and should link these tasks to the organisation's change goals and priorities. Activity planning should also gain top management approval, should be cost-effective, and should remain adaptable as feedback is received during the change process. It must therefore determine the final and intermediate objectives, and these must be tied to a specific timetable in order to avoid uncertainty amongst those who have to carry out the changes.
- *Commitment planning* – this activity involves identifying key people and groups whose commitment is needed for change to occur and deciding how to gain their support. It can be seen in the case of Dolphin Electronics that, at an early stage, the company identified that certain groups would need to be given specific attention if their behaviour, which was seen as being crucial to success, was to be modified.
- *Management structures* – because organisational transition tends to be ambiguous and to need direction, special structures, such as project teams with an appropriate reporting relationship to senior

management, need to be created to manage the change process. These management structures should include people who have the power to mobilise resources to promote change, who have the respect of the existing leadership and advocates of change, and who are in a position to guide the change process.

- *Post audit* – after the changes have taken place, a post audit should be carried out to establish: (a) that the objectives have really been met; and (b) what lessons can be learned and how can these be incorporated into future projects.
- *Training* – this is a key part of any change project and takes a number of forms. The obvious one is in relation to new skills that might be necessary. However, as the Dolphin Electronics study showed, training can play a part in creating awareness of the need to change behaviour. One aspect of this might be team-building sessions. Also, there is a need to give general awareness training to those in the organisation who might only be indirectly affected. To ensure that the various types of training are targeted at the right people or groups, a training programme, starting before implementation and continuing afterwards, should be established, showing who needs training, the form of the training and when it will take place.

7 Involvement

One of the issues which stands out from the case studies in Chapters 5, 7 and 8 is that involvement plays a crucial role in the success or otherwise of a change project. Achieving a successful change can be and, usually is, a long and complex task. Always, there will be difficult obstacles to overcome, most of which should have been anticipated, but others which are unexpected. To overcome these, and to develop and maintain the momentum necessary to ensure the project is successful, requires the commitment and support of all concerned, especially those who are most closely affected. In effect, it requires them to take ownership of the process so that it is 'their' project and 'their' success. This will not be achieved unless they can be involved in its planning and execution. Involvement in this respect has three facets:

- *Information and progress reporting* – letting those who will be affected by the change process know from the early stages what is happening, how it might or definitely will affect them, and giving them reports on the progress being made.

- *Communication* – establishing a two-way dialogue. This involves not only providing information, but also listening to the response and taking it seriously. This has a number of benefits. The change management team will very quickly pick up significant worries and concerns and will be able to respond to these; they will also be made aware of aspects that need to be taken into consideration which have been overlooked; and assumptions which have been made will be tested and sometimes challenged.

- *Actual involvement* – not everyone can be involved in all aspects of planning and execution, but it may be possible to ensure that those most closely affected are involved in some, if not all, aspects. Where possible, responsibility for aspects of the change project should be given to those who will be directly affected by the result.

These three elements of involvement relate to different groups in the organisation. The whole organisation should be given information on planned change, but it may only be necessary to establish a dialogue with those most closely affected. As for actual involvement, this usually only extends to those most closely affected, but will depend to a degree on how an individual/group is affected by the proposed changes.

8   Sustaining the momentum

Even in the best-run organisations, it sometimes happens that initial enthusiasm for change wanes, and progress becomes slower and can grind to a halt. In organisations which are less well run, the momentum may not even be present in the beginning (Fort Construction is clearly an example of this). In such situations, people will return to the methods and types of behaviour which they are familiar with. Given that momentum does not arise of itself nor will continue without encouragement, organisations need to consider how to build and sustain it. The points already made above regarding planning and implementation, and especially involvement, are clearly part of this. However, in addition, organisations should:

- *Provide resources for change* – to achieve any change will normally require additional resources, both financial and human. In cases where staff are required to keep up the same level of output during the transition phase, it may require considerable additional resources to achieve this. It is important that these extra resources are budgeted for and allocated as necessary, whether for the provision of training, senior management time or whatever. Nothing is guaranteed to be more demoralising than having to make changes without the necessary resources or support.

- *Give support to the change agents* – an enormous responsibility falls upon the change management team. They have not only to plan and oversee the change project, but also to motivate others and deal with difficulties, and sometimes very personal problems. However, just as they have to support others, so too must they receive support themselves. Otherwise they may be the ones who become demoralised and no longer in a position to motivate others.

- *Develop new competences and skills* – change frequently demands new knowledge, skills and competences. Increasingly, managers are having to learn new leadership styles, staff are having to learn to work as teams, and all are expected to be innovators. This requires more than just training and retraining. It may also include on-the-job counselling and coaching. Therefore, organisations need to consider what is required, who requires it and – the difficult part – how to deliver it in a way which encourages rather than threatens staff.

- *Reinforce desired behaviour* – in organisations, people generally do those things which bring rewards or avoid criticism. Consequently, one of the most effective ways of sustaining momentum for change is to reinforce the kinds of behaviour required to make it successful. Sometimes this may be monetary – linking increased pay or bonuses to particular types of activity or progress. Sometimes it may be symbolic – senior managers themselves adopting certain types of behaviour such as moving their desk into the same communal office as the rest of their department. Sometimes it may be through recognition – whereby senior managers openly single out individuals or groups for particular praise. Such activities are particularly important during the early stages of change, when achieving an identifiable and openly-recognised success helps participants develop a positive attitude about the change project.

9 Continuous improvement

It is quite clear that, even after change has been implemented, improvements can still be made. Indeed, it is argued that the most successful companies are the ones which are committed to continuous improvement (Peters, 1989; Wickens, 1987). This involves individuals and groups continuously examining their work to see how it can be improved. This approach goes beyond simple employee suggestion schemes. Instead, employees are encouraged to meet and actively discuss ways of improving their performance. Many companies use Quality Circles or improvement groups to facilitate this. Other companies have appointed improvement managers (sometimes the Japanese term for this type of improvement activity, 'kaizan', is used). However, the intention is the same: to make gradual improvements in performance through a continuous series of small-scale, low-cost/no-cost improvements which are driven by those in the area affected (Partnership Sourcing, 1991). This is not seen as an alternative to radical change or individual change projects, but as an adjunct to ensure that improvement is continuous rather than a discontinuous or one-off event.

Conclusions

Managing change successfully has never been nor can ever be easy or problem-free, and as can be seen from the above discussion of the case studies, it is very often made more difficult than it should be. Smith *et al.* (1982) pointed out that most people regard change with suspicion and are therefore prepared to be antagonistic from the outset. However, both the theory and practice of managing change give some justification for believing that this is neither inevitable nor an immutable facet of human nature. Rather, it depends on the employees' past experiences and present expectations of the organisation in which they work.

A number of the case studies have shown what happens when change is contemplated either for the wrong reasons, for confused reasons, or for reasons which are deliberately aimed at disadvantaging those involved; or when the process is badly managed and key elements, such as employee involvement, are omitted. Some of the case studies also show that the process of change can be well managed and can be accomplished, if not with ease, then certainly with a great deal less difficulty than other companies appear to have encountered. If the reasons for change are seen to be legitimate, if there is openness and involvement, if the overall culture of the organisation is conducive, commitment and ownership are generated rather than resistance and alienation.

From the theory and practice of change, we have established nine guidelines. These cover elements which create the conditions for successful change – an organisation's vision, strategy and culture; and guidelines which assist in the actual implementation of particular change projects. In some companies, the conditions for successful change already exist, and therefore what is necessary is for the individual change projects to be carried out in a well-planned fashion. In other organisations, much more radical change is initially required to create the conditions for successful change, such as the appropriate culture and strategies. This is neither a quick nor a straightforward process, as the case of PCI revealed, but it can be accomplished in both large and small companies – FFT, Seaside Biscuits and G K Printers are good examples.

Also, once created, the necessary conditions can be sustained – not without considerable effort – over long periods of time, as shown by ING. Yet creating the necessary conditions is not automatic, it is time-consuming and some companies never get past the starting line.

Indeed, it should be apparent from the guidelines for managing change that actually implementing change is or should be the least time-consuming part of the whole change process. It is the preparation – the planning and organising of change, as well as consolidating and building on the change – that takes, or should take, the majority of the time. Burnes and Weekes (1989) argued that the companies who achieved successful change tended to spend some 90 per cent of their time in planning and organising change and only some 10 per cent of their time implementing it. This approach, they contend, allows companies to implement change in a relatively rapid and problem-free fashion. However, this is only possible if the planning and preparation for change have been thorough and detailed.

In contrast, Burnes and Weekes (1989) point to less successful companies who tried either to rush or to skimp on the planning and preparation. In these cases, implementation was the most time-consuming element of the change process. This was because these companies were ill-prepared, and, as a consequence, 'unexpected' problems kept cropping up. Not only did this make change in these companies a lengthy affair, but it also meant that, in many instances, objectives were never reached and completion never achieved.

A good analogy for the preparation and implementation of change is that of a family moving house. The actual move may take less than a day, but the decision to move in the first place and the subsequent planning and organising of the move can be time-consuming in the extreme. Key questions to be considered are:

- Why move?
- What are the alternatives to moving?
- Where to move to?
- What type of accommodation is required?
- How much to pay?
- When to move?
- How to move?

Also, if the move is to be successful, it is important that everyone in the family has their say on these issues and feels that their comments and suggestions have been seriously considered, if not always accepted. Otherwise, one disgruntled family member can make life hell for the rest. Only when the key issues have been decided upon to everyone's satisfaction can the family actually move. Even when the move is over, there is still the need to settle in to the new home, and convince one and all that the move was necessary and that the new home is preferable to the old. Hopefully, they will feel positive about their future and accept the new home as their own.

Nevertheless, this does not mean that improvements cannot be made to the new home. Indeed, one sign that the family consider the move to have been a success is their wish to spend time and energy improving the property and changing the decor to their taste. Also, as every home-owner knows, improving and redecorating a house is a continuous process. Clearly, to re-emphasise the point, the planning and organising of the move are the time-consuming elements. The actual move, though not its consequences, should be and needs to be relatively quick if success is to be achieved.

Relating this analogy to the case study companies in this book, it can be seen that some decided to move house with little thought or preparation. The result was that they were less than happy with the change. In other cases, more thought was given to the need to move in the first place but key members of the family were left in the dark or misled. Once again the result was far from satisfactory. However, in several cases, the planning and preparation were excellent and the changes were accomplished to everyone's satisfaction, though some unforeseen occurrences had to be dealt with on the way.

Clearly, as the case studies show, the main responsibility in creating the conditions for, planning and organising, and sustaining successful change lies with the managers, especially at the most senior level. They are the ones who can establish a vision, create strategies, and initiate change. Others in the organisation can obviously assist in this process, but unless the leadership is committed and competent, the efforts of the others will almost certainly be in vain. As the next chapter will argue, the presence of competent, committed management can be neither taken for granted nor lightly treated.

10

Changing managers: management competence and organisational culture

Introduction

The aim of this book has been to help the reader understand the process and management of change. A key objective has been to set the management of change in its historical and theoretical contexts in order to show how these have influenced how organisations are structured and managed. To this end, the origins and development of organisations and management have been discussed, and the crucial cleavages between theory and practice, and between one theory and another, have been highlighted. Attention has been devoted to the future challenges and developments which face organisations; especially showing how these are shaped by, and often need to overcome, past and present organisational and managerial practices.

The one clear theme which runs throughout is that change – both stand-alone and radical – has been, and will continue to be, an ever-present feature of organisational life. This presents management, especially at the senior level, with its most important task: to identify and achieve successfully the changes necessary for their organisations to function efficiently, effectively and competitively in the rapidly changing environment of the 1990s and beyond. This last, and concluding, chapter will examine the ability of managers to achieve this.

Most importantly, it must be appreciated that while managerial competence is a basic requirement for achieving successful change, this alone is not enough. Rather, managers' efforts are constrained or facilitated by their own personal beliefs and values, and the culture of the organisation in which they operate. Indeed, to create the type of flexible, dynamic and effective organisations that are required in the 1990s, creating the right organisational culture is a prime task of management, and one of the major changes they have to effect.

This investigation of change management concludes by identifying, and showing a way out of, the major dilemma that this task creates for organisations and managers. Most managers have been trained and work in organisations whose structures and cultures still owe much to the work of Taylor and the other Classical theorists. As a result, many managers, whilst recognising the need for change, are extremely reluctant to give their staff additional flexibility, autonomy and skills. Yet, unless they make such changes, their organisations are unlikely to reach the required level of competitiveness. Therefore, in order to achieve organisational success, managers must change their attitudes and beliefs. The key method for achieving this will be management development programmes which imbue managers with the knowledge and skills necessary to judge the appropriateness of their own, and their organisations', attitudes and beliefs. Managers must accept that it is their responsibility, and no one else's, to develop the abilities necessary to bring success. If they do not, they run the real risk of either their own career or their organisation suffering terminal decline. Consequently, managing change, in many cases, will mean changing managers – by developing them if possible or replacing them if necessary.

The manager's role

Definitions

It has never been easy to define the role of managers, though this has not prevented a great number of attempts to do so over the years (Barnard, 1938; Brewer and Tomlinson, 1964; Carlson, 1951; Constable and McCormick, 1987; Handy *et al.* 1987; Horne and Lupton, 1965; Kotter, 1982; Mintzberg, 1973 and 1975; Silverman and Jones, 1976; Stewart, 1976). As Hales (1986) found when he reviewed many of these studies, the information available presents managers, and others, with a confusing and conflicting picture of what managers should do and how they should do it.

Definitions of the role of a manager have ranged from attempts to list basic tasks:

> *[The manager] plans, organises, directs and controls, on proprietors' or own behalf, an industrial, commercial or other*

undertaking, establishment or organisation, and co-ordinates the
work of departmental managers or other immediate subordinates.
(Dakin and Hamilton, 1990:32)

to more ambitious attempts to define the essence of the manager's
role:

[The manager has the] task of creating a true whole that is larger
than the sum of its parts, a productive entity that turns out more
than the sum of the resources put into it. (Drucker, 1985:53)

Drucker (1985) also likened the manager to the conductor of a sym-
phony orchestra. As conductor, the manager is the one through whose
effort, vision and leadership the various instrumental parts, that are
so much noise by themselves, become the living whole of music. In
this instance, the manager is also the composer as well as the conductor.

Handy (1986), in contrast, likened the manager to a general practitioner: the manager is the first recipient of problems. The manager's
role is, therefore, to identify the symptoms in any situation; to diagnose the disease or cause of the trouble; to decide how it might be
dealt with, through a strategy for health; and to start the treatment.

Such analogies are useful in that they create a picture of the manager's role, but they can also be misleading. Conducting is an art
form; is management an art form? Or, as Handy's analogy implies, is
it a science in the same way that medicine is a science? As Part One of
this book showed, the clash between those who see management as a
rational, science-based process, and those who believe it to be more intuitive and less rational, is not new.

Duncan (1975) tried to resolve this conflict by taking a holistic view
of the job of the manager. He identifies three distinct levels of management activity: *philosophical* (goal formation); *scientific* (goal
accomplishment and evaluation); and *art* (implementation of decisions).
At the philosophical level, in forming goals the manager, Duncan argues, is mainly concerned with the effects of the actions and reactions
of other individuals and groups within the wider economic and social
context within which the organisation is set. At this level, managers
and their associates formulate clear and precise strategies that will
encompass all envisaged effects that can result from the set goals, not
only on the various pressure groups within its internal and external
environment, but also on competitors and regulatory agencies. It is
also at this level that the ethics of managerial behaviour, values and
priorities of the organisation are formulated and established. At the

scientific level, management develops plans, methods and techniques for achieving set goals, and establishes procedures for monitoring and evaluating progress.

The 'art' level is concerned with the implementation of decisions; this is the level at which tactical and administrative decisions are made to deploy the organisation's resources and attain the optimum degree of operational efficiency. This level is an 'art' because, according to Duncan, there appears to be a particular talent necessary to persuade others that management-generated goals and decisions should be accepted.

Whilst not necessarily agreeing with his definitions, especially in terms of strategy formulation, Duncan's three-level approach is extremely useful in that it shows, as Mullins (1989) argues, that management is both a science and an art. By its very nature, management is forced to deal with both rational, science-based activities, such as the design and operation of manufacturing systems, and less rational, more intuitive activities, especially those concerning managing and motivating people. The extent to which a manager is involved in any of these activities, however, will depend on the kind of organisation the manager works for, the type of job the manager has and, crucially, the manager's level in the organisation's hierarchy (Hales, 1986). Position in the hierarchy, formally at least, is likely to exert the greatest influence on the role given to and expected of the manager. The three main hierarchical levels are:

- *Top management* – the policy-making group responsible for the overall direction of the company.
- *Middle management* – responsible for the execution and interpretation of policies throughout the organisation and for the successful operation of assigned divisions or departments.
- *First level or supervisory management* – directly responsible to the middle management group for ensuring the execution of policies by their subordinates. They are also responsible for the attainment of objectives by the units they control, through practices and procedures approved and issued by top or middle management.

Superficially, at least, these three categories appear to mirror Duncan's three levels. However, on a closer examination, it becomes more difficult to match them because each category can encompass all three levels. This can be seen more clearly by examining what it is that managers actually do, as averse to what academics say they should do.

How managers spend their time

There have been a number of important studies conducted to determine how managers spend their time (Brewer and Tomlinson, 1964; Child and Ellis, 1973; Kotter, 1982). Perhaps the most widely known and duplicated work in this area is by Mintzberg (1973 and 1975). Synthesising his results and the previous research on the role of managers, he concluded that:

- Although much managerial work is unprogrammed, all managers do have regular, ordinary duties to perform.
- Rather than being systematic, reflective thinkers and planners, managers simply respond to the pressures or demands of their jobs.
- Managerial activities are characterised by brevity, variety and discontinuity.
- Managers' jobs are remarkably similar and their work can be described in terms of three very important roles: interpersonal, informational and decision making.

Interpersonal roles

The three key functions in this respect are as follows:

- *Figurehead* – as the formal representative of the organisation;
- *Liaison* – forming connections with other organisations;
- *Leader* – in relation to members of a group within the organisation.

Informational roles

Those in managerial positions have unique opportunities to obtain and disseminate information. The three key functions involved are as follows:

- *Monitor* – as monitors, managers seek, receive and store information which can be used to the advantage of the company;
- *Disseminator* – the manager must broadcast this useful information to the organisation;
- *Spokesperson* – on behalf of the organisation, the manager communicates information to other relevant groups and bodies, both internal and external.

Decision-making roles

A key part of any manager's job is to take decisions. In this respect, the manager is required to fulfil the following roles:

- *Entrepreneur* – looking for ways to improve the operation of the organisation or for new product/market opportunities;
- *Disturbance-handler* – managers must handle crises effectively;
- *Resource allocator* – responsible for constructing budgets and allocating resources;
- *Negotiator* – according to Mintzberg, managers spend a great deal of their time as negotiators, because only they have the necessary information and the authority to carry out this role.

Mintzberg (1975) argues that differences in the roles of managers are due to the relative importance of the roles at different hierarchical levels and in different functional specialities. He contends that Chief Executive Officers (CEOs), for example, focus considerable attention on external roles like liaison, spokesperson and figurehead, that link the organisation to its work environment. At lower levels, work is more focused, more short term in outlook, and the characteristics of brevity and fragmentation are more pronounced. As a result of this, the external managerial roles are less important, and real-time internal roles (disturbance-handler and negotiator) concerned with daily operating problems and maintaining the work flow become relatively more important. Furthermore, he maintains that interpersonal roles are more important to sales managers; staff managers give more attention to informational roles; and production managers attend to decisional roles. Mintzberg's observations have been supported by a number of other studies (Kotter, 1982; Silverman and Jones, 1976; Stewart, 1976).

Hales (1986:102), in reviewing the research on the manager's role, concluded that:

> *Much of what managers do is, of necessity, an unreflective response to circumstances. The manager is less a slow and methodical decision maker, more a 'doer' who has to react rapidly to problems as they arise, 'think on his feet', take decisions in situ and develop a preference for concrete activities. This shows in the pace of managerial work and the short time span of most activities ...*

Therefore, in examining the role of managers, it can be seen that there is a discrepancy between the literature detailing what managers should do and what the managers actually do. Indeed, as Mintzberg (1975:49) pointed out, this discrepancy even extends to managers' own observations on their role:

> *If you ask a manager what he does, he will most likely tell you he plans, organizes, co-ordinates and controls. Then watch what he does. Don't be surprised if you can't relate what you see to those four words.*

However, the above discussion to an extent deals with the past and not the future. Not only have organisations and the role of managers changed considerably in the last 200 years but, according to Handy (1989) and others, they will change even more dramatically in the next few years. Kanter (1989) argued that archetypical images of managers tend to derive from two basic models: the 'corpocrat' and the 'cowboy'. The former is the corporate bureaucrat, the conservative re-source preserver who lives by, and controls the organisation, through established and detailed rules. The latter, the 'cowboy', is a maverick who challenges the established order, who wants to seize every oppor-tunity, question every rule and who motivates and controls through personal loyalty. Kanter (1989:361) argues that in future organisa-tions will require managers who combine the best of both the corpo-crat and cowboy:

> *Without the bold impulses of the take-action entrepreneurs and their constant questioning of the rules, we would miss one of the most potent sources of business revitalization and development. But without the discipline and coordination of conventional man-agement, we could find waste instead of growth, unnecessary risk instead of revitalization.*

Managerial competence in practice

A review of the case studies

It is the responsibility of management to create the strategic frame-work within which desired changes are identified and prioritised. Chapter 5 illustrated very clearly the difficulty this poses. The case of both ING and FFT highlighted two important lessons for management with regard to developing and implementing strategies successfully.

The first lesson is that strategy development and execution is es-sentially a long-term process. In ING's case, the strategy has de-veloped and been consistently implemented over 20 to 30 years. At

FFT, the period has been shorter, a mere decade, but the strategy arose from the need to awaken 'the sleeping giant'; this required a long-term and consistent approach from management.

The second lesson arises from this. Sometimes it appears to be beyond the competence or willingness of a company's management either to undertake the scale of change necessary or to pursue a change policy consistently for the necessary time period. In such instances, as with FFT, a change of management at the most senior level may be required.

It appeared to be the case at PCI that a change of senior management was required to overcome its perceived shortcomings. However, merely changing the Chief Executive proved insufficient to do this. Despite the new Chief Executive's best efforts to change the company, he failed: partly because he did not carry his team with him, and partly because of his early departure. Clearly the two were related, though whether success would have come if he had stayed longer is difficult to say. Nevertheless, it does reinforce the point made above that strategic change is an essentially long-term process and requires consistency and commitment from management.

The PCI case also shows the importance of teamwork, or rather the problems caused when it is lacking. The case of Seaside Biscuits makes the same point in a positive fashion. The managers there were a disparate and individualistic group, until they took part in an Action Learning exercise designed to develop a company strategy. Not only did they construct a strategic plan, but in the process came to work as a team and developed a strong common view of what they needed to do. Therefore, the same people who had disagreed about what should and could be done were transformed. They found that once common agreement was reached, changes that seemed impossible or not worthwhile were suddenly both available and beneficial.

On the surface, therefore, the four case studies of strategic management in Chapter 5 bear out the argument that the role and competence of management constitute the key factor in successfully managing change. Certainly, the case of PCI would appear to indicate that somewhere, whether it be the new CEO, his management team or the level of management above him, there was a failure initially to identify the company's real problems and then to tackle them effectively. In the same way, FFT could be portrayed as a company where more competent management replaced less competent management. Following this line of argument, ING could be viewed as an organisation where management competence was a continuing trait which the company nurtured and prized.

However, how does such an argument account for Seaside Biscuits' experience? The company did not change its management, but there was a noticeable and crucial change in the effectiveness of senior managers, brought about by a change in their attitude. Unless Seaside Biscuits is an anomaly, which is always a possibility, then either management competence is not the key issue in managing change, or competence needs to be viewed in a wider context than just the attributes of individual managers. This is an important, if not crucial, issue which will now be explored further by examining the case studies in Chapters 7 and 8.

The case studies in Chapter 7 related to changes which were necessary in order to achieve the companies' strategic objectives; though, as Pope Vehicles revealed, just because a change arises for strategic reasons, success is not guaranteed. However, it is interesting to note that in the case of G K Printers, a management which appeared to have drifted along for some years was suddenly galvanised into developing and successfully implementing a pro-active strategic plan. This is not to say that the company's management had been incompetent in the past, but like those at FFT it had certainly been passive.

At G K, unlike the companies in Chapter 8, the changes which took place were not blind or copying actions but the product of a well-thought-out strategic plan. As with Seaside Biscuits, an event took place, in this instance the threat of closure, which transformed a hitherto passive management into one which developed a talent for strategic thinking and managing change. What changed was the managers' perceptions of what could and should be done. As with Seaside Biscuits, there was a change of attitude amongst the managers, aided by the workforce, which created the conditions for their innate competence to flourish. It should also be noted that none of the people at G K were professional managers in the sense that they had received formal management training; all, apart from a later recruit, had grown up with the business.

At Dolphin Electronics managers, and the great majority of staff, were highly trained, as opposed to the situation at G K. This was reflected in their attitude towards each other and the company's commitment to training and education. The competence of the management at Dolphin was evident in the way they both planned the company's future and executed change projects. This is not to say they were always totally successful. In the case study it can be seen that they fell short of their objective, but they knew why they had failed and what needed to be done to rectify the situation.

In many respects there are strong similarities between Dolphin Electronics and Pope Vehicles, in terms of the professionalism of staff and their approach to strategic planning. Yet, management at Pope, in effect, sabotaged their own success by failing to consult and involve those affected by the introduction of CAD; staff were taken for granted and their justified concerns ignored. This was compounded by a lack of senior management involvement in, and oversight of, the change project, despite its apparent strategic importance. Pope did not totally fail in its aims, but progress was far slower and the end product much less satisfactory than the company had, correctly, expected.

In examining the competence displayed by the managers in the case studies in Chapter 7, what is striking is that it appears to have been higher in G K than at Pope. Indeed, in terms of what was actually achieved, it could be argued that G K's management performed better than managers at Dolphin Electronics. However, what is noticeable at both these companies, in contrast with Pope Vehicles, is that they are people-centred, rather than technology-centred – people are seen as their biggest asset. Once again, the issue of effectiveness appears to have less to do with management competence per se, and is more concerned with approach, attitude and perhaps, culture.

Chapter 8 presented three studies of change projects which, unlike those in Chapter 7, were not driven by strategy or overall objectives. Indeed, none of the companies practised strategic management, and all had difficulty in identifying and prioritising the types of changes they needed to make in order to enhance their competitiveness. Also, unsurprisingly, they all experienced serious difficulties in carrying out change projects. Nevertheless, the companies were of a size to attract competent managers, and indeed possessed them.

Fort Vehicles had competent and experienced management. However, the process of introducing their new manufacturing equipment was very badly handled. The company may have been correct in its assertion that it vitally needed such equipment (though in the absence of any strategic overview it is difficult to evaluate this assertion), but this was not reflected in the way it was introduced. Its task was not made easier by their owner's decision to transfer the equipment at short notice. However, the way Fort responded to the situation, as though the new equipment was an inconvenience which would go away if ignored, borders on the unbelievable.

The actions of MEW also have elements of unreality about them. To commit the expenditure of large sums of money on what could be construed as a whim or guesswork, is difficult to comprehend. Then to handle the introduction and use of the CAD/CAM system as MEW did – without consulting users, putting the system in a separate department – is also baffling. Yet the strangest twist of all was the decision to get rid of the system after so much money, time and effort had been poured into it.

Certainly, this does appear to be a clear case of managerial incompetence. But, on past performance, the same managers appear to have been very competent in building up the company. It is true that they operated in a 'soft' market; however, so did their competitors, many of whom achieved less than MEW. The key issues in MEW's case emerge as its fatalistic attitude – 'what will be, will be' seems to have been its management's motto – and its addiction to fire-fighting immediate problems, rather than taking a more considered and strategic approach, which might have eliminated the source of so many of these problems. Both these attitudes are clearly reflected in the CAD/CAM situation. 'Get the system in and then we'll sort it out' seems to have been the basis of MEW's pre-introduction planning. Then, when it eventually became evident that this approach had failed, the fatalism emerged: 'We did our best but circumstances were against us' was the management's refrain.

Similar attitudes can be detected in the Global Financial Services case study. The company viewed reacting to events and copying the opposition as perfectly suitable procedures. Likewise it saw nothing amiss in its attitude towards staff in the Financial Services Division; they were considered second-class citizens who needed strong management to keep them working effectively. It was this approach to change and staff which led Global to spend £300,000 on a computer system which was supposed to improve the company's image with its customers and give it better control over staff. That neither seems to have been achieved was not, apparently, considered to be a cause for alarm or concern by senior managers. If this is so, the management of Global can surely be accused of incompetence; or can they?

Another explanation is that the main issue at Global, and in the other companies, is not management competence as such. Rather, it is whether or not the environment in which the managers operate allows them to deploy their competence effectively. As can be seen from all the case studies, what prevented success in some of the companies, and aided it in others, was the attitude and values – culture – of the individual organisations. It was their organisation's culture which allowed some managers to work effectively and others less so, rather than their individual competence. Undoubtedly management competence is important but, as argued below, the effectiveness of individuals and groups depends to a large extent on the culture of the organisation in which they operate.

Organisational culture

Putting the discussions above into perspective, it can be seen that managers do not perform their duties in a vacuum. Their work and the way it is done are governed, directed and tempered by a set of values, beliefs, customs and systems which they – or those above them – create and sustain. Organisations, as noted by Silverman (1970), are societies in miniature. Therefore, if they are 'little societies', they can be expected to show evidence of their own cultural characteristics. However, culture does not spring up automatically and fully formed from the whims of management. Allaire and Firsirotu (1984) argued that it is the product of a number of different influences: the ambient society's values and characteristics, the organisation's history and past leadership, and factors such as industry and technology.

Culture, as Eldridge and Crombie (1974:78) state, refers 'to the unique configuration of norms, values, beliefs, ways of behaving and so on, that characterise the manner in which groups and individuals combine to get things done.' Culture defines how those in the organisation should behave in a given set of circumstances. It affects all, from the most senior manager to the humblest clerk. Their actions are judged by themselves and others in relation to expected modes of behaviour. Culture legitimises certain forms of action and proscribes other forms.

This view is supported by Turner (1971) who observed that cultural systems contain elements of 'ought' which prescribe forms of behaviour or allow behaviour to be judged acceptable or not. However, culture is not static: as the external and internal factors which influence culture change, so culture will change. But given that culture is locked into the beliefs, values and norms of each individual in the organisation, and because these are difficult constructs to alter, cultural change will be slow, unless perhaps there is some major shock to the organisation. Therefore, situations will arise where an organisation's culture may be out of step with changes that are taking place in the structure and practices of the organisation. In this situation, rather than facilitating the efficient operation of the organisation, it may obstruct it. As Handy (1986:188) commented:

> *Experience suggests that a strong culture makes a strong organisation, but does it matter what sort of culture is involved? Yes, it*

*does. Not all cultures suit all purposes or people. Cultures are
founded and built over the years by the dominant groups in an
organisation. What suits them and the organisation at one stage
is not necessarily appropriate for ever – strong though that culture may be.*

In addition, Salaman (1979) pointed out that whilst there may be a
dominant culture in an organisation, just like the ambient society,
there will also be sub-cultures. These may be peculiar to the organisation or may cut across organisations. An example of the latter are professional groups, such as accountants, who have their own norms,
customs, values and traditions which are peculiar to their profession
rather than to the organisations that employ them. This may also be
the case with other white- and blue-collar staff. These sub-cultures
will exist in a complex and potentially conflicting relationship with
the dominant culture. However, if that dominant culture is seen by
some groups to have lost its appropriateness (and thus legitimacy),
then potential conflicts can become actual conflicts. The reverse can
also be the case; cultural values and methods of operation which one
group adopts may be seen as out of step with 'the way we've always
done things'. This in turn can lead to an undermining of the authority
of managers and specialists – endangering the efficient operation of
the organisation. This is particularly likely to be the case where radical change is taking place. Many companies, such as GKN, Black &
Decker and the Rover Group, have been and are restructuring
themselves to increase their competitiveness in the face of growing international competition, especially from the Japanese. However,
unless they also make compatible changes in their culture, the results
could be less favourable than they expect.

Handy (1986) attempted to categorise types of culture and how
these relate to particular organisational forms. Two of the main types
of culture he identified are role and task. A role culture is appropriate
to bureaucracies, organisations with mechanistic, rigid structures and
narrow jobs. Such cultures stress the importance of procedures and
rules, hierarchical position and authority, and security and predictability. In essence, role cultures create situations in which those in
the organisation stick rigidly to their job description (role) and any exceptions are passed on to the next layer up in the hierarchy.

Task cultures, on the other hand, are job- or project-orientated; the
onus is on getting the job in hand (the task) done rather than prescribing how it should be done. Such types of culture are appropriate to
organically-structured organisations where flexibility and teamwork
are encouraged. Task cultures create situations in which speed of

reaction, integration and creativity are more important than adherence to particular rules or procedures, and where position and authority are less important than the individual contribution to the task in hand.

It follows from this, as argued earlier, that individual competence and effectiveness should be viewed in terms of the context and culture of the particular organisation in which they are deployed.

In mechanistically-structured organisations with role cultures, an individual's competence will be judged in terms of how well they perform within the confines of their role – whether he or she sticks to the rules. In an organically-structured organisation with a task culture, competence and effectiveness will be judged by results rather than methods. Someone judged effective in a mechanistically-structured organisation may not be judged so in an organically-structured one if they continue to operate in the same way as before, or vice versa.

Similarly, in organisations in transition, where the culture is out of step with structure and policies, different groups may adopt contradictory views of effectiveness. In these situations, there is likely to be no commonly agreed view of who is or is not effective or competent. Nor is it just a matter of opinion. Clearly, practices and procedures which work in one situation will not, possibly because of resistance or non-cooperation, work in another. Perhaps this is the worst situation of all, where organisations are in transition and old ways are being discredited but new ones have yet to gain legitimacy.

Changing circumstances, whether this be competitive pressure, the emergence of new technologies or products, or the entry into, and exit from, the organisation of individuals or groups, all contribute in a complex and unpredictable manner to the evolution of culture and changes in structures. These changes are inevitable (and probably necessary to sustain the organisation) but they can lead to conflict between the old and the new, and between groups and individuals who have to adjust to them. If change is too fast or causes too great a disjuncture, then rather than sustaining the organisation, it will lead to a disintegration of the common goals and ways of working which have previously existed. This can result in sectional groupings, who previously acquiesced to their own cultures being subsumed by the dominant culture, beginning to pursue what they see as the best practices in the new situation. This is not to deny the ever-present nature of organisational politics, but to argue that, in the absence of a dominant culture, groups and individuals will pursue their own interests more vigorously, and their actions will no longer be constrained by having to be legitimised in relation to that culture.

This emphasises the necessity for each organisation to achieve harmony between structure and culture and ensure that both are compatible with its strategic needs. For many organisations, though by no
means all, this will mean developing flexible, organic structures allied
to what Handy (1986) refers to as task-orientated cultures. However,
this is unlikely to be easy. Campbell and Warner (1988) testified to
the continuing influence of Taylorism, arguing that it has become the
major influence on managerial practice in the Anglo-Saxon world.
McGregor (1960) argued that managers hold one of two basic views of
human nature; either they subscribe to Theory X – which is akin to
the Tayloristic view – or they subscribe to Theory Y – which is akin to
the organic/task view. Nevertheless, like Campbell and Warner, he
believed it was the negative view of human nature, the Tayloris-
tic/Theory X view, which dominated. Nor are they alone in this, many
researchers, over the years, have come to a similar conclusion (Kelly,
1982; Littler, 1978; Locke, 1982; Mumford, 1979; Rose, 1988). Therefore, attempts to develop and adopt new, non-Tayloristic structures
and cultures may fail at the first hurdle, because they will meet with
managerial resistance and rejection.

The implications for managers

As already argued, organisations need to recognise that changing circumstances may require the adoption of new structures and practices.
At present, increased uncertainty, changes in technology, and changes
in organisational size are all combining to push organisations towards
more flexible structures and jobs in order to be efficient and effective.
The result of these changes can be that in some organisations the
existing culture is in conflict with its competitive needs. Therefore, as
argued by Burnes (1991), in such cases the relationship between
structure and culture needs to be restored to a mutually supportive
one, if the organisations are to operate efficiently and effectively.

The significance of this for managers is profound. For not only are
managers going to find that their competence and effectiveness may
be judged differently than in the past, but also that they are the
people responsible for managing the changes taking place and restor-
ing the balance between structure and culture. Nor is this just an
issue in organisations going through major transitions: even managers in stable organisations have to bear this in mind.

The implications of the relationship between structure and culture
for organisational change are twofold. Firstly, individual change

projects in stable organisations must be in tune with the existing structure–culture nexus; otherwise they will meet with resistance and rejection, because they will be seen as inappropriate and lacking legitimacy by the majority of the members of the organisation. Secondly, it may well be, as argued earlier, that the real problem is that the structure–culture nexus which served an organisation well in the past is no longer appropriate or effective in its present circumstances. In such a situation, radical rather than incremental change is required. But attempts to change only the structure – which is the easier option – without compensating changes in culture are likely only to add to uncertainty, friction and conflict rather than resolve it.

The obvious answer, of course, is for changes in structure and culture to take place simultaneously. According to some writers (Cummings and Huse, 1989; Robbins, 1986), this may be feasible. However, when viewed more closely, it can be argued that the core elements of culture are embedded deep in people's consciousness and cannot easily or quickly be changed. In an organisational context, changing the deep-seated values and beliefs that govern the working of an entire group of people must, of necessity, require the conviction, commitment and active support of senior management.

However, the difficulty with this, as argued above, is that culture is created, promoted and nurtured by these same senior managers, and it is a product of a number of influences such as the organisation's history, past leadership, industry and technology (Allaire and Firsirotu, 1984). In fact, according to Schein (1985), the only thing of real importance that managers do is to create and manage culture, and the unique talent of leaders is their ability to work with culture. What these observations signify for managers, therefore, is a culture change dilemma, in that they are the ones most likely to have been fully inculcated with the existing culture, which is consequently the governing factor in their ways of feeling, thinking and acting. To demand a change from them is to require of them a whole new philosophy of life, and for most people – especially those who have spent most of their adult life in learning and gaining experience at work – this demand is usually painful. Personal uncertainty is unbalancing, and many people, especially those in a position of power, will resist change which threatens to disturb their state of equilibrium.

Research has shown (Block, 1981; Bryant, 1979; Lawrence, 1973; Smith et al. 1982) that there are certain individuals who are particularly likely to resist the types of changes (in beliefs, attitudes and behaviour) associated with creating new cultures. These are people who rely heavily on their own personal experience in making decisions, who assume that prior conditions will continue to prevail, who take the position that there is always one best way of doing things, and who have little propensity to take risks. When in a managerial position, such people tend to adopt the characteristics of, to use Kanter's (1989) terms, the corpocrat rather than the cowboy. On the other hand, there are those, Kanter's cowboys, who are more inclined to be innovative, and who actively seek to make changes.

However, it has already been argued that in Anglo-Saxon countries, such as Britain, the more conservative and less innovative (Tayloristic) type of manager tends to be more prevalent. It would also seem reasonable to assume that this is especially likely to be the case in organisations whose cultures and structures no longer equip them for the environments and markets in which they operate. (The more innovative type of manager is less likely to have allowed such a situation to occur, because she/he would have been more inclined to take action to develop and change the structure–culture nexus in order to maintain its appropriateness.) The dominance of the corpocrat-type manager who resists change is perhaps the reason why many instances of cultural change appear to require the removal of a large proportion of senior executives before progress can be made (Cummings and Huse, 1989). However, as with FFT and PCI, such managerial changes are only likely to occur in a crisis situation (Grinyer *et al.* 1988) and, therefore, for most companies who are not in such a situation, the replacement of senior managers in order to facilitate radical change is possibly not an option.

The presence of managers who are deeply imbued with, and committed to, an organisation's existing culture is one of the main reasons why there is considerable debate as to whether something as deepseated as culture can be changed, at least in the short term (Frost *et al.* 1985). For example, Meek (1988:469) argued that:

> *Culture as a whole cannot be manipulated, turned on and off, although it needs to be recognised that some [organisations] are in a better position than others to influence aspects of it ... Culture should be regarded as something an organisation 'is', not something it 'has': it is not an independent variable nor can it be created, discovered or destroyed by the whims of management.*

This may be the reason why many of those advocating culture change tend to focus on its surface elements, such as norms and artifacts, and also why categorisations and definitions of culture tend to be very sketchy and difficult to put into practice (Handy, 1986; Peters and Waterman, 1982; Robbins, 1986). It should be said, however, that successful cases of cultural change have been reported. In these instances, the process appears to have been fraught with difficulties and taken anything from six to 16 years to achieve (Uttal, 1983). Nevertheless, difficult though it may be to change, organisational culture is crucial to the effectiveness of managers and all other groups, and, therefore, one of the key tasks of management is to create, sustain and, if necessary, reconstruct an appropriate culture for their organisation (Handy, 1986; Schein, 1985).

Conclusions: culture and competence

As this chapter has argued, the willingness and ability of organisations to develop and implement strategy-driven change programmes is dependent on the nature of their existing culture, and the competence and receptiveness of their management, particularly at the most senior level. Given the earlier discussion of these, it would appear that many organisations will need to make substantial changes both in their cultures and in their management if they are to survive and prosper. Such changes are not be treated as separate from, or as precursors to, a strategy-driven change programme; rather they must be seen as an integral and vital part of such a programme. Nevertheless, it is crucial that these two aspects of such a change programme, above all, are well thought out and implemented.

Changing culture

There are some writers, of whom Peters and Waterman (1982) are the prime example, who take a very prescriptive view of changing culture: all that is necessary, they imply, is for organisations to accept their (i.e. Peters and Waterman's) recommendations as to the type of culture that is required for success. Once their formula has been accepted as the goal, all the organisation has to do is to imbue their members with it. However, this approach has been criticised as being simplistic and putting forward recommendations which are far too general to be of use to individual organisations (Gordon, 1985; Hassard and Sharifi, 1989; Nord, 1985: Uttal, 1983).

Schein (1985) takes a more considered and organisation-specific approach. He believes that before any attempt is made to change an organisation's culture, it is first necessary to understand the nature of its existing culture and how this is sustained. According to Schein, this can be achieved by analysing the values that govern behaviour, and uncovering the underlying and often unconscious assumptions which determine how those in the organisation think, feel and react. Difficult though he acknowledges this is, he argues that it can be achieved by:

- Analysing the process of recruitment and induction for new employees.
- Analysing responses to critical incidents in the organisation's history, as these are often translated into unwritten, but nevertheless very strong, rules of behaviour.
- Analysing the beliefs, values and assumptions of those who are seen as the guardians and promoters of the organisation's culture.
- Discussing the findings from the above with those in the organisation, and paying especial attention to anomalies or puzzling features which have been observed.

Schein's approach, therefore, is to treat culture as an adaptable and tangible learning process. His approach emphasises the way in which an organisation communicates its culture to new recruits. It illustrates how assumptions are translated into values and how values influence behaviour. Schein seeks to understand the mechanisms used to propagate culture, and how new values and behaviours are learned. Once this mechanism is uncovered, he argues, it can then form the basis of a strategy to change the organisation's culture.

Schwartz and Davis (1981), on the other hand, adopt a different stance with regard to culture. They suggest that when an organisation is considering any form of change, it should compare the strategic significance (the importance to the organisation's future) of the change with the cultural resistance that attempting to make the particular change will meet. They term this the 'cultural risk' approach. They offer a step-by-step method for identifying the degree of cultural risk involved in any particular change project. From this, they argue, it is then possible for an organisation to decide with a degree of certainty whether to ignore the culture, manage round it, attempt to change the culture to fit the strategy, or change the strategy to fit the culture. Although Schwartz and Davis' method relies heavily on managerial judgment, they maintain that it makes for a methodical approach to identifying, at an early stage, the potential impact of strategic change on an organisation's culture, and vice versa.

It should, of course, be pointed out that though Schein's and Schwartz and Davis' approaches are different, this does not mean they are in conflict or are not compatible. Indeed, both could be considered as different aspects of the same task: deciding whether culture needs to be changed, and, if it does, in what way. However, this still begs the question: How can organisational culture be changed?

No one should dispute the difficulty of changing an organisation's culture. In discussing approaches to achieving this, Cummings and Huse (1989) identified what they considered to be the crucial steps necessary to bring about cultural change. These are as follows:

1 *A clear strategic vision* – effective cultural change should start from a clear vision of the firm's new strategy and of the shared values and behaviour needed to make it work. This vision provides the purpose and direction for cultural change.
2 *Top management commitment* – cultural change must be managed from the top of the organisation. Senior managers and administrators need to be strongly committed to the new values and the need to create constant pressure for change.
3 *Symbolic leadership* – senior executives must communicate the new culture through their own actions. Their behaviour needs to symbolise the kind of values and behaviour being sought. For example, at Nissan's UK car plant, all the directors have their desks in the same open-plan offices as their staff.
4 *Supporting organisational changes* – cultural change must be accompanied by supporting modifications in organisational structure, human resource systems, information and control systems, and management style. These organisational features can help to orientate people's behaviours to the new culture. As part of creating a new participative culture at Lucas Car Braking Systems, there has been radical restructuring of the company into mini factories, small work teams and the elimination of individual bonus payments.
5 *Selection and induction of newcomers and termination of those who cannot adapt to the new ways* – one of the most effective methods for changing culture is to change organisational membership. People can be selected and terminated in terms of their fit with the new culture. This is especially important in key leadership positions, where people's actions can significantly promote or hinder new values and behaviours. (Cummings and Huse, 1989:428–30.)

These five steps illustrate the symbiotic relationship between culture and structure in organisations. They also show how neither can be changed without a clear strategic vision. Therefore, whether an organisation sets out to create a new culture, or a new strategy which results in major and radical restructuring of the organisation, the inescapable fact is that all three – strategy, culture and structure – must be considered together.

In relation to culture, the work of Schein (1985), Schwartz and Davis (1981) and Cummings and Huse (1989) provides organisations with the guidelines and methods for evaluating the need for and managing cultural change. Schein's work shows how an organisation's existing culture, and the way it is reinforced, can be revealed. Schwartz and Davis' work shows how the need for cultural change can be evaluated and the necessary changes identified. Finally, the work of Cummings and Huse (1989) shows how cultural change can be implemented.

None of the above writers suggests that changing cultures is either an easy or short-term activity, however, they all argue that it is possible. Given that many organisations need to undertake major transformations in their structures, practices and cultures if they are to remain viable, the key question is not: 'Can they change their cultures?' but, 'Will they change their cultures?'

In a synthesis of the literature on organisational culture, Hassard and Sharifi (1989) came to a similar conclusion as the above writers with regard to the approach that organisations should adopt when changing culture. In particular, Hassard and Sharifi (1989:11) stress two crucial aspects of this process:

- Before a major [cultural] change campaign is commenced, senior managers must understand the implications of the new system for their own behaviour: and senior management must be involved in all the main stages preceding change.
- In change programmes, special attention must be given to the company's 'opinion leaders'.

Once again, this raises the role of managers, especially senior managers. If managers are in tune with and supportive of the proposed changes, a key element of successful cultural change will be in place. However, in many companies this may not be the case. It follows that in order to identify the need for and implement major organisational change, managers may need to alter radically the way they have operated in the past. In effect they need to change themselves, their value systems and beliefs, before they can change the rest of the organisation. Therefore, changing organisations and managing change cannot be seen in isolation from changing managers. Yet, from the case studies in this book, and from the history of organisational development outlined in Part One, it is clear that some managers find this almost impossible, and left to themselves will continue to do so. This raises the question of how organisations and managers can overcome this.

Changing managers

Changing managers, whether by replacement or development, is not an easy or certain task. One major obstacle to be overcome is identifying what it is that managers should be changed to. Kanter (1989) attempted to provide a guide to the attributes required of managers in the future, who she terms post-entrepreneurial managers. Kanter (1989:361–5) identified seven skills and sensibilities that this new breed of manager must cultivate:

> *First, they must learn to operate without the might of the hierarchy behind them. The crutch of authority must be thrown away and replaced by their own personal ability to make relationships, use influence, and work with others to achieve results.*
>
> *Second, they must know how to 'compete' in a way that enhances rather than undercuts co-operation. They must be oriented to achieving the highest standard of excellence rather than to wiping out the competition.*
>
> *Third, and related, [they] must operate with the highest ethical standards. While business ethics have always been important from a social and moral point of view, they also become a pragmatic requirement [of competitiveness].*
>
> *A fourth asset for [post-entrepreneurial managers] is to have a dose of humility sprinkled on their basic self-confidence, a humility that says that there are always new things to learn. Just as ... athletes must be willing to learn, willing to accept the guidance of coaches, constantly in training, and always alert to the possibility of an improvement in their techniques, so must [managers] be willing to learn.*
>
> *Fifth [they] must develop a process focus – a respect for the process of implementation as well as the substance of what is implemented. They need to be aware that how things are done is every bit as important as what is done.*
>
> *Sixth [they] must be multifaceted and ambidextrous, able to work across functions and business units to find synergies that*

multiply value, able to form alliances when opportune but to cut ties when necessary, able to swim equally effectively in the mainstream and in newstreams. There is no room for narrow or rigid people in the new business environment.

Seventh [this new breed of managers] must gain satisfaction from results and be willing to stake their own rewards on them. The accomplishment itself is really the only standard for [them].

Nevertheless, useful though such a list of characteristics may be, it still does not identify the methods that organisations, and managers themselves, can use to create managers who fit this new model. Whilst the case studies in Chapter 5 showed that some managers possessed the attributes to achieve continuing change in their organisations (ING), and that others could transform their own attitudes and beliefs (Seaside Biscuits), in other companies – FFT and PCI – the managers themselves had to be replaced. The difficulty that existing managers appear to face in changing cultures is borne out by research which has suggested that newly recruited executives are in a better position to change cultures than existing ones (Tushman and Virany, 1986). This was a point also made by Cummings and Huse (1989) above. The reason for this is obvious: some managers find it very difficult to give up the habits and beliefs which they have grown up with over a lifetime of management. New managers, recruited for the types of attitudes and beliefs which companies wish to promote, find it much easier to create new cultures because they do not carry the cultural baggage which existing managers do.

The message from this is clear. Managing change successfully does and will involve changing managers: either they will adopt new attitudes and value systems or they will be replaced by managers who can. It is a stark message, but one which is becoming increasingly evident throughout British industry (Grinyer *et al.* 1988): radical transformation of companies often means replacing their existing senior managers. Therefore, the challenge to managers at all levels, but especially at a senior level, is to create the organisational cultures which allow competence, whether it be managerial or technical, to flourish, and in doing this to change their own values and beliefs.

However, if the majority of organisations have managers who are imbued with inappropriate values and beliefs, as seems the case, where are the new managers to come from? If the managers with the desired traits and attitudes are in the minority, then in the short term or even the long term, replacing managers will not be an option for many companies. Many organisations will have to live with their existing managers. Unless companies are prepared to accept managers who are unequal to the challenges facing them, an alternative must be sought. The main, if not only, option is to develop, and so change, existing managers.

Perhaps because of the shortage of fully-grown and appropriate managerial talent, there has been a growing interest in management development in recent years (Sissons and Storey, 1988; Storey, 1989 and 1990). Indeed, both ING and FFT saw management development as an important part of their strategic plans.

Management development has been defined in a number of ways:

> ... *a conscious and systematic decision–action process to control the development of managerial resources in the organisation for the achievement of organisational goals and strategies. (Ashton et al. 1975:5)*

> ... *that function which, from deep understanding of business goals and organisational requirements, undertakes: (a) to forecast needs, skill mixes and profiles for many positions and levels; (b) to design and recommend the professional, career and personal development programmes necessary to ensure competence; (c) to move from the concept of 'management' to the concept of 'managing'. (Beckhard, 1985:22)*

> ... *an attempt to improve managerial effectiveness through a planned and deliberate learning process. (Mumford, 1987: 29)*

The above help to define management development, but they do not indicate what the objectives of such programmes are. To an extent this is understandable, given that different organisations will initiate such programmes for different reasons. However, it should be noted that more and more companies are pursuing management development as a key device for bringing about organisational change and, in particular, as a way to manage culture change and organisational renewal (Lippitt, 1982; Marsh, 1986; Morgan, 1988; Pearson, 1987; Storey, 1989).

If management development programmes are to be successful in developing effective managers and improving the performance of organisations, then it is self-evident not only that they will vary from company to company, but also that they will need to vary from individual to individual. This makes it important to determine the training needs of individual managers accurately, in order to ensure that it is these that determine the nature of the management development programme, rather than vice versa. Unfortunately, there is plenty of evidence that this is often not the case, and that management development programmes tend to be standard packages which everyone is sent on, regardless of how appropriate they are in relation to the needs of the individual and the objectives of the organisation that employs them (Mangham Working Party, 1987; Sissons, 1989; Storey, 1989; Thornberry, 1987).

Though there are many reasons why such programmes are inappropriate, the main problems appear to be twofold. Firstly, many organisations do not know sufficiently well what their strategic objectives are and, therefore, what they require of their managers in the future. The lack of strategic management in many organisations is an issue discussed at length earlier and requires no further elaboration here, except to say that, in its absence, organisations are prone to accept the latest managerial fashion which, no matter how appropriate as a general guide, is unlikely to match their exact needs. The above guidelines provided by Kanter (1989) fall into this category. They may or may not be an accurate generalisation of the post-entrepreneurial style of management; however, at best, they are only generalisations which need to be tempered by and adjusted to the needs of each organisation and each manager.

The second reason relates to the difficulty in assessing the needs of individual managers, and shaping these into a tailor-made programme of development and training. Whilst it is relatively easy to identify a manager's training requirements in terms of technical skills (such as accountancy, engineering, etc.), the difficulty comes in trying to identify the skills a manager needs in order to be an effective manager. This chapter has already shown that it is difficult to define the role of a manager and that, in any case, this will vary from organisation to organisation and will certainly change over time.

In order to overcome this second problem, some organisations are moving away from standard packages of off-the-job training, which some see as an expensive waste of time (Newstrom, 1985; Wilkinson and Orth, 1986), to more individually-tailored and job-related programmes. These types of personalised programmes have a number of common characteristics:

- The use of assessment and assessment centres to identify potential managers and the developmental needs of existing managers (Long, 1986).
- Regular coaching by a more senior manager, a mentor, to allow the manager to talk over problems and issues and learn from the experience of the senior manager (Willbur, 1987).

- Self-development, this appears to have come to the fore as a reaction to disappointing results from formal training courses. The purpose of self-development is to allow managers to identify and develop a programme to meet their own needs. Obviously, managers are more likely to feel that such a programme is better suited to their needs; they may consequently be more committed to it and may get more out of it than a standard programme (Burgoyne and Germaine, 1984).

As with all general developments, this move away from formal, off-the-job training programmes to more personalised, on-the-job programmes needs to be viewed critically. Certainly, drawbacks have been identified, particularly the need to avoid isolation if self-development is too heavily relied upon (Stuart, 1986). Also, as Storey (1989) pointed out in a major review of the management development literature, drawing a distinction between on-the-job and off-the-job training may miss the main issue, which is the requirement to assess development and training needs of individual managers accurately and to relate these to the organisation's strategic objectives.

Final note

It is clear from what has gone before that the role of managers in the 1990s and beyond will be significantly different from the past, at least in successful companies. To all intents and purposes, successful companies are rejecting, and will continue to reject, the rigid and negative views of human potential as put forward by the Classical school. Nor are they seeing their relations with the external world as necessarily deterministic or conflictual. Rather, they seek to develop partnerships both internally and externally. These partnerships are based on long-term strategic business needs and reflect a commitment to developing human potential rather than minimising it or replacing people with machines.

To achieve this requires new internal structures, practices and procedures and new types of external relationship; i.e. change on all fronts. Nor will these changes be one-off affairs or searches for permanent solutions. Rather, change will be continuous and dynamic – external and internal relationships, alliances and structures will form, operate and dissolve as competitive pressures and strategic necessity dictate.

However, fundamental to all this will be the need for changes in attitudes, beliefs and values – a change in culture – by all those concerned. As this chapter, and indeed the entire book has clearly shown, changes in structures are much easier to achieve than changes in culture, but without the latter, the former are likely to fail. Therefore, changing individual beliefs and organisational culture is crucial, but as many have recognised (Burnes, 1991; Cummings and Huse, 1989; Hassard and Sharifi, 1989; Kanter, 1989; Morgan, 1988), this can only be achieved by management, especially senior management. It is they who are the guardians of the organisation's culture, it is they who have the power and authority to initiate change, and it is they who must initiate and consistently support cultural change.

Yet, to state this one final time, here is the paradox. Those who are in the best position to change culture are also the ones most likely to be inculcated with the old ways and attitudes that pervade organisations. It is managers, especially senior ones, who create and sustain culture and perhaps they have the most to lose by changing it. Therefore, it may well be that management as a group are the ones who will most resist attempts to change culture. If this is the case, then ultimately they will either be replaced or their organisations will cease to exist. Neither of these are inevitable. Managers can change their attitudes and ways of working, and organisations can be transformed. However, this will not be achieved by imposing the latest managerial fashion or theory, significant and beneficial though these may be. Nor will it be achieved by managers copying 'successful' organisations; though there are important lessons that can be learnt from them. These types of action are essentially mindless copying and, as such, an abdication of managerial responsibility.

Managers owe an obligation to the other stakeholders in their organisations to examine their organisation and its needs consciously and systematically. In this they should draw on organisation theory. They should also examine what other organisations do. But they must recognise that all theories have their drawbacks and limitations, and that what works for one organisation in its particular situation may not, and probably will not, work for all organisations.

In the end, managers have to exercise judgment, and make choices. These choices then have to be implemented, monitored and, where necessary, adjusted or changed. Managers may, and indeed should, consult and involve outside experts and facilitators in managing change. Nevertheless, it is the responsibility of managers to make the choices and initiate the necessary changes. This requires skill, knowledge and commitment, but it starts with a recognition that change is continuous and cannot be avoided or sidestepped. Managers, therefore, have to take responsibility for equipping themselves with the knowledge and skills to deal with this. They have to accept that managing change is their responsibility and that the choices are theirs. Only in this way will they be able to develop strategic perspectives and complementary organisational cultures; and shape and reshape their organisations to compete in an increasingly competitive world.

Bibliography

Abell, D F (1977). *Using PIMS and Portfolio Analysis in Strategic Market Planning: A Comparative Analysis.* Intercollegiate Case Clearing House, Harvard Business School: Boston, Mass., USA.

Abell, P (1975). 'Organisations as technically constrained bargaining and influence systems.' In P Abell (ed): *Organisations as Bargaining and Influence Systems.* Heinemann: London.

Abodaher, D (1986). *Iacocca.* Star: London.

Allaire, Y, and Firsirotu, M E (1984). 'Theories of organizational culture.' *Organization Studies,* 5 (3), 193–226.

Anderson, C, and Paine, F (1978). 'PIMS: a re-examination.' *Academy of Management Review,* 3 (3), 602–12.

Andrews, K R (1980). *The Concept of Corporate Strategy.* Irwin: Homewood, Illinois, USA.

Ansoff, H I (1965). *Corporate Strategy.* McGraw-Hill: New York, USA.

Argenti, J (1974). *Systematic Corporate Planning.* Nelson: London.

Argyris, C (1970). *Intervention Theory and Method.* Addison-Wesley: Reading, Mass., USA.

Argyris, C (1973). 'Peter Blau.' In G Salaman and K Thompson (eds): *People and Organizations.* Longman: London.

Ashton, D; Easterby-Smith, M; and Irvine C (1975). *Management Development : Theory and Practice.* MCB: Bradford.

Ashton, T S (1948). *The Industrial Revolution 1760–1830.* Oxford University Press: Oxford.

Babbage, C (1835). *On the Economy of Machinery and Manufacture.* Knight: London.

Barnard, C (1938). *The Functions of the Executive.* Harvard University Press: Cambridge, Mass., USA.

Beach, S D (1980). *Personnel.* Macmillan: London.

Beckhard, R (1985). 'Whither management development?' *Journal of Management Development,* 4 (2).

Bell, R M (1974). *The behaviour of labour, technical change, and the competitive weakness of British manufacturing.* Technical Change Centre: London.

Bennett, R (1983). 'Management Research.' *Management Development Series* 20: Geneva.

Bennis, W G (1959). 'Leadership theory and administrative behaviour.' *Administrative Science Quarterly,* 4, 259–301.

Bennis, W G (1966). 'The coming death of bureaucracy.' *Think,* November-December, 30–5.

Bernstein, L (1968). *Management Development.* Business Books: London.

Bessant, J (1983). 'Management and manufacturing innovation: the case of information technology.' In G Winch (ed): *Information Technology in Manufacturing Processes.* Rossendale: London.

Bessant, J, and Haywood, B (1985). *The introduction of flexible manufacturing systems as an example of computer integrated manufacture.* Brighton Polytechnic: Brighton.

Bigge, L M (1982). *Learning Theories for Teachers.* Gower: Aldershot.

Blackler, F, and Brown, C (1986). 'Alternative models to guide the design and introduction of new information technologies into work organisations.' *Journal of Occupational Psychology,* 59 (4), 287–314.

Blake, R R, and Mouton, J S (1969). *Building a Dynamic Corporation Through Grid Organisation Development.* Addison-Wesley: Reading, Massachusetts, USA.

Blake, R R, and Mouton, J S (1976). *Organizational Change by Design.* Scientific Methods: Austin, Texas, USA.

Blau, P M (1970). 'The formal theory of differentiation in organizations.' *American Sociological Review,* 35, 201–18.

Blau, R M, and Schoenherr, R A (1971). *The Structure of Organizations.* Basic Books: New York, USA.

Block, P (1981). *Flawless Consulting: A Guide to Getting Your Expertise Used.* Learning Concepts: Austin, Texas, USA.

Bowers, D G, Franklin, J L, and Pecorella, P (1975). 'Matching problems, precursors and interventions in OD: a systematic approach.' *Journal of Applied Behavioural Science,* 11, 391–410.

Bowman, C, and Asch, D (1985). *Strategic Map.* Macmillan: London.

Bracker, J (1980). 'The historical development of the strategic management concept.' *Academy of Management Review,* 5 (2), 219–24.

Brewer, E, and Tomlinson, J W C (1964). 'The manager's working day.' *Journal of Industrial Economics,* 12, 191–7.

Bryant, D (1979). 'The psychology of resistance to change.' *Management Services,* March, 9–10.

Buchanan, D A (1984). 'The impact of technical implications and managerial aspirations on the organization and control of the labour process.' *Paper presented to the second Annual Conference on the Control and Organisation of the Labour Process.* UMIST/Aston, 28–30 March.

Buckley, W (1968). *Modern Systems and Research for the Behavioral Scientist.* Aldine Publishing: Chicago, USA.

Bullock, R J, and Batten, D (1985). 'It's just a phase we're going through: a review and synthesis of OD phase analysis.' *Group and Organization Studies,* 10, December, 383–412.

Burawoy, M (1979). *Manufacturing Consent: Changes in the Labour Process under Monopoly Capital.* University of Chicago Press: Chicago, USA.

Burgoyne, J and Germaine, C (1984). 'Self development and career planning: an exercise in mutual benefit.' *Personnel Management,* 16 (4), April, 21–3.

Burke, W, Michael, R S, Luthems, F, Odiorne, S, and Hayden, S (1981). *Techniques of Organisational Change.* McGraw-Hill: London.

Burke, W (1980). *Organisation Development.* Little, Brown and Co: Toronto, Canada.

Burnes, B (1988). *Strategy for Success: Case Studies in Advanced Manufacturing Technologies.* EITB: Watford.

Burnes, B (1989). *New Technology in Context.* Gower: Aldershot.

Burnes, B (1991). 'Managerial competence and new technology: don't shoot the piano player – he's doing his best.' *Behaviour and Information Technology,* 10 (2), 91–109.

Burnes, B, and Weekes, B (1989). *AMT: A Strategy for Success?* NEDO: London.

Burns, T, and Stalker, G M (1961). *The Management of Innovation.* Tavistock: London.

Butler, V G (1985). *Organisation and Management.* Prentice-Hall: London.

Byars, L L (1984). *Strategic Management: Planning and Implementation.* Harper and Row: London.

Campbell, A, and Warner, M (1988). 'Organization of new forms of manufacturing operations.' In M Wild (ed): *International Handbook of Production and Operations Management.* Cassells: London.

Carlson, S (1951). *Executive Behaviour.* Strombergs: Stockholm.

Chandler, A D (1962). *Strategy and Structure: Chapters in the History of American Industrial Enterprise.* MIT: Cambridge, USA.

Child, J (1972). 'Organizational structure, environment and performance: the role of strategic choice.' *Sociology,* 6 (1), 1–22.

Child, J (1984). *Organization.* Harper and Row: Cambridge.

Child, J, and Ellis, T (1973). 'Predictors of variation in managerial roles.' *Human Relations,* 26, 2, 227–250.

Clark, P (1972). *Action Research and Organisational Change.* Harper and Row: London.

Clegg, C W (1984). 'The Derivation of Job Design.' *Journal of Occupational Behaviour,* 5, 131–46.

Clegg, C W, and Symon, G (1991). 'Technology-led change: a case study of the implementation of CADCAM.' *Journal of Occupational Psychology,* 64 (4), 273–90.

Constable, J, and McCormick, R (1987). *The Making of British Managers.* British Institute of Management/Confederation of British Industry: London.

Crosby, P B (1979). *Quality is Free.* McGraw-Hill: New York, USA.

Cummings, T G, and Huse, E F (1989). *Organization Development and Change.* West: St Paul, Minnesota, USA.

Cuthbert, N (1970). 'Readings from Henri Fayol, General and Industrial Management.' In A Tillett, T Kempner and G Willis (eds): *Management Thinkers.* Pelican: Harmondsworth.

Dakin, S R, and Hamilton, R T (1990). 'How "general" are your general managers?' *Management Decision,* 28 (2), 32–7.

Dale, B G, and Cooper, C L (1992). *TQM and Human Resources: An Executive Guide.* Blackwell: Oxford.

Dastmalchian, A (1984). 'Environmental dependencies and company structure in Britain.' *Organization Studies,* 5 (3), 222–41.

Davis, R (1928). *The Principles of Factory Organization and Management.* Harper and Row: New York, USA.

Deming, W E (1982). *Quality Productivity and Competitive Position.* MIT Press: Cambridge, Mass., USA.

Dess, G G, and Davis, P S (1984). 'Porter's (1980) generic strategies as determinants of strategic group membership and original performance.' *Academy of Management Journal,* 27 (3), 467–88.

Drucker, P F (1974). *Management: Tasks, Responsibilities, Practices.* Harper and Row: London.

Drucker, P F (1985). *Innovation and Entrepreneurship.* Pan: London.

Duncan, W J (1975). 'Organisations as political coalitions: a behavioral view of the goal function process.' *Journal of Behavioral Economics,* 5, Summer, 25–44.

Dunphy, D D, and Stace, D A (1988). 'Transformational and coercive strategies for planned organizational change: beyond the OD model.' *Organization Studies,* 9 (3), 317–34.

Edwardes, M (1983). *Back from the Brink.* Collins: London.

Eldridge, J E T, and Crombie, A D (1974). *A Sociology of Organizations.* George Allen and Unwin: London.

Elliot, K, and Lawrence, P (1985). *Introducing Management.* Penguin: Harmondsworth.

Fawn, J, and Cox, B (1985). *Corporate Planning in Practice.* Strategic Planning Society: London.

Fayol, H (1949). *General and Industrial Management* (trans). Pitman: London.

Ford, T M (1981). 'Strategic planning – myth or reality? A chief executive's view.' *Long Range Planning,* 14, December, 9–11.

Fortune (1990). 'Global 500: The World's Biggest Industrial Corporations.' *Fortune,* July 30.

Fox, J M (1975). 'Strategic planning: a case study.' *Managerial Planning,* 23, May/June, 32–8.

Freeman, C (1988). 'The factory of the future: the productivity paradox, Japanese just-in-time and information technology.' *ESRC PICT Policy Research Paper 3.*

French, W L and Bell, C H (1984). *Organization Development.* Prentice-Hall: Englewood Cliffs, New Jersey, USA.

Frost, P, Moore, L, Louis, M, Lundberg, C, and Martin, J (eds) (1985). *Organizational Culture.* Sage: Beverly Hills, USA.

Gilbreth, F B, and Gilbreth, L M (1914). *Applied Motion Study.* Sturgis and Walton: New York, USA.

Glueck, W F (1978). *Business Policy and Strategic Management.* McGraw-Hill: New York, USA.

Gordon, G (1985). 'The relationship of corporate culture to industry sector and corporate performance.' In R Kilmann, M Saxton and R Serpa (eds): *Gaining Control of the Corporate Culture.* Jossey-Bass: San Francisco, USA.

Grant, A (1983). *Against the Clock.* Pluto: London.

Grinyer, P H, Mayes, D G, and McKiermon, P (1988). *Sharpbenders: The Secrets of Unleasing Corporate Potential.* Blackwell: Oxford.

Hales, C P (1986). 'What do managers do? A critical review of the evidence.' *Journal of Management Studies,* 22 (1), 88–115.

Hall, D T, and Nougaim, K E (1968). 'An examination of Maslow's need hierarchy in an organizational setting.' *Organizational Behaviour and Performance,* 3, February, 12–35.

Hamel, G, and Prahalad, C K (1989). 'Strategic intent.' *Harvard Business Review,* May–June, 63–76.

Handy, C (1986). *Understanding Organizations.* Penguin: Harmondsworth.

Handy, C (1989). *The Age of Unreason.* Arrow: London.

Handy, C, Gow, I, Gordon, C, Randlesome, C, and Moloney, M (1987). *The Making of a Manager.* NEDO: London.

Harrigan, R K (1980). *Strategy for Declining Businesses.* Lexington Books: Lexington, Mass., USA.

Harrison, R (1970). 'Choosing the depth of an organisational intervention.' *Journal of Applied Behavioural Science,* 6, 181–202.

Hassard, J, and Sharifi, S (1989). 'Corporate culture and strategic change.' *Journal of General Management,* 15 (2), 4–19.

Hax, C A, and Majluf, N S (1982). 'Competitive cost dynamics.' *Interfaces,* 12, October, 50–61.

Hax, C A, and Nicholson, S M (1983). 'The use of the growth share matrix in strategic planning.' *Interfaces,* 13, February, 46–60.

Heller, F (1970). 'Group feed-back analysis as a change agent.' *Human Relations,* 23 (4), 319–33.

Hendry, C (1979). 'Contingency Theory in practice, I.' *Personnel Review,* 8 (4), 39–44.

Hendry, C (1980). 'Contingency Theory in practice, II.' *Personnel Review,* 9 (1), 5–11.

Hickson, D J, Pugh, D S, and Pheysey, D C (1969). 'Operations technology and organisation structure: an empirical reappraisal.' *Administrative Science Quarterly,* 14, 378–97.

Hickson, D J, and Butler, R J (1982). 'Power and decision-making in the organisational coalition.' *Research report presented to the Social Science Research Council.*

Hobsbawm, E J (1968). *Industry and Empire.* Pelican: Harmondsworth.

Hofer, C H, and Schendel, D E (1978). *Strategy Formulation: Analytical Concepts.* West: St Paul, Minnesota, USA.

Horne, J H, and Lupton, T (1965). 'The work activities of "middle managers" – an exploratory study.' *Journal of Management Studies,*' 2 (1), 14–33.

Hoskin, K (1990). 'Using history to understand theory: a re-consideration of the historical genesis of "strategy"'. *Paper prepared for the EIASM Workshop on Strategy, Accounting and Control,* Venice.

Howarth, C (1988). 'Report of the Joint Design of Technology, Organisation and People Growth Conference' – Venice pp. 12–14. October. *Information Services News and Abstracts,* 95 November/December, Work Research Unit: London.

Huse, E F (1980). *Organization Development and Change.* West: St Paul, Minnesota, USA.

Hussey, D E (1978). 'Portfolio analysis: practical experience with the Directional Policy Matrix.' *Long Range Planning,* 11, August, 2–8.

Johnson, G and Scholes, K (1988). *Exploring Corporate Strategy.* Prentice Hall: Hemel Hempstead.

Juran, J M (1988). *Quality Control Handbook.* McGraw-Hill: New York, USA.

Kahn, H, and Weiner, A (1978). *The Year 2000.* Macmillan: London.

Kanter, R M (1989). *When Giants Learn to Dance: Mastering the Challenges of Strategy, Management, and Careers in the 1990s.* Unwin: London.

Kearney, A T (1989). *Computer Integrated Manufacturing: Competitive Advantage or Technological Dead End?* Kearney: London.

Kelly, J E (1982). *Scientific Management, Job Redesign, and Work Performance.* Academic Press: London.

Kempner, T (1970). 'Frederick Taylor and Scientific Management.' in A Tillett, T Kempner and G Wills (eds) *Management Thinkers.* Pelican: Harmondsworth.

Kerr, C, and Fisher, L (1957). 'Plant Sociology: The Elite and the Aborigines.' In M Komarovsky (ed): *Common Frontiers of the Social Sciences.* Greenwood: Westport, Connecticut, USA.

Keshavan, K, and Rakesh, K S (1979). 'Generating future scenarios – their use in strategic planning.' *Long Range Planning,* 12, June, 57–61.

Kotler, P (1978). 'Harvesting strategies for weak products.' *Business Horizons,* 21 (4), August, 15–22.

Kotter, J (1982). *The General Manager.* Free Press: New York, USA.

Kuhn, T S (1962). *The Structure of Scientific Revolutions.* University of Chicago Press: Chicago, USA.

Landes, D S (1969). *The Unbound Prometheus.* Cambridge University Press: Cambridge.

Landsberger, H A (1958). *Hawthorne Revisited: 'Management and the Worker'. Its Critics and Developments in Human Relations in Industry.* Cornell University Press: New York, USA.

Lanford, H W (1972). *Technological Forecasting Methodologies: A Synthesis.* American Management Association: New York.

Lawler, E E, and Suttle, J L (1972). 'A causal correlation of the need hierarchy concept in an organizational setting.' *Organization Behaviour and Human Performance,* 7, April, 265–87.

Lawrence, P R, and Lorsch, J W (1967). *Organization and Environment.* Harvard Business School: Boston, USA.

Lawrence, R P (1973). 'How to deal with resistance to change'. In W Dalton, R P Lawrence and E Grenier (eds): *Organisational Change and Development.* Dorsey: Homewood, Illinois, USA.

Leemhuis, J P (1990). 'Using scenario development strategies at Shell.' In B
   Taylor and J Harrison (eds): *The Manager's Casebook of Business Strategy.*
   Butterworth-Heinemann: Oxford.
Leifer, R, and Huber, G P (1977). 'Relations amongst perceived
   environmental uncertainty, organisation structure and
   boundary-spanning behaviour.' *Administrative Science Quarterly,* 22,
   235–47.
Leontiades, M (1986). *Managing the Unmanageable.* Addison-Wesley:
   Reading, Mass., USA.
Levine, A L (1967). *Industrial Retardation in Britain 1880–1914.* Basic
   Books: New York, USA.
Lewin, K (1958). 'Group decisions and social change.' In G E Swanson, T M
   Newcomb, and E L Hartley (eds): *Readings in Social Psychology.* Holt,
   Rhinehart and Winston: New York, USA.
Linneman, R E, and Klein, H E (1979). 'The use of multiple scenarios by US
   industrial companies.' *Long Range Planning,* 12, February, 83–90.
Lippitt, R, Watson, J, and Westley, B (1958). *The Dynamics of Planned
   Change.* Harcourt, Brace and World: New York.
Lippitt, G (1982). 'Management development as the key to organisational
   renewal.' *Journal of Management Development,* Vol 1, No 2.
Litschert, R, and Nicholson, E (1974). 'Corporate long range planning groups
   – some different approaches.' *Long Range Planning,* 7, August, 62–6.
Little, R (1984). 'Conglomerates are doing better than you think.' *Fortune,* 28
   May, 60.
Littler, C R (1978). 'Understanding Taylorism.' *British Journal of Sociology,*
   29 (2), 185–202.
Locke, E W (1982). 'The ideas of Frederick W Taylor.' *Academy of
   Management Review,* 7 (1), 14–24.
Long, P (1986). *Performance Appraisal Revisited.* IPM: London.
Lorsch, J W (1970). 'Introduction to the structural design of organizations.' In
   G W Dalton, P R Lawrence and J W Lorsch (eds): *Organization Structure
   and Design.* Irwin-Dorsey: London.
Lovell, R (1980). *Adult Learning.* Croom Helm: London.
Lu, D J (1987). *Inside Corporate Japan.* Productivity Press: Cambridge,
   Massachusetts, USA.
Malaska, P, Malmivirta, M, Meristo, T, and Hansen, S O (1984). 'Scenarios in
   Europe – who uses them and why?' *Long Range Planning,* 17, October,
   45–9.
Mangham Working Party (1987). *The Mangham Working Party Report: A
   Survey of the In-house Activities of Ten Major Companies.* British Institute
   of Management/Confederation of British Industry: London.
Mansfield, R (1984). 'Formal and informal structures.' In M Gruneberg and T
   Wall (eds): *Social Psychology and Organizational Behaviour.* Wiley:
   Chichester.
Marglin, S A (1976). 'What do bosses do?' In A Gorz (ed): *The Division of
   Labour: the Labour Process and Class Struggle in Modern Capitalism.*
   Harvester: Brighton.

Marsh, N (1986). 'Management development and strategic management change.' *Journal of Management Development,* 5 (1).

Maslow, A H (1943). 'A theory of human motivation.' *Psychology Review,* 50, 370–96.

Massie, J L (1965). 'Management Theory.' In J G March (ed): *Handbook of Organizations.* Rand McNally: Chicago, USA.

Mathias, P (1969). *The First Industrial Nation.* Methuen: London.

Mayo, E (1933). *The Human Problems of Industrial Civilization.* Macmillan: New York, USA.

McGregor, D (1960). *The Human Side of Enterprise.* McGraw-Hill: New York, USA.

McKracken, J K (1986). 'Exploitation of FMS technology to achieve strategic objectives.' *Paper to the 5th International Conference on Flexible Manufacturing Systems.* Stratford-Upon-Avon.

McNamee, B P (1985). *Tools and Techniques of Strategic Management.* Pergamon: Oxford.

McNulty, C A R (1977). 'Scenario development for corporate planning.' *Futures,* 9 (2), 128–38.

Meek, V L (1988). 'Organizational culture: origins and weaknesses.' *Organization Studies,* 9 (4), 453–73.

Miewald, R D (1970). 'The greatly exaggerated death of bureaucracy.' *California Management Review,* Winter, 65–9.

Miles, R E and Snow, C C (1978). *Organisational Strategy, Structure and Process.* McGraw-Hill: New York, USA.

Miller, E (1967). *Systems of Organisation.* Tavistock: London.

Mintzberg, H (1973). *The Nature of Managerial Work.* Harper and Row: New York, USA.

Mintzberg, H (1975). 'The manager's job: folklore and fact.' *Harvard Business Review,* 53 (4), 49–61.

Mintzberg, H (1979). *The Structure of Organizations.* Prentice-Hall: Englewood Cliffs, New Jersey, USA.

Mintzberg, H (1987). 'Crafting Strategy.' *Harvard Business Review,* 19 (2), 66–75.

Mintzberg, H, and Quinn, J B (1991). *The Strategy Process: Concepts, Contexts, and Cases.* Prentice-Hall: London.

Mitroff, I I, and Mason, R O (1981). *Challenging Strategic Planning Assumptions.* Wiley: New York, USA.

Morgan, G (1986). *Images of Organizations.* Sage: Beverly Hills, California, USA.

Morgan, G (1988). *Riding the Waves of Change.* Jossey-Bass: San Francisco, USA.

Mullins, L (1989). *Management and Organisational Behaviour.* Pitman: London.

Mumford, A (1987). 'Myths and reality in developing directors.' *Personnel Management,* 19 (2), February, 29–33.

Mumford, E (1979). 'The design of work: new approaches and new needs.' In J E Rijnsdorp (ed): *Case Studies in Automation Related to the Humanisation of Work.* Pergamon: Oxford.

Myers, C S (1934). *An account of the work carried out at the National Institute of Industrial Psychology during the years 1921–34.* NIIP: London.

Naylor, T H (1979). *Simulation Models in Corporate Measuring.* Draeger: New York, USA.

Naylor, T H (1981). 'Strategic planning models.' *Managerial Planning,* 30, July/August, 3–11.

NEDO (1987). *Signposts to Success.* NEDO: London.

New, C (1989). 'The challenge of transformation.' In B Burnes and B Weekes (eds): *AMT: A Strategy for Success?* NEDO: London.

Newstrom, J (1985). 'Modern management: does it deliver?' *Journal of Management Development,* Vol 4, No 1.

Nord, W (1985). 'Can organizational culture be managed: a synthesis.' In R Kilmann, M Saxton and R Serpa (eds): *Gaining Control of Corporate Culture.* Jossey-Bass: San Francisco, USA.

Norse, D (1979). 'Scenario analysis in interfutures.' *Futures,* 11 (5), 412–22.

Ohmae, K (1986). *The Mind of the Strategist.* Penguin: Harmondsworth.

Ohmae, K (1990). Untitled article in Special Report 1202, The Management Briefing. *The Economist:* London.

Parsons, T (1947). 'Introduction.' In M Weber (ed): *The Theory of Social and Economic Organization.* Free Press: Glencoe, Illinois, USA.

Partnership Sourcing (1991). *Case Studies in Partnership Sourcing.* Partnership Sourcing Ltd: London.

Pascale, R T, and Athos, A G (1982). *The Art of Japanese Management.* Penguin: Harmondsworth.

Patel, P, and Younger, M (1978). 'A frame of reference for strategy development.' *Long Range Planning,* 11, April, 6–12.

Pavlov, I P (1927). *Conditioned Reflexes* (trans). Oxford University Press: London.

Pearson, A E (1987). 'Muscle-build the Organization.' *Harvard Business Review,* 65 (4), 49–55.

Pearson, B (1977). 'How to manage turnarounds.' *Management Today,* April, 75.

Pelling, H (1960). *American Labor.* Chicago University Press: Chicago, USA.

Perez, C (1983). 'Structural change and the assimilation of new technologies in the economic and social systems.' *Futures,* 15, 357–75.

Perrow, C (1967). 'A framework for the comparative analysis of organizations.' *American Sociological Review,* 32, 194–208.

Perrow, C (1970). *Organizational Analysis: a Sociological View.* Tavistock: London.

Perrow, C (1983). 'The organizational context of human factors engineering.' *Administrative Science Quarterly,* 28, 521–41.

Peters, T J, and Waterman, R H (1982). *In Search of Excellence: Lessons from America's Best-Run Companies.* Harper and Row: London.

Peters, T J (1989). *Thriving on Chaos.* Pan: London.

Pettigrew, A M (1980). *The politics of organisational change.* In N B Anderson (ed): *The Human Side of Information Processing.* North Holland: Amsterdam, Netherlands.

Pettigrew, A M (ed) (1988). *The Management of Strategic Change.* Blackwell: Oxford.

Pfeffer, J (1981). *Power in Organizations.* Pitman: Cambridge, Mass., USA.

Pollard, S (1965). *The Genesis of Modern Management.* Pelican: Harmondsworth.

Porter, M (1980). *Competitive Strategy.* Free Press: New York, USA.

Pugh, D S (ed) (1984). *Organization Theory.* Penguin: Harmondsworth.

Pugh, D S, Hickson, D J, Hinings, C R, and Turner, C (1969a). 'The context of organization structures.' *Administrative Science Quarterly,* 14, 91–114.

Pugh, D S, Hickson, D J, and Hinings, C R, (1969b). 'An empirical taxonomy of structures of work organisation.' *Administrative Science Quarterly,* 14, 115–26.

Pugh, D S, and Hickson, D J (1976). *Organizational Structure in its Context: The Aston Programme 1.* Saxon House: Farnborough.

Quinn, J B (1980). 'Managing strategic change.' *Sloan Management Review,* 21 (4), 3–20.

Robbins, S P (1986). *Organizational Behavior: Concepts, Controversies, and Applications.* Prentice-Hall: Englewood Cliffs, New Jersey, USA.

Robbins, S P (1987). *Organization Theory: Structure, Design, and Applications.* Prentice-Hall: Englewood Cliffs, New Jersey, USA.

Roethlisberger, F, and Dickson, W J (1938). *Management and the Worker.* Wiley: New York, USA.

Roll, E (1930). 'An early experiment in industrial organisation: Boulton and Watt, 1775–1805' Reprinted in M Berg (ed) (1979): *Technology and Toil in Nineteenth Century Britain.* CSE Books: London.

Rose, M (1988). *Industrial Behaviour.* Penguin: Harmondsworth.

Rubin, I (1967). 'Increasing self-acceptance: a means of reducing prejudice.' *Journal of Personality and Social Psychology,* 5, 233–38.

Salaman, G (1979). *Work Organisations.* Longman: London.

Schein, E H (1969). *Process Consultation.* Addison-Wesley: Reading, Mass., USA.

Schein, E H (1985). *Organizational Culture and Leadership: A Dynamic View.* Jossey-Bass: San Francisco, USA.

Schmuck, R, and Miles, M (1971). *Organizational Development in Schools.* National Press: Palo Alto, California, USA.

Schwartz, H, and Davis, S (1981). 'Matching corporate culture and business strategy.' *Organizational Dynamics,* 10, 30–48.

Scott, W R (1987). *Organizations: Rational, Natural and Open Systems.* Prentice-Hall: Englewood Cliffs, New Jersey, USA.

Selznick, P (1948). 'Foundations of the theory of organization.' *American Sociological Review,* 13, 25–35.

Silverman, D (1970). *The Theory of Organizations.* Heinemann: London.

Silverman, D, and Jones, J (1976). *Organizational Work.* Macmillan: London.

Simon, H A (1957). *Administrative Behaviour: A Study of Decision-making Processes in Administrative Organizations.* Macmillan: New York, USA.

Sissons, K (ed) (1989). *Personnel Management in Britain.* Blackwell: Oxford.

Sissons, K and Storey, J (1988). 'Developing effective managers: a review of the issues and an agenda for research.' *Personnel Review,* 17 (4), 3–8.

Skinner, B F (1974). *About Behaviourism*. Cape: London.

Sloan, A P (1986). *My Years with General Motors*. Penguin: Harmondsworth.

Smith, A (1776). *The Wealth of Nations, Vol 1*. Methuen (1950 edition): London.

Smith, S, and Tranfield, D (1987). 'The implementation and exploitation of advanced manufacturing technology – an outline methodology.' *Change Management Research Unit, Research Paper No 2,* Sheffield Business School.

Smith, J (1987). 'Elton Mayo and the hidden Hawthorne.' *Work, Employment and Society,* 1 (1), 107–20.

Smith, J G (1985). *Business Strategy*. Blackwell: Oxford.

Smith, M, Beck, J, Cooper, C L, Cox, C, Ottaway, D, and Talbot, R (1982). *Introducing Organizational Behaviour*. Macmillan: London.

Steiner, G A (1969). *Top Management Planning*. Macmillan: London.

Stewart, R (1976). *Contrasts in Management*. McGraw-Hill: London.

Storey, J (1989). 'Management development: a literature review and implications for future research – Part 1: conceptualisations and practices.' *Personnel Review,* 18 (6), 3–19.

Storey, J (1990). 'Management development: a literature review and implications for future research – Part 2: profiles and context.' *Personnel Review,* 19 (1), 3–11.

Stuart, R (1986). 'Social learning.' *Management Decision,* 24, (6), 32–5.

Taguchi, G (1986). *Introduction to Quality Engineering*. Asian Production Organization: Dearborn, Michigan, USA.

Taylor, F W (1911a). *Shop Management*. Harper (1947 edition): New York, USA.

Taylor, F W (1911b). *The Principles of Scientific Management*. Harper (1947 edition): New York, USA.

Terry, P T (1976). 'The Contingency Theory and the development of organisations.' *Paper presented to the British Sociological Association.*

Thickett, M (1970). 'Gilbreth and the measurement of work.' In A Tillett, T Kempner and G Willis (eds): *Management Thinkers*. Pelican: Harmondsworth.

Thompson, J (1967). *Organizations in Action*. McGraw-Hill: New York, USA.

Thompson, A A Jnr, and Strickland, A J (1983). *Strategy Formulation and Implementation*. Business Publications Inc: Illinois, USA.

Thornberry, N E (1987). 'Training the engineer as project manager.' *Training and Development Journal,* 41 (10).

Tillett, A (1970). *Industry and Management*. In A Tillett, T Kempner and G Willis (eds): *Management Thinkers*. Pelican: Harmondsworth.

Toffler, A (1970). *Future Shock*. Random House: New York, USA.

Trist, E L; Higgin, G W; Murray, H; and Pollock, A B (1963). *Organisational Choice*. Tavistock: London.

Turner, B (1971). *Exploring the Industrial Subculture*. Macmillan: London.

Turner, I D (1989). 'Strategy and Organisation'. *Manager Update,* 1 (i) 1–9.

Tushman, M, and Virany, B (1986). 'Changing characteristics of executive teams in an emerging industry.' *Journal of Business Venturing,* 37–49.

Udy, S H Jnr (1959). '"Bureaucracy" and "Rationality" in Weber's Organization Theory.' *American Sociological Review,* 24 (December), 791–5.

Ure, A (1835). *The Philosophy of Manufactures.* Frank Cass (1967 edition): London.

Ure, A (1836). *The Cotton Manufacture of Great Britain Volume 1.* Johnson (1970 edition): London.

Uttal, B (1983). 'The corporate culture vultures.' *Fortune,* 17, 66–72.

Voss, C A (1985). 'Success and failure in advanced manufacturing technology.' *Warwick University Working Paper.*

Warner, M (1984). 'New technology, work organisation and industrial relations.' *Omega,* 12 (3), 203–10.

Watson, T J (1986). *Management Organisation and Employment Strategy: New Directions in Theory and Practice.* Routledge and Kegan Paul: London.

Weber, M (1928). *General Economic History.* George Allen and Unwin: London.

Weber, M (1946). *From Max Weber: Essays in Sociology* (trans). Oxford University Press: London.

Weber, M (1947). *The Theory of Social and Economic Organization* (trans). Free Press: Glencoe, Illinois, USA.

Wheelen, T L, and Hunger, D J (1989). *Strategic Management and Business Policy.* Addison-Wesley: Reading, Mass., USA.

White, S, and Mitchell, T (1976). 'Organization development: a review of research content and research design.' *Academy of Management Review,* 1 (2), 57–73.

White, R E (1986). 'Generic business strategies: organisational context and performance.' *Strategic Management Journal,* May/June, 217–31.

Whyte, W H (1960). *The Organization of Man.* Penguin: Harmondsworth.

Wickens, P (1987). *The Road To Nissan.* Macmillan: London.

Wilkinson, H E, and Orth, D C (1986). 'Soft skill training in management development.' *Training and Development Journal,* 40 (3).

Willbur, J (1987). 'Does mentoring breed success?' *Training and Development Journal,* Vol 41, No 11.

Womack, J P, Jones, D T, and Roos, D (1990). *The Machine That Changed the World.* Rawson Associates: New York, USA.

Wood, S (1979). 'A reappraisal of the contingency approach to organization.' *Journal of Management Studies,* 16, 334–54.

Wood, S (ed) (1989). *The Transformation of Work.* Unwin Hyman: London.

Woodward, J (1965). *Industrial Organization: Theory and Practice.* Oxford University Press: London.

Woodward, J (1970). *Industrial Organization: Behaviour and Control.* Oxford University Press: London.

Zentner, R D (1982). 'Scenarios, past, present and future.' *Long Range Planning,* 15, June, 12–20.

Zinn, H (1980). *A People's History of the United States.* Longman: London.

Zwerman, W L (1970). *New Perspectives in Organization Theory.* Greenwood: Westport, USA.

Index